The Burden-Sharing Dilemma

A VOLUME IN THE SERIES

Cornell Studies in Security Affairs

Edited by Austin Carson, Alexander B. Downes, Kelly M. Greenhill, and Caitlin Talmadge

Founding Series Editors: Robert J. Art, Robert Jervis, and Stephen M. Walt

A list of titles in this series is available at www.cornellpress.cornell.edu.

The Burden-Sharing Dilemma

Coercive Diplomacy in US Alliance Politics

BRIAN D. BLANKENSHIP

Cornell University Press

Ithaca and London

Copyright © 2023 by Brian D. Blankenship

All rights reserved. Except for brief quotations in a review, this book, or parts thereof, must not be reproduced in any form without permission in writing from the publisher. For information, address Cornell University Press, Sage House, 512 East State Street, Ithaca, New York 14850. Visit our website at cornellpress.cornell.edu.

First published 2023 by Cornell University Press

Library of Congress Cataloging-in-Publication Data

Names: Blankenship, Brian D., 1990– author.
Title: The burden-sharing dilemma : coercive diplomacy in US alliance politics / Brian D. Blankenship.
Description: Ithaca : Cornell University Press, 2023. | Series: Cornell studies in security affairs | Includes bibliographical references and index.
Identifiers: LCCN 2023005582 (print) | LCCN 2023005583 (ebook) | ISBN 9781501772474 (hardcover) | ISBN 9781501772481 (pdf) | ISBN 9781501772498 (epub)
Subjects: LCSH: Alliances. | Diplomacy. | United States—Foreign relations—1945–1989.
Classification: LCC JZ1314 .B53 2023 (print) | LCC JZ1314 (ebook) | DDC 327.1/160973—dc23/eng/20230216
LC record available at https://lccn.loc.gov/2023005582
LC ebook record available at https://lccn.loc.gov/2023005583

Contents

Acknowledgments	*vii*
List of Abbreviations	*ix*
Introduction: Why Is Burden-Sharing a Contentious Issue in US Alliances?	*1*
1. The Strategic Logic of Coercive Burden-Sharing	*12*
2. "A Legitimate Role in the Defense of the Alliance, but on a Leash": West German Burden-Sharing, 1961–1974	*35*
3. "Between Scylla and Charybdis": Japanese Burden-Sharing, 1964–1976	*66*
4. "They Live at Our Sufferance": South Korean Burden-Sharing, 1964–1980	*87*
5. "Is Iceland Blackmailing Us?": Icelandic Burden-Sharing, 1949–1960	*111*
Conclusion: The Enduring Challenges of Burden-Sharing in US Alliances	*120*
Appendix: Selected US Economic Statistics, 1950–1980	*141*
Notes	*143*
References	*173*
Index	*189*

Acknowledgments

I am enormously thankful to have had so many mentors, colleagues, friends, and family that helped me along the journey to completing this book, one way or another. I owe particular thanks to my mentors during my undergraduate studies at Indiana University and my graduate studies at Columbia University, most notably Richard Betts, Allison Carnegie, Page Fortna, Sumit Ganguly, Robert Jervis, Tonya Putnam, Armando Razo, Dina Spechler, Jack Snyder, Johannes Urpelainen, Gerald Wright, and Keren Yarhi-Milo. I owe a special debt of gratitude to Robert Jervis, whose work and wise counsel has left a lasting impact on my thinking and my research, this book being no exception. I am also extraordinarily grateful for the feedback I received on earlier iterations of the book from my mentors and colleagues during my postdoctoral fellowships at Dartmouth's Dickey Center for International Understanding and at the Council on Foreign Relations, including Stephen Brooks, Jeffrey Friedman, James Lindsay, Jennifer Lind, Nicholas Miller, Daryl Press, Sheila Smith, Paul Stares, Benjamin Valentino, and William Wohlforth.

Since beginning on the tenure track at the University of Miami, I have had the good fortune of having supportive colleagues who have offered wise advice and feedback on this project and many others, including Cali Curley, Jennifer Connolly, Louise Davidson-Schmich, June Dreyer, Xue Gao, Laura Gomez-Mera, Namhoon Ki, Casey Klofstad, Greg Koger, Costa Pischedda, Mike Touchton, and Joe Uscinski. Outside the University of Miami, I have benefited from my conversations with a number of scholars, including Josh Alley, Jonathan Caverley, Tim Crawford, Mayumi Fukushima, Andres Gannon, James Goldgeier, Dotan Haim, Koji Kagotani, Kelly Matush, Roseanne McManus, Mike Poznansky, Josh Shifrinson, Jennifer Spindel, Katsuya Tsukamoto, and Tristan Volpe. I would also like to extend a special thanks to

ACKNOWLEDGMENTS

Tongfi Kim, Alexander Lanoszka, Sara Bjerg Moller, and Paul Poast for participating in my book workshop and offering invaluable feedback—not least of all the suggestion for this book's title—without which the book would not be what it is today.

This book owes a great debt to the editors at Cornell University Press and the Cornell Studies in Security Affairs series, particularly Michael McGandy, Jacqulyn Teoh, and Stephen Walt, as well as an anonymous reviewer, for their insightful comments on the manuscript and for shepherding it through the process of review and publication. I am grateful as well to the editors and anonymous reviewers at *Security Studies*, particularly Ron Krebs and Jennifer Erickson, for their feedback on an earlier iteration of the manuscript. I thank Taylor and Francis for granting me permission to adapt material from my article "The Price of Protection: Explaining Success and Failure in US Alliance Burden-Sharing Pressure," *Security Studies* 30, no. 5 (2021): 691–724, available online: http://www.tandfonline.com/10.1080/09636412.2021.2018624. I also thank Oxford University Press for allowing me to adapt material from my article "Promises under Pressure: Statements of Reassurance in US Alliances," *International Studies Quarterly* 64 (2020): 1017–30. This project was made possible in no small part thanks to the generous support I received from the Smith Richardson Foundation and Columbia's Weatherhead East Asian Institute, in addition to the institutional support I received from Columbia University, Dartmouth's Dickey Center for International Understanding, the University of Miami, and the Council on Foreign Relations.

Over the years I have been fortunate to have made a number of friends and colleagues who not only have provided insights, feedback, and advice but also, and perhaps even more importantly, have kept me in good spirits: Seung Cho, Ben Denison, Renanah Joyce, Raymond Kuo, Erik Lin-Greenberg, Jeff Lax, Shawn Lonergan, Cullen Nutt, Asli Saygili, and Joon Yang. I owe a debt of gratitude to my friends outside of academia as well for reminding me of life beyond work: Shadman Ahmed, Nathan Berbesque, Alex Brueggman, Spencer Chenhall, Ryan Huffman, Salman Iqbal, Warwick Mannington, Ryan Smith, and Al Wood.

Last but hardly least, I would like to thank my family. My sister, Brooke Blankenship, and my mother, Mary Ellen Blankenship, have been a constant source of support. Without the sacrifices of my parents, I doubt I would have been able to take advantage of the opportunities to advance my education, and this book would not exist. While he was not able to read this book, I have little doubt that my father, Curtis Blankenship, would have kept his copy close to him. Finally, I would like to say a few words of appreciation for my wife, Olivia Warschaw, as well as Nora Warschaw-Alexander, Gary Warschaw, Arpie Meneshian, and Jonah Warschaw, who immediately made me feel like part of the family. Olivia has been the most supportive, loyal partner I could possibly have. I could not have managed the journey without her.

viii

Abbreviations

ANZUS	Australia-New Zealand-United States Alliance
ATOP	Alliance Treaty Obligations and Provisions
CINC	Composite Index of National Capability
DNSA	Digital National Security Archive
EDIP	European Defense Improvement Program
FMS	Foreign Military Sales
FRG	Federal Republic of Germany
FRUS	*Foreign Relations of the United States*
GDP	gross domestic product
GIUK	Greenland-Iceland-United Kingdom
GNP	gross national product
GRFL	Gerald R. Ford Presidential Library
HNS	host-nation support
JCP	Japanese Communist Party
JSP	Social Democratic Party of Japan
LDP	Liberal Democratic Party (Japan)
MBFR	Mutual and Balanced Force Reductions
MDT	Mutual Defense Treaty (US-South Korea)
MLF	Multilateral Force
MST	Mutual Security Treaty (US-Japan)
NATO	North Atlantic Treaty Organization
NDPO	National Defense Program Outline
NIE	National Intelligence Estimate
NPT	Nuclear Nonproliferation Treaty
NSC	National Security Council
NSDM	National Security Decision Memorandum

ABBREVIATIONS

NSSM	National Security Study Memorandum
REFORGER	Return of Forces to Germany
RMNL	Richard M. Nixon Presidential Library
ROK	Republic of Korea
SALT	Strategic Arms Limitations Treaty
SDF	Self-Defense Forces (Japan)
SDP	surplus domestic product

The Burden-Sharing Dilemma

Introduction

Why Is Burden-Sharing a Contentious Issue in US Alliances?

A recent US president once complained that Washington's allies do not pay their fair share for defense. "Free riders aggravate me," he stated bitterly. "You have to pay your fair share."[1]

This president was not Donald Trump, who repeatedly made headlines by casting doubt on his willingness to protect US allies unless they made sufficient defense contributions.[2] Rather, it was his predecessor, Barack Obama. Indeed, Obama's secretary of defense went so far as to warn US partners that "there will be dwindling appetite and patience . . . to expend increasingly precious funds on behalf of nations that are apparently unwilling to devote the necessary resources . . . to be serious and capable partners in their own defense."[3]

Obama and Trump were hardly the first US leaders to solicit greater burden-sharing from US allies. In late 1953, President Eisenhower's secretary of state John Foster Dulles warned that unless Europe became more self-reliant, the United States would undertake "an agonizing reappraisal of basic United States policy" toward its commitment to the Continent.[4] In much the same way, John F. Kennedy threatened to withdraw US troops from West Germany to secure compensation for the costs of stationing them in the country, declaring that "we cannot continue to pay for the military protection of Europe while the NATO states are not paying their fair share and [are] living off the 'fat of the land.'"[5] Across numerous administrations, the need for allied burden-sharing has been a constant refrain in US foreign policy.

But there is striking variation in the success and, in fact, the incidence of US burden-sharing pressure. In some cases, burden-sharing pressure efforts succeed—Jimmy Carter, for instance, persuaded South Korea to increase its defense spending to 6 percent of gross national product when he leveraged the possibility of troop withdrawals.[6] At other times, they fail—US pressure on the United Kingdom to retain its military presence in Asia during the 1960s amounted to little.[7] And then there are those cases, perhaps most puzzling of

1

INTRODUCTION

all, where US officials have notably declined to seek greater allied contributions to the common defense. During the early 1970s, for example, the Nixon administration refrained from seeking a substantially greater Japanese military role despite the explicit ambition of the Nixon Doctrine to delegate more responsibility to allies to defend themselves.[8] Similarly, US policymakers have repeatedly balked at the prospect of a united, independent European defense capability since the end of the Cold War.[9]

This book attempts to understand such variation in burden-sharing within US alliances. It investigates why the United States sometimes puts pressure on its allies to bear more of the collective burden (and sometimes doesn't) and when these burden-sharing pressures succeed (or don't). To that end, it advances two central claims. First, US decisions to encourage allied burden-sharing at all are the product of calculations about both the benefits and the risks of greater allied self-reliance. Burden-sharing is useful insofar as it can purchase a similar amount of collective military power at lower US cost. But in some cases—particularly those in which allies have a realistic capability to go their own way—the United States actually prefers that its allies *not* assume more responsibility for their own defense, since doing so can reduce their dependence on US protection and, by extension, US influence. Second, if the United States elects to encourage allied burden-sharing, its success depends on whether allies fear that it will abandon them. The more credible its threat of abandonment, and the more allies depend on its protection, the more successful it will be.

Each claim challenges strands of conventional wisdom on burden-sharing. The first rethinks the assumption that larger allies disproportionately contribute to collective defense and are always encouraged to do so.[10] I suggest that patrons like the United States actually have good reason not to encourage their largest allies to spend more on defense—namely, to prevent them from becoming too independent. The second claim confronts the notion that the United States' ability to pressure allies into greater burden-sharing is inherently precluded by its disproportionately great power and vast network of overseas troop deployments. I show that the United States is in fact sometimes able to wield the threat of abandonment to encourage greater burden-sharing even among allies that host a substantial US troop presence. Thus, even though great powers like the United States may be constrained in their ability to solicit allied military contributions, they are far from helpless in doing so. The operative constraint on alliance burden-sharing is in some cases not the United States' ability to secure it, but simply its willingness to seek it.

What We Know (and Don't Know) about Burden-Sharing

Burden-sharing refers broadly to actions by which an alliance member contributes to the alliance's capacity to carry out its objectives. These contribu-

2

tions can take a number of military or nonmilitary forms, such as deploying forces to active conflicts, hosting military bases, providing logistical support, or supplying aid.[11] In this book, I focus on burden-sharing in the form of allies' efforts to provide for their own defense and enhance their own military capabilities.

Burden-sharing is core to the functioning of alliances. By enabling states to pool resources, burden-sharing crucially ensures that alliances can achieve their collective goals, as they are unlikely to succeed in deterring and defeating adversaries unless their members possess sufficient capabilities. A lack of burden-sharing, or free-riding, can cause an alliance to fail to achieve its objectives if the patron is unwilling or unable to contribute enough by itself, and it can create discord in the alliance by generating resentment among members who feel taken advantage of.[12] Burden-sharing additionally facilitates the self-preservation of great powers. Scholars have long argued that overinvesting in military power sows the seeds of great powers' long-term decline by diverting resources from more productive investments and innovation.[13] They offer evidence that even financing military spending through debt does not avoid painful fiscal trade-offs, as doing so can cause inflation and contribute to economic crises.[14] These problems are especially challenging in asymmetric alliances between a more powerful great power patron and weaker partners, as the patron's greater capacity to provide security for the alliance makes it tempting for weaker partners to seek a free ride.[15] Securing allied burden-sharing thus allows a patron to ensure that its commitments do not exceed its resources, and that adversaries can be deterred at a sustainable cost.

The literature on burden-sharing, however, is generally pessimistic about its prospects in asymmetric alliances, largely portraying burden-sharing by smaller allies as an objective that great power patrons seek but have difficulty attaining. This pessimism partly has to do with the predominant view that alliances between great powers and weaker states feature an asymmetric exchange, wherein the former provides security for the alliance while the latter gives up some degree of foreign policy autonomy. From this perspective, the capacity for burden-sharing in asymmetric alliances is limited almost by definition; the great power already tacitly agrees to the costs of providing security in exchange for weaker states' aligning their foreign policies with its own.[16] Another cause for pessimism has to do with an understanding of alliances based on the logic of public goods, which emphasizes that larger alliance members tend to contribute disproportionately more to collective defense since it is their contributions that ultimately matter most. From this perspective, smaller allies rationally free-ride, and alliances with more members tend to feature more free-riding.[17] Others likewise suggest that the global US military footprint and other assurances of US protection encourage allies to free-ride.[18] Alexander Lanoszka, for instance, suggests that Washington's efforts to discourage nuclear proliferation forced it to fortify its commitment

INTRODUCTION

to allies' defense, thereby diminishing the United States' ability to encourage allied burden-sharing.[19]

This literature also tends not to focus on allies' ability to influence each other's contributions through coercive bargaining. To the extent that they do consider burden-sharing as a bargaining outcome, they adopt, at most, a tacit bargaining framework in which allies' military expenditures change in response to changes in the patron state's defense spending.[20] But we know very little about what this bargaining process looks like in practice, or about the conditions that encourage states to pressure their partners to contribute more and the factors that lead to success. Indeed, the studies that do approach burden-sharing through a bargaining framework mostly focus on particular cases and do not present a general theory that can systematically explain variation in burden-sharing across time and cases.[21]

These studies thus leave gaps in our understanding of variation in burden-sharing. They cannot fully explain why France withdrew from NATO's military command in 1966, despite being among NATO's largest members; why Germany, since the end of the Cold War, has been among NATO's lowest spenders on defense as a percentage of its gross domestic product (GDP); or why, by contrast, comparably smaller NATO members in the 2010s—notably Estonia, Latvia, Lithuania, and Poland—have punched above their weight. Moreover, they cannot fully explain why allies who hosted many US troops nevertheless spent a great deal on defense. Empirical research on the subject has produced mixed results and does not conclusively show that signals of alliance commitment negatively impact burden-sharing—some studies find that the presence of US troops has a negative effect on burden-sharing, but others find no such effect.[22] While there are cases in which US protection almost certainly discouraged allies from making significant efforts toward self-defense—perhaps most famously Japan, whose constitution's Article 9 imposes restrictions on its military, and Iceland, whose membership in NATO came with the assurance that it would not need to have a military—there are yet other cases in which allies hosting tens or hundreds of thousands of US troops still contributed a great deal to their own security, such as West Germany and South Korea.

Existing literature likewise has difficulty explaining why the United States has in other cases been reluctant to seek more burden-sharing from its partners. In addition to seeking just a modest military contribution from Japan, US officials only grudgingly accepted the need for West German rearmament during the early Cold War so that it could assist NATO in counterbalancing Soviet power in Central Europe.[23] Similarly, US policymakers were lukewarm about European proposals for a more united European defense policy during the 1990s and 2000s, and even the Trump administration balked at proposals for a European defense fund.[24]

What one is left with, then, are two puzzles. The first is that while in many cases the United States has been able to actively shape its partners' military

INTRODUCTION

contributions—even in seemingly unlikely cases where allies hosted considerable numbers of US troops—other times it has failed to do so. The second is that in some cases the United States has actually preferred that its allies not maximize their military capabilities, even when doing so could have allowed it to conserve its own resources.

The Argument in Brief

These puzzles raise the following question: Under what conditions is the United States willing and able to encourage allied burden-sharing? The answer lies in what I call *alliance control theory*. Alliance control theory predicts that patrons like the United States will calibrate their burden-sharing pressure toward allies in consideration of three factors—an ally's latent military potential, the external threat environment, and the patron's resource constraints. It shows that a substantial amount of variation in asymmetric alliance burden-sharing is the result of bargaining between the patron and its weaker allies.[25] Although alliances can discourage allies from investing in their own defense, a patron can mitigate this tendency by combining assurances of support with threats of abandonment. The extent to which the patron's protection can be made conditional on allies' burden-sharing efforts, in turn, depends on whether the patron is both willing to ask them to contribute more and able to credibly threaten to abandon them if they do not.

In deciding to seek allied contributions, a patron must balance competing priorities. On the one hand, burden-sharing allows a patron to secure military power for collective defense against shared adversaries without bearing the costs of doing so itself. For this reason, patrons can be expected to encourage allied burden-sharing when the alliance's external threat environment is severe and when their own resources are constrained. On the other hand, asking allies to shoulder more responsibility for defending themselves reduces both the value of the alliance to them and their dependence on the patron's protection. As such, patrons are likely to tailor their efforts at securing allied contributions not only to maximize cost savings, but also to minimize the risk of empowering allies to go their own way and exit the alliance. Patrons, in other words, are likely to take a "Goldilocks" approach to allied burden-sharing. While the smallest allies have little to contribute, and so pose the least risk of defection, larger allies, who have more to contribute, pose the greatest risks, since they have greater potential to fend for themselves outside of the alliance. Counterintuitively, then, it is not the allies who have the greatest potential to provide resources for collective defense that face the most pressure to contribute. Rather, it is moderately sized allies who are strong enough to make meaningful contributions, but not so strong that they can choose to leave the alliance given sufficient investments in defense.

5

INTRODUCTION

If a patron does choose to seek greater burden-sharing, its success then depends on whether allies fear being abandoned by it. Two factors shape the effectiveness of patron burden-sharing pressure: whether a patron's threat of abandonment is credible, and how badly allies need protection. A patron can more believably threaten to walk away from its alliances when it faces strains on its resources and pressure to retrench from domestic actors, which constrain its ability to maintain its commitments. Its threat of abandonment is also likely to carry more weight for allies who perceive a greater level of external threat and thus can less easily afford to lose the patron's protection.

Patrons, in sum, face a burden-sharing dilemma—they must balance discouraging free-riding and encouraging allies to remain loyal to the alliance through a reduction of allies' incentives and capabilities to act independently.[26] Stated differently, patrons in asymmetric alliances must find a trade-off between *control*—their ability to influence allies' preferences and persuade them to act in ways that align with their own—and *cost-sharing*—their ability to reduce the costs of military readiness for themselves and shift those costs onto their partners. Although patrons can never fully overcome this dilemma, they can nevertheless mitigate it by making their protection conditional on allied burden-sharing and manage it by exercising caution in their attempts to secure burden-sharing.

Scope Conditions and Limitations

This book examines coercive burden-sharing efforts that aim at getting allies to assume more responsibility for their own defense by enhancing their own military capabilities. I focus on this form of burden-sharing not only because it is among the most frequently discussed indicators of allied contributions in existing literature, but also because the pool of military power available to an alliance plays a central role in determining the success or failure of an alliance and in shaping the military missions it can successfully carry out.[27] Although the book indirectly touches on other forms of burden-sharing insofar as they can substitute for military buildups, it does not aim to explain variation in US efforts to encourage such other forms of burden-sharing. To be sure, the causal processes that drive all forms of burden-sharing are likely to overlap—one might expect fear of abandonment to drive allied contributions in other domains, for example. Yet, the key difference between these forms is the double-edged nature of encouraging allies to enhance their military capabilities; this form of burden-sharing empowers allies to go their own way, whereas others do not. The theory of burden-sharing pressure that this book develops thus accounts only for the unique dilemmas inherent to this form of contribution.

My theory is thus not meant to judge which allies are free-riding or not. Isolating any one form of alliance contribution and using it as the standard by which to judge all members' contributions risks missing the multitude of other contributions that allies make.[28] Some allies are better suited to some contributions than others; larger, wealthier allies, for example, can more effectively supply material resources, while smaller, poorer allies may be limited to making nonmaterial contributions such as military bases. Moreover, allies can elect to contribute to collective defense missions for reasons unrelated to patron pressure.[29] This book makes a narrower claim to explain the conditions under which a patron attempts to pressure partners to invest in their own defense and why these attempts succeed or fail.

Additionally, this book looks at burden-sharing in the context of asymmetric alliances, here defined as formal agreements between two or more states in which at least one partner agrees to be involved in case other signatories come under attack, and in which one member (the patron) is significantly more powerful than the others.[30] Its empirical content focuses on alliances formed within the bipolar and unipolar systems that emerged after 1945. This period saw an explosion of asymmetric alliances led by the United States or the Soviet Union—a marked difference from the period preceding World War II, during which alliance formation was characterized more by symmetric alliances between great powers within a multipolar system.[31] The bipolar and unipolar systems of the Cold War and post–Cold War periods thus represent ideal grounds for studying the dynamics of asymmetric alliances. That said, I examine only asymmetric alliances formed by the United States during this period, and not those by the Soviet Union. The coercive nature of Soviet alliances, coupled with these allies' greater concern with internal rather than external threats, make comparisons across the two alliance blocs difficult.[32] Nevertheless, my conclusion discusses the extent to which my findings can shed light on the dynamics of burden-sharing in Soviet alliances.

Focusing on post-1945 US alliances potentially limits the generalizability of this book's findings in several ways, since there are certain characteristics of the United States and its alliances that are peculiar to them. The first is that the United States and most of its allies are democracies. This detail raises the question of whether US alliances are shaped by the democratic peace, which could mean that US willingness to use threats is particularly constrained by normative affinity between democracies.[33] Yet, this possibility may be moot—many argue that the democratic peace can be attributed more to democracies' transparency and ability to signal their intentions or to democracies being tougher opponents in wartime rather than to shared norms and values.[34] That aside, democratic politics may also shape perceptions of US reliability. The literature on democratic alliance credibility stresses that democratic allies may be more (or less) trustworthy than nondemocratic allies given their transparency, checks and balances, and regular leadership turnover.[35] Thus, as a democratic patron, the United States' willingness and ability to use threats of abandonment may be distinctive.

INTRODUCTION

Second, the United States is geographically remote from the vast majority of its allies (and adversaries), and thus its ability to directly dominate or conquer wayward allies is much less than that of a contiguous, continental power such as the Soviet Union.[36] Therefore, assurances of support and threats of abandonment may play a greater role in US alliances than in alliances of coercion in which a patron uses force to keep its allies in line. Moreover, having local partners may be especially important for the United States given the expenses that a geographically remote power must incur to project power, so burden-sharing may be more important in US alliances.[37] Its distance from allies might similarly give US threats of abandonment inherent credibility, given the difficulty of projecting power and the margin of safety afforded to it by the Atlantic and Pacific Oceans.[38]

Third, US security guarantees are underwritten by the United States' nuclear capabilities. This capacity may reduce the need for conventional forces in the alliance and make allies reluctant to make costly investments in conventional military power.[39] Nuclear alliances may thus be tough cases for encouraging allied conventional burden-sharing. Yet, even as the fear of nuclear retaliation may deter large-scale conflict, it may not necessarily reduce—or may even increase—the risk of lower-scale conflicts where the threat of nuclear retaliation is less credible, a phenomenon Glenn Snyder refers to as the "stability-instability paradox."[40] Conventional forces may thus still be necessary for deterring and winning these sorts of conflicts. Mutual nuclear deterrence may also render nuclear threats less credible and conventional forces nearly as important as they would be in the absence of nuclear weapons.[41] As such, the United States might just as easily encourage allied conventional burden-sharing in alliances underwritten by nuclear deterrence. Indeed, the destructive capacity of nuclear weapons may increase allies' fears of being abandoned and thus their vulnerability to US pressure, as they may question whether the United States would risk nuclear war to protect them.[42]

Finally, US alliances since 1945 have tended to last longer than other countries'.[43] On average, alliances formed since World War II last just over twenty years; those formed between 1815 and 1944, fewer than ten years. In comparison, allliances of the United States have lasted an average of more than forty years.[44] The reasons for this disparity have not been the subject of much study, but there are a number of potential explanations. These include the influence of the nuclear revolution, which, by reducing the likelihood of war, may have effectively frozen some alliances in place as instruments of long-term deterrence; the influence of bipolarity and unipolarity; the greater number of democracies over time, which research suggests have longer-lasting alliances; and the greater institutionalization of alliances.[45] In any case, this expanded time horizon has implications for burden-sharing; an acceptable division of burdens in one time period can break down as allies' perception of threat, their ability to contribute, and their interest in the alliance shift. Moreover, political and military planning over an extended time period re-

8

quires careful attention to managing collective resources for dealing with existing and potential threats, and to ensuring that burdens are divided acceptably and sustainably over the long term.[46]

Contributions of the Book

This book advances the study of alliance politics on several fronts. It shows, first, that existing literature underestimates great power patrons' ability to persuade their allies to shoulder a greater portion of the collective defense burden. I demonstrate that great power patrons are often surprisingly capable of encouraging allies to contribute more, even when those allies receive considerable signals of support such as troop deployments. In the case of the United States, there are three reasons for this capability. First, US assurances are not distributed randomly, and many of the same factors that drive the need for reassurance—such as when allies doubt their patron's reliability or perceive a high level of external threat—also make them predisposed to burden-share. Indeed, the very fact that allies need to be reassured suggests that they may be vulnerable to their patron's pressure.[47] Second, even if the United States provides signals of support, allies may nevertheless fear that that support could be withheld at a later date. Finally, the United States can in some cases use the possibility of reduced protection to motivate allies, pairing threats to punish an ally if it does not comply with assurances that the ally will not be punished if it does.[48]

At the same time, my findings show that existing literature overestimates the degree to which patrons actually want their allies to contribute more. Often, the challenge of alliance burden-sharing is not a question of whether a patron can extract burden-sharing concessions from its allies, but of whether it is willing to tolerate the risks of doing so. The conventional wisdom on alliance burden-sharing, based on the logic of collective goods, suggests that larger partners in an alliance inevitably pay a disproportionate share of the alliance's defense burden.[49] Yet, when one considers burden-sharing in the broader context of the alliance and as an outcome of alliance bargaining, a central challenge for the patron becomes evident: allies who can contribute more can also do more for themselves and go their own way, pursuing policies that the patron may oppose and ultimately weakening the alliance. In other words, an ally's capacity for self-reliance poses the risk of alliance abandonment—a possibility underplayed in existing literature, which tends to view an ally's ability to find other partners as the primary cause of alliance abandonment, and which thus tends to underestimate the risk of alliance exit in bipolar and especially unipolar systems.[50] Thus, if a patron is deliberately seeking to suppress its larger allies' military capabilities for the purposes of maintaining influence over them, then the notion that larger allies must always or should always be encouraged to contribute disproportionately more of their resources toward the alliance's common defense does not hold. In the final analysis, burden-sharing is not an unalloyed good, since it may result in diminishing returns for the collective good. Inequitable burden-sharing in US alliances should therefore not be seen as a predetermined result of collective goods logic that the United States perpetually resists, but rather as a conscious choice.

This book also bears broader implications for understanding alliance management while pointing to the limits of alliance treaties as commitment devices. Based on the assumption that the presence of a formal alliance treaty is one of the strongest assurances of support and indicators of friendly relations among states, the literature on alliances has long focused on understanding the causes and consequences of alliance formation. It has also emphasized how alliance treaty design—for example, whether a treaty imposes strict conditions on supports or limits on behavior, is bilateral or multilateral, and is vague or precise—enables allies to lock in their leverage over partners.[51] But the formation of an alliance is only the starting point; a great deal of bargaining takes place after an alliance treaty is signed. Moreover, a treaty's ability to actually constrain partners and lock in bargaining leverage is limited, no matter how foolproof its initial design, since partners' interests, capabilities, and intentions, along with the external environment, can change in ways that make the alliance less useful or shift bargaining power among members. While this book does not discount the importance of studying alliance formation or alliance treaty design, it does show, through the lens of burden-sharing, that what happens after alliances are formed between great power patrons and their weaker protégés is equally important. And by paying more attention to burden-sharing rather than treaty design, the book demonstrates that patrons are able to maintain their bargaining leverage over the long term by willingly accepting or even encouraging a degree of free-riding.

Finally, this book contributes to our understanding of alliances as tools of restraint and control. Scholars have long argued that alliances can restrain allies from launching offensive wars—both against each other, by fostering transparency and building trust, and against third parties, by allowing partners to mediate and use the threat of withholding support to dissuade adventurous allies.[52] But an understudied mechanism by which alliances can restrain and control partners is by reducing their incentives for independent military arming or engaging in security competition with their neighbors, thus ameliorating local security dilemmas that could otherwise foster conflict.[53] This book explores this mechanism precisely by identifying the conditions under which great power patrons are more likely to seek a way to limit their allies' military power.

The next chapter of this book elaborates on alliance control theory, explaining the conditions under which the United States is willing and able to persuade its allies to increase their burden-sharing contributions. I argue that in asymmetric alliances there is a tension between control and cost-sharing, which the United States manages by using a mix of reassurance and threats of abandonment. The chapter concludes with a discussion of alternative explanations and the book's methodology. The next four chapters present case studies of the United States applying burden-sharing pressure on West Germany, South Korea, and Japan during the 1960s and 1970s, and on Iceland during the 1950s. These chapters draw on declassified government documents and secondary historical texts. The book then concludes with a summary of the findings as well as a discussion of policy implications and avenues for future research.

CHAPTER 1

The Strategic Logic of Coercive Burden-Sharing

This chapter lays out my theory of coercive burden-sharing in asymmetric alliances, alliance control theory. The theory offers an explanation for the variation in US burden-sharing pressure—its occurrence, its success, its failures—that is present across the history of US foreign relations. Of all the various forms burden-sharing can take, the theory focuses on burden-sharing in the form of allied military improvements. It predicts the measures patrons such as the United States will take in the face of a dilemma that emerges when they pursue this particular form of burden-sharing—namely, balancing the desire for burden-sharing with the fear that too much burden-sharing will encourage allies to go their own way.

Given this dilemma, the theory expects that patrons will be strategic with their burden-sharing pressure. While they will seek more burden-sharing during periods when their own resources are under strain, and from allies that face higher levels of threat, they will also be cautious in soliciting contributions from allies that have the latent capability to become self-reliant. The theory also expects that when patrons do elect to seek more burden-sharing, their success depends on whether the allies take seriously the threat to abandon them.

In this chapter, I present the theory's empirically testable hypotheses, compare them to those of alternative explanations, and then describe the empirical approach I take to test the theory. First, however, I detail the theory's assumptions and causal logic, elaborating on both the burden-sharing dilemma and the policy levers patrons can use to manage it.

Alliance Control Theory I: Burden-Sharing in Asymmetric Alliances

Alliance control theory is built on five assumptions particular to asymmetric alliances.[1] Taken together, these assumptions have implications for a pa-

12

tron's willingness and ability to secure greater levels of burden-sharing from its allies.

ASSUMPTIONS

The first assumption is that a junior ally (the protégé) seeks protection from its stronger partner (the patron), while the patron wants its allies to remain loyal and pursue policies consistent with its interests. This assumption is based on the logic of asymmetric alliances described by James Morrow and hierarchical relationships described by David Lake, where great powers provide protection to weaker states, which, in exchange, give up a degree of their foreign policy autonomy to align their policies more closely with the patron's preferences.[2]

Second, patrons constantly gauge the extent of their investment in foreign commitments, and are sensitive to the costs of those commitments. Should they overcommit their own resources, patrons run the risk of becoming unable to successfully respond to challengers. They may also have to divert resources from domestic investments and consumption, thereby potentially undermining their own economic growth.[3]

Third, all else being equal, a patron prefers that its allies survive and maintain their territorial integrity. Put another way, a patron prefers that other great powers do not dominate other regions or the patron's own region—hence the desire for ally survival.[4] If an adversary who is considerably more powerful than its neighbors and rivals shows signs of aggressive intent, then the patron may have little choice but to become more directly involved in deterring and containing the aggressor to ensure the survival and territorial integrity of its allies and, by extension, its own position vis-à-vis the adversary.

Fourth, an ally's willingness to defer to the patron's interests is shaped by its dependence on the patron's protection. Existing literature on alliance bargaining shows that states highly dependent on their partners have weak bargaining leverage; the opposite is true for states that are not as dependent on their partners.[5] Thus, a patron will presumably have more success bargaining on a variety of issues—burden-sharing included—with allies who have more need for its protection.[6]

The final assumption is that neither the patron nor its allies knows each other's intentions with absolute certainty, and that those intentions can change.[7] Although alliance treaties are often seen as one of the strongest means by which partners can signal their commitments to support each other, their ability to reduce uncertainty is imperfect for several reasons.[8] To begin with, the terms of an alliance are rarely so unambiguous that they remove all doubt about whether a partner would be obligated to act or whether it could instead justify nonintervention by appealing to the situation's extenuating circumstances.[9] Even if patrons do follow through, the

CHAPTER 1

timing and amount of their support is subject to discretion.[10] NATO's Article 5, for example, obliges each member only to undertake "such action as it deems necessary" in the event that one of its partners comes under attack, while other US alliance treaties ask only that signatories act in ways consistent with their "constitutional processes."[11] The terms of alliances also tend to be quite static. Out of the 551 alliances listed between 1946 and 2016 in the Alliance Treaty Obligations and Provisions (ATOP, version 4.0) dataset, only twenty-seven entered into a "second phase" with altered provisions, and only three were US alliances.[12] Furthermore, alliances can be abrogated, and members' interests, capabilities, and intentions can change over time and may be difficult to discern.[13] Indeed, research suggests that alliances are less likely to be honored the longer they last, and that leadership turnover can reduce alliance reliability.[14] Finally, the primary obligation of an alliance—support during wartime—is not an ongoing process where compliance can be verified. A patron's willingness to carry out its promise can be determined only after it is too late.

THE BURDEN-SHARING DILEMMA

These assumptions underlie two trade-offs that great power patrons like the United States must face when they seek to manage the distribution of costs in their alliances. The first, related to the alliance security dilemma famously discussed by Glenn Snyder, involves the built-in tension between a patron's signals of alliance commitment and its allies' willingness to burden-share.[15] Patrons often need to signal that they are committed to their allies' defense, as such signals of support have been shown to play an important role in deterring third-party adversaries, maintaining alliance cohesion by discouraging allies from seeking substitutes for the alliance, and discouraging nuclear proliferation.[16] At the same time, such signaling may prompt allies to do less to shore up their own military capabilities.[17] Patrons thus must balance providing assurances of support and ensuring that allies remain willing to burden-share. This trade-off may be especially stark in asymmetric alliances where, given the disparity in their relative power, a patron's allies are more likely to receive more security from the alliance than they provide back to it.[18]

The second and perhaps more fundamental trade-off a patron faces is that of *control* versus *cost-sharing*—or, more precisely put, of balancing the desire to preserve its influence over its allies and the desire to reduce alliance costs for itself. Protection is the patron's quid pro quo in the alliance, and if allies are expected to pay for their own protection, they are likely to question the value of the partnership. So, while demanding more contributions from allies can enable the patron to cut its own costs, doing so may also reduce the value that allies perceive in remaining in the alliance and ultimately encourage allies to consider outside options that reduce their dependence on the alliance. Additionally, the more allies build up their own military capabilities, the less they inherently need support from their patron, as the capabilities they developed in service of the alliance also empower them to act independently.[19] With more independent military power, allies become more capable of conducting independent foreign policies. In the extreme, they can leave the alliance and even pose a threat to their neighbors. Short of that, allies that become more self-reliant inevitably become less susceptible to the patron's influence and are likely to demand greater freedom of action in their foreign policies. The Trump administration discovered as much, to its chagrin, when its calls for greater NATO burden-sharing resulted in European members' desire for more autonomous capabilities. As French president Emmanuel Macron put it: "What I don't want to see is European countries increasing the budget in defense in order to buy Americans' [sic] and other arms or materials coming from your industry. I think if we increase our budget, it's to have [sic] to build our autonomy and to become an actual sovereign power."[20]

In my theory, patrons navigate these trade-offs—which I refer to as the "burden-sharing dilemma"—by trying to strike a balance between burden-sharing's risks and benefits. Too little burden-sharing, and a patron risks overextension; too much, and it risks unraveling its alliances. In the final analysis, the dilemma cannot be "solved"; a patron cannot, for example, ask allies to fend entirely for themselves while also expecting them to spurn all alternative means of meeting their security needs and to acquiesce to all its foreign policy preferences. No matter how the patron chooses to manage its dilemma, whether by allowing or even encouraging allies to free-ride or by seeking greater cost-sharing, its policy choices are likely to be marked by some ambivalence.

That said, I expect its willingness to seek burden-sharing, and its success in securing it, to vary systematically. In the next section, I expound on the policy levers patrons can use to navigate the burden-sharing dilemma—levers that themselves stem from the assumptions I described above.

POLICY LEVERS TO NAVIGATE THE BURDEN-SHARING DILEMMA

In managing the burden-sharing dilemma, a patron faces two choices. The first is whether to solicit burden-sharing at all. Given the assumption that a patron is able to maintain greater leverage over allies that are more dependent, a patron may opt to permit and even encourage a degree of free-riding in order to render allies more dependent on its protection. In other words, a patron may take the approach of *selectively encouraging burden-sharing* to manage the risk of empowering allies to go their own way. Even in cases where allies have enormous military potential, a patron can maintain allied dependence by exploiting the time it would take allies to actually develop an independent military capability. Because of the difficulties and delays in scaling up domestic arms production, fielding, equipping, and training a

CHAPTER 1

large, competent force, and synergizing different complex military platforms by integrating them into doctrine, allies are likely to experience delays in converting their potential power into actual power.[21] During that interval, allies are likely to still be highly dependent on their patron's protection. A patron may thus elect to encourage allied free-riding in order to dissuade an ally from building up its military capabilities and, by the same token, keep it dependent on the patron's protection.

It is worth noting here that encouraging burden-sharing selectively is not necessarily the only way to mitigate allies' capability for independent action. A patron might also try to integrate allies' military forces with its own, whether via multinational blending of forces or through joint command, or to encourage allies to specialize in capabilities that limit their independence.[22] In practice, though, neither integration nor specialization can definitively solve the burden-sharing dilemma. Integration is neither permanent nor absolute. Even in the case of West Germany, whose military was more deeply integrated into and submerged within NATO than that of any other country, other members of the alliance were under no illusions that having West German military forces assigned to NATO without an independent command structure was a permanent, irreversible solution to weakening West German military capability—after all, the West Germans could have developed such an infrastructure over time.[23] Specialization likewise offers only a partial solution, as there is no single capability that can alone be denied to allies that would render them dependent on US protection. The best candidates are capabilities that allow for long-distance power projection, such as strategic airlift—indeed, as many observers note, this is an area where the capabilities of US partners are often quite deficient.[24] However, even allies lacking the capability for long-distance power projection may still be capable of self-defense or power projection on a more local scale.

Should a patron elect to encourage burden-sharing, the second choice it must make is how. Given the assumption that neither the patron nor its ally is ever able to know the other's intentions with absolute certainty, the ally may continue to fear that its patron will abandon it, even if the patron is providing considerable assurances of support. The patron may thus be able to exploit an ally's chronic fear of abandonment to persuade it to increase its burden-sharing efforts, deploying both assurances of support and threats of reducing its protection if the ally does not comply. Put another way, a patron does not necessarily have to withdraw its support altogether in order to offset the ally's temptation to view its protection as a substitute for its own defense. Instead, the patron can effectively use *conditional pressure*, combining assurances of continued protection if they do comply with threats of abandonment—whether troop withdrawals, limits on the amount of assistance, a delay in assistance, and so forth—if they don't.[25] Far from being at odds, then, assurances of support and coercive burden-sharing often go to-

16

gether, because the factors that drive the former may also make it easier for the patron to implement the latter.

Conditional pressure is difficult to implement in practice, as it requires combining signals that communicate opposing messages—simultaneously demonstrating interest in an ally's security while also expressing a willingness to abandon them. Nevertheless, combining threats and assurances is likely to make the patron's pressure more effective, as if it does not include assurances of protection alongside its threats of abandonment, allies have less incentive to comply overall.[26] Conditional pressure is also less risky than actually withdrawing protection. Actually withholding support, such as by withdrawing troops or making public statements distancing the patron from its commitment to an ally, can be perilous, both because allies are likely to search for other means of security if they do not receive sufficient security from the alliance and because adversaries are likely to perceive disunity as an opportunity to seek policy concessions.[27]

The extent of burden-sharing in alliances is thus shaped by whether a patron such as the United States wants to encourage burden-sharing, as well as whether its threat of abandonment is sufficiently potent to motivate allies to comply with its pressure. The following section addresses both the conditions under which the United States, as a patron, is more or less likely to seek greater burden-sharing from its allies, and the conditions under which it is more or less successful in doing so.

Alliance Control Theory II: Explaining Variation in Burden-Sharing Pressure

Alliance control theory identifies three factors that explain variation in the use and success of US burden-sharing pressure. The first is *allies' latent military power.* While the United States is unlikely to ask its smallest allies to make substantial military contributions, since they have less capacity to provide them, its largest allies may face similarly low levels of burden-sharing pressure for a different reason—because their capacity for self-reliance is sufficiently high that unilateral arming carries the risk that they will no longer need the alliance. The second is the *external threat environment.* A severe threat environment increases both the likelihood of US burden-sharing pressure, owing to the greater need for collective defense, and the likelihood that this pressure will succeed, owing to allies' greater dependence on US protection. The third factor is *patron resource constraints*—that is, the extent to which the United States faces constraints on the resources it can devote to its foreign commitments. The more constrained its resources, the more Washington will turn to allies to provide for their own defense, and the more likely it is that allies will fear abandonment.

CHAPTER 1

INDEPENDENT VARIABLE: ALLIES' LATENT MILITARY POWER

In my theory, allies' latent military power refers to the resources that could be converted into military power.[28] Latent military power stems from the ability to mobilize *manpower* and *materiel*.[29] As such, the most important indicators for latent military power include population and material wealth.[30] The commonly used Correlates of War Composite Index of National Capability (CINC), for example, includes population, iron and steel production, and energy consumption, though it also includes indicators of actual military power such as personnel and defense expenditures.[31] Michael Beckley argues in favor of an indicator of latent military power that multiplies aggregate GDP by GDP per capita, as the latter is an indicator of economic efficiency and thus how much of a country's total economic output is free for use after taking care of the domestic population's needs.[32] Therese Anders, Christopher Fariss, and Jonathan Markowitz similarly advocate for a measure of "surplus domestic product" (SDP) that subtracts from GDP the costs of providing the subsistence needs of the population, using the World Bank's three-dollars-a-day poverty threshold.[33]

For my purposes, I rely on two main indicators of latent military power: total population and surplus domestic product. Population shapes countries' manpower potential as well as the potential size of their economies. Surplus domestic product, much like GDP, provides a measure of the overall size of the economy and thus the aggregate material wealth that could be put toward military purposes. But unlike GDP, it has the advantage of considering the costs of providing for the population's subsistence needs, and thus it provides a better picture of resources that could actually be mobilized for military power. In any case, country rankings using SDP are similar to those using GDP, except with respect to countries with very low GDP per capita such as South Korea prior to the mid-1970s. The rankings are also similar using Beckley's measure of GDP multiplied by GDP per capita, though the latter arguably overweights GDP per capita since it leads to some relatively small but wealthy countries, being quite high in the global rankings during various periods.[34]

Latent military power shapes both the potential benefits and risks that an ally's burden-sharing contributions could present to an alliance. On the one hand, the benefits of military burden-sharing by richer, larger allies are greater than those of smaller, poorer allies, because the former have more potential to assume responsibility for their own defense and relieve the patron's burdens.[35] Potentially powerful allies are natural targets to which a patron can delegate burdens and responsibilities.[36] Weak allies, in contrast, are less able to contribute to their own or other states' defense, and their efforts to do so may be self-defeating. Because an ally with fewer resources can less easily afford to divert resources to defense, forcing it to do so may stunt its economic growth and foster resentment, both from the ally toward

18

the patron and from the ally's domestic audiences toward its incumbent government—all without ultimately producing significantly greater capabilities for the alliance.[37] Weak states frequently align with a stronger patron to avoid excessive military burdens, so demanding self-reliance removes their motivation for being in the partnership and risks friendly governments being replaced by hostile ones.[38] Indeed, one of the primary sources of bargaining leverage for weak states is the threat that they might collapse without their patron's support.[39] After the devastation of World War II, for example, US policymakers feared that friendly governments in Europe and East Asia might be replaced—whether by election or revolution—with ones more friendly to Moscow. As a result, the United States resorted to using foreign aid and investment to bolster the stability of friendly governments and reduce the appeal of left-wing parties. In Europe, this effort most notably took the form of the Marshall Plan, which provided upward of $10 billion (or more than $150 billion in 2022 dollars) to rebuild the region's economies.[40] For the same reason, US officials hesitated to demand military self-reliance before allies could recover.[41]

On the other hand, burden-sharing by larger, richer allies poses its own risks. The more powerful the ally, the more inherently capable it is of looking after its own defense and shedding its dependence on the patron. Allies with greater military potential can more easily pursue a nonaligned, autonomous foreign policy, whether by relying on their own military power or by aligning with other states. While they may not be able to defeat a great power by themselves, powerful allies may be able to deter attack because they can more credibly threaten to impose significant costs on an invader.[42] Larger and stronger allies also have more sizable internal markets and are likely to be less dependent on foreign trade—whether with their patron, another great power, or others.[43] They are thus better equipped to engage with adversaries on more semi-equal terms and are not as vulnerable to bullying or coercion which might otherwise make them reluctant to negotiate bilaterally or to proceed without the patron's protection. As such, they can more easily pursue neutrality without having to bandwagon or make asymmetric concessions.[44] Additionally, wealthy and conventionally powerful allies may have an easier time obtaining nuclear weapons, both because they have more resources to devote to the task and because they can more effectively deter preventive conventional attacks on their nuclear programs.[45] On the extreme end of the spectrum, such allies may even become sufficiently powerful that they can afford to effectively go their own way. France, for example, leveraged its position as not only one of the more powerful members of NATO but also one that possessed nuclear weapons, in order to establish autonomy from the United States, withdrawing from NATO's unified military command in 1966 and maintaining an option of "nonbelligerence" in the event of a NATO–Warsaw Pact conflict in Central Europe.[46] Even if an effectively self-sufficient ally chooses to remain in the

CHAPTER 1

alliance, the patron's ability to coerce it will be quite limited. Thus, a patron may counterintuitively be reluctant to encourage burden-sharing from the very allies that have the most potential to contribute.

The implications of burden-sharing by weaker and stronger allies that I have sketched out above suggest a nonlinear relationship between allies' military potential and the amount of the resources they devote to their own defense—one where both smaller allies and larger allies face relatively less burden-sharing pressure than those of more moderate size. In effect, a patron faces a Goldilocks problem when it comes to allies' latent military power. Smaller allies have little to contribute, so the patron has less incentive to seek burden-sharing from them. But as allies grow larger and more capable of standing on their own, the risks of burden-sharing begin to rise steeply, since allies who have more military power at their disposal may choose to direct it toward objectives that do not necessarily align with those of the patron—such as expanding or preserving a colonial empire, engaging in competition or coercion with nonshared adversaries, or behaving more aggressively toward mutual adversaries—or simply leave the alliance unilaterally. I would thus expect to see a greater level of burden-sharing pressure directed toward allies whose latent military power is "just right"— neither too small to make a difference for the alliance as a whole, nor so large that they have the potential to exit the alliance and fend for themselves. This points to the following hypothesis:

Hypothesis 1. A patron's willingness to encourage allies to shoulder more responsibility for their own defense is nonlinear depending on allies' latent military potential, with smaller and larger allies facing less pressure than moderate-sized allies.

INDEPENDENT VARIABLE: EXTERNAL THREAT ENVIRONMENT

When the level of shared threat is higher, the patron's interest in allied military contributions is likely to be higher as well because the need for collective defense capabilities is greater.[47] That is, when the alliance faces a powerful, revisionist adversary, the patron may have little choice but to encourage its allies to contribute more. This expectation is consistent with a balance-of-threat logic, which suggests that states are more likely to seek out partners with whom to share military burdens when they perceive a higher level of threat.[48]

Similarly, allies' perception of threat from shared adversaries is likely to increase their need for the patron's protection, which makes it less likely that they will go their own way even if they invest more in defense.[49] By contrast, allies who are not facing a high level of threat have more flexibility to refuse the patron's requests and even to pursue neutrality, and they are likely to have priorities that diverge from those of their partners, such as competing with rivals that their allies do not share.[50] New Zealand, for example, refused to allow US nuclear-armed submarines during the mid-1980s, even at the price of being expelled from the Australia-New Zealand-United States (ANZUS) alliance in 1986.[51] And much to the chagrin of the United States, Australia's rivalry with Indonesia during much of the Cold War absorbed resources and attention that could have otherwise been used to resist Communist expansion in Southeast Asia.[52]

Shared external threat is also likely to increase the success rate of US burden-sharing pressure, albeit unevenly. Because an external threat makes allies more dependent on the alliance and raises the costs of fighting without the patron's assistance, allies with a higher perception of external threat should be more susceptible to a patron's threats of abandonment.[53] At the same time, however, external threat is also likely to bind the patron to its allies, as the patron is by definition the most disproportionately powerful member of the alliance and its ability to pass the buck to its allies is limited.[54] When the patron perceives a high level of threat from an adversary, it has less incentive to remain aloof from its allies, lest it risk tempting the adversary to take its chances and attack a seemingly disunited alliance that does not have the patron's full commitment.[55] As a result, allies can effectively exploit the patron's inability to drive a hard bargain with them. Michael Handel captures this dynamic when he notes that during the Cold War, "the readiness on the part of the super powers to pay almost any price to keep their primacy and alliance systems intact create[d] a situation in which weak states could enjoy defense and protection while at the same time reducing their own defense expenditures."[56] In the aftermath of the Soviet invasion of Afghanistan, for example, US policymakers found it quite difficult to persuade NATO allies to increase their military spending because the US commitment to resisting Soviet expansion offered little reason for them to do so.[57] The result was stagnant NATO military spending.[58] By contrast, allies' abandonment fears are likely to be more severe when they suspect that their patron does not take an adversary as seriously as they do.[59] The concern voiced by many US Persian Gulf partners in the wake of the 2015 Joint Comprehensive Plan of Action with Iran is a case in point.[60]

The degree to which shared external threat increases allies' abandonment fears and, by extension, the success of patron burden-sharing pressure, depends on the balance between patron and ally perceptions of the threat (see figure 1.1). If the ally's perception of threat is higher and the patron's is lower, the patron's burden-sharing pressure is more likely to succeed. Conversely, if the patron's perception of threat is higher than the ally's, then the patron's burden-sharing pressure is less likely to succeed.

The challenge in making empirical predictions is that these two scenarios are likely to be correlated, so parsing the net effect of the threat environment (i.e., whose perception of threat is greater) is difficult. Many objective indicators of threat, such as the adversary's capabilities and behavior, do not vary between the ally and its patron, making their net effect theoretically

CHAPTER 1

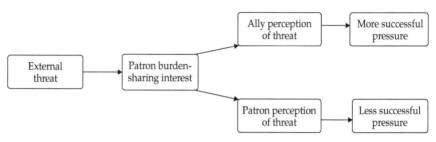

Figure 1.1. Causal mechanisms by which external threat shapes the likelihood and success of patron burden-sharing pressure.

indeterminate. While allies may come to different subjective conclusions about adversary intentions based on the same information, it is difficult to theorize ex ante why, as perceptions of adversary intentions are likely to depend on a variety of idiosyncratic, contingent factors such as leaders' personal assessments and ideology.[61] Ultimately, a theory of perception of intentions is beyond the scope of this book, and I am agnostic about the factors that drive differences in perceptions of adversary intentions; I simply expect that allies who share the patron's adversaries and perceive a higher level of threat from them are on average more likely to burden-share than those who do not share the patron's adversaries and perceive a lower level of threat.

One solution to these problems of theoretical indeterminacy and empirical inference is to focus on variation in allies' geography. Geography may explain variations in allies' susceptibility to threats of abandonment because proximity to a shared adversary varies across allies whereas the patron's position is constant. Allies geographically closer to shared adversaries can be expected to perceive the most threat and as such are more likely to respond to patron burden-sharing pressure. Focusing on variation in allies' geography by no means suggests that other indicators of threat are unimportant. Rather, because the net effects of such other indicators of threat are difficult to theorize ex ante and empirically test, exploiting variation in geography offers a clearer test of the effects of ally threat perception on the success of US burden-sharing pressure.

Allies who share a land border with adversaries are uniquely vulnerable since they lack the buffer of either a body of water or another country. Projecting power over water via amphibious or airborne assault is notoriously difficult, as doing so requires packing forces into a smaller number of ships or planes that are vulnerable to being destroyed en route, as well as investing in the production of not only the transports themselves, but also sufficient air and naval power to protect them. Land invasions, by contrast, involve forces that can more easily disperse and move on foot.[62] Allies who are separated from adversaries by a body of water are thus likely to have a lower perception of threat. In the same vein, having buffer states between themselves and an adversary is likely to make allies feel more secure.[63] If the buffer state is a neutral, then the adversary might be reluctant to attack. If the buffer state is an alliance member, then that state can serve as the point of forward defense and absorb the attack itself. In either case, having a buffer offers time for the ally to mobilize its own capabilities and for patron reinforcements to arrive. Allies bordering shared adversaries by land, by contrast, face a challenge: even if the likelihood of patron abandonment is very low, the costs of being abandoned are extremely high. In fact, even if the risk of abandonment is zero, they nevertheless will have to fend off the adversary until the patron's reinforcements arrive.

A great deal of research shows that contiguity is one of the strongest determinants of rivalry, conflict, and state death.[64] By the same logic, contiguity can be used to account for US success in burden-sharing pressure. During the Cold War, for example, vulnerable allies such as South Korea, Turkey, and West Germany tended to be quite susceptible to US burden-sharing pressure. Turkey, for one, hosted a substantial number of US forces, but nevertheless fielded one of the largest militaries in NATO.[65] US allies not directly proximate to the Communist bloc often found it easier to resist US pressure. Portugal, for example, contributed little to NATO for much of the 1950s through the 1970s, as it was more concerned with protecting its overseas empire.[66]

The preceding discussion thus suggests the following hypotheses:

Hypothesis 2a. A patron is more likely to encourage allies to shoulder more responsibility for their own defense when the level of shared external threat is higher.

Hypothesis 2b. A patron is more likely to succeed in encouraging allied burden-sharing among allies that perceive a greater level of threat from shared adversaries.

EMPIRICAL PREDICTIONS

As shown in table 1.1, combining the predicted effects of the previous two independent variables yields six ideal-type outcomes related to the use and success of patron burden-sharing pressure. The left half of the table denotes allies in more severe threat environments—those proximate to powerful shared adversaries. In general, these allies can be expected to face more US pressure for conventional military burden-sharing for two reasons: because they are essential for frontline defense and deterrence, and because their dependence on the alliance for protection makes it unlikely that becoming more capable will cause them to go their own way. This dependence also increases the chances that US pressure succeeds, as the consequences of being abandoned are greater for these allies.

As indicated from the top to the bottom of the table, the amount of pressure these allies face varies based on their latent military power. In the upper-left quadrant (high latent military power, high threat environment)

Table 1.1 Examples of each ideal-type burden-sharing outcome

		Threat environment	
		Less benign	*More benign*
Latent military power	**High**	**Cautious Success** Reluctance to encourage a powerful ally to arm itself is partially overcome by the need to compete with shared rivals.	**Grudging Cheap-Riding** Reluctance to encourage a powerful ally to arm itself coupled with more benign threat environment produces limited conventional burden- sharing, partially substituted by other contributions (economic, political).
	Moderate	**Favorable Bargaining** High patron interest in burden-sharing coupled with more severe threat environment produces substantial amounts of successful burden-sharing pressure.	**Unfavorable Bargaining** High patron interest in burden-sharing coupled with more benign threat environment produces moderate amounts of burden-sharing pressure with limited success.
	Low	**Cost Imposition** Ally's limited ability to make conventional contributions is balanced by need to deter adversary attack, leading to moderate amounts of successful burden-sharing pressure focused on making it difficult for adversaries to quickly invade and occupy.	**Benign Neglect** Little patron interest in conventional defense burden-sharing; focus instead is on other, especially nonmaterial forms of burden-sharing (e.g., basing).

Note: Each cell describes the empirical prediction for an ally's burden-sharing outcome, given each combination of the ally's latent military power (y-axis) and external threat (x-axis).

are "Cautious Success" cases. These are defined by the tension between a reluctance to encourage powerful allies to become more self-reliant and the desire to secure resources to compete with common adversaries. I would expect to see evidence that patrons considered the risks of burden-sharing, but ultimately elected to encourage moderate amounts of military contributions. At the same time, I would also expect to see patrons seek substitute contributions beyond enhancing defense capabilities, especially resource-intensive economic contributions such as foreign aid. Perhaps the most notable example here is the Federal Republic of Germany (FRG) during the Cold War. As I discuss in chapter 2, the United States ultimately backed West German rearmament, but did so in a limited way that reduced the likelihood of a revival of German militarism by subsuming German military power under NATO command and arming West Germany with US military equipment. It also funneled German contributions into areas like providing foreign aid to Greece as well as compensating Washington for the cost of stationing US forces on German territory.

In the center-left quadrant are "Favorable Bargaining" cases, characterized by allies with moderate latent military power but within a severe threat environment. Here I would expect maximal patron interest in burden-sharing without the reservations of the "Cautious Success" quadrant. I would also expect that this pressure will generally succeed, owing to these allies' greater fears of abandonment. Chapter 4 shows that the United States put enormous pressure on South Korea to become self-sufficient in defending against North Korea throughout the 1970s, in large part because its meteoric economic growth in the 1960s and 1970s rapidly made the country much richer.

Finally, in the bottom-left quadrants are "Cost Imposition" cases. Because these allies' capacity to meaningfully contribute to collective defense is limited, the patron's efforts to encourage contributions are likely to be limited. However, even though the chances of successful defense against a powerful, determined adversary are low, adversaries may be deterred by the threat of extended, costly conflict.[67] As a result, the patron is likely to encourage these allies to invest in capabilities that can allow them to impose costs on adversaries that would at the very least allow them to delay until reinforcements arrive. Estonia, for example, has pursued this strategy since Russia's annexation of Crimea in 2014. NATO stations only a single multinational battlegroup in the country and relies largely on the promise of follow-on reinforcements to arrest and roll back Russian advances while Estonian forces resist and harass Russian forces.[68]

The right half of the table includes allies in more permissive threat environments. In these cases, I would predict comparatively less US pressure for conventional defense contributions and more pressure for other forms of contributions, ranging from providing foreign aid to hosting military bases. In general, these allies' military contributions can be expected to lean heavily toward power projection in terms of both having military forces that can be

CHAPTER 1

deployed to assist frontline states in the event of conflict and offering rights of transit or facility use to other allies' military forces. The upper-right quadrant, "Grudging Cheap-Riding" (high latent military power, low threat environment), features the same level of ambivalence as the Cautious Success category but without the countervailing pressures of the threat environment. In these cases, I would predict that the patron's reluctance to seek allied self-reliance would be as strong if not stronger than its desire for cost-sharing, resulting in fairly modest conventional military burden-sharing pressure with limited success, as well as an attempt to funnel these allies' contributions toward nonmilitary means. In the center-right quadrant are "Unfavorable Bargaining" cases. In comparison to Grudging Cheap-Riding, I would expect to see higher patron interest in defense burden-sharing, but with similarly low rates of success.

Japan is the classic case of Grudging Cheap-Riding. As chapter 3 details, US policymakers have long been ambivalent about Japanese rearmament. Even in the early 1970s during the height of the Nixon Doctrine, which encouraged allies to assume responsibility for their own defense, US policymakers balked at the prospect of a self-sufficient Japan that no longer needed US protection. Australia, in contrast, frequently exhibited characteristics of an Unfavorable Bargaining case. While it made a number of contributions throughout the Cold War, contributing some forces to the Vietnam War and offering use of its territory and facilities for the transit and refueling of US vessels, its support was often fickle. US policymakers were frustrated that Australia committed only a few thousand forces to Vietnam, and they pressed it—with little success—to play a greater security role in countering Communist expansion in Southeast Asia.[69] In fact, in the early 1970s, Australia became one of the most vocal critics of US conduct in Vietnam, and its government was slow to condemn Australian maritime unions' ban on US shipping in 1973, which was instituted to protest the bombing of North Vietnam.[70]

Finally, in the bottom-right quadrant are "Benign Neglect" cases, which refer to allies who have little in the way of latent military power and are in fairly benign threat environments. As a result, the United States is likely to seek little in the way of conventional defense burden-sharing. Instead, these allies are likely to be asked to provide nonmaterial contributions like basing. Chapter 5 shows that Iceland effectively faced no pressure to provide contributions beyond basing, while New Zealand similarly made little military contribution aside from offering military access. Both countries frequently proved to be reluctant hosts: whereas Iceland leveraged the threat of eviction to extract foreign aid packages, New Zealand declined to host US nuclear submarines in the mid-1980s, which resulted in the United States suspending its obligations to New Zealand under the ANZUS alliance in 1986.[71]

INDEPENDENT VARIABLE: PATRON RESOURCE CONSTRAINTS

Allies' latent military potential and their external threat environment can explain variation in the use and success of US burden-sharing pressure among its allies.[72] A third variable can also explain this variation over time: the degree to which the United States faces constraints on its own resources. For a patron, the core benefit of allied burden-sharing is reducing its own costs. Therefore, it will naturally tend to seek contributions from allies when its own burdens become less tenable, in order to bring its obligations in line with its diminished resources. Great powers can do only as much as their resources allow, and attempting to maintain their current level of military might and foreign commitments during periods of reduced resources can run the risk of overextension and exhaustion from being stretched too thin—as well as invite predation from competitors.[73] It is during times of resource constraints that great powers are likely to be sensitive to the costs of overseas engagement and face trade-offs between spending on domestic priorities and upholding foreign military commitments.[74]

Resource constraints can be the result of objective material factors such as shrinking revenue or resources being devoted to other priorities, or of political constraints such as domestic pressure to reduce defense spending, withdraw military forces from abroad, or avoid military entanglements. The most significant sources of material constraints stem from costly wars abroad and the size and health of the patron's economy. War saps the manpower and financial resources a patron can devote to its allies' defense, both while the conflict is ongoing and in its immediate aftermath. Maintaining foreign commitments at existing levels thus may become less tenable due to budgetary and manpower limitations brought about by the loss of blood and treasure in foreign wars.[75] A patron is likely to be quite reluctant to intervene on allies' behalf while it is already militarily engaged elsewhere, and it will seek to recoup its costs and regather its strength after suffering losses and expending resources.[76]

A patron's ability to provide security in its alliances also depends on its domestic economy. Scholars have long viewed differential growth rates as central to the rise and fall of great powers.[77] The overall health of the patron's economy and its share of global economic output dictate the amount of revenue the patron can collect and use to fund foreign commitments. The smaller and more strained its economy, the more it will struggle to manage its alliances. Thus, its motivation for seeking allied burden-sharing is likely to be higher when its position in the balance of power is weaker, whether because its share of global economic output has declined or because it experiences negative economic conditions at home.[78] Moreover, wars and economic hardship are related. A growing body of scholarship on the economic consequences of war suggests that foreign wars and economic hardship frequently go hand

CHAPTER 1

in hand, with sustained foreign conflict triggering tax increases, cuts in spending elsewhere, ballooning deficits, and/or rising inflation, depending on how the war is financed.[79]

Domestic pressure for military retrenchment—whether in the form of removing troops from abroad, cutting military spending, or an unwillingness to use force abroad—likewise increases the need for allied burden-sharing as a substitute for the patron's own ability to provide security for the alliance. Such political constraints are likely to be partially downstream of material constraints. Domestic audiences' tolerance for expending resources on foreign commitments will be strained when these costs become too high or encroach on competing domestic priorities. A long line of research suggests that protracted, costly wars diminish domestic political support in the United States for foreign entanglements.[80] Domestic audiences—including the public and the US Congress—often become war weary and want to avoid becoming involved in yet another military entanglement so soon after the last. Additionally, the size and health of the patron's economy restricts its freedom of action. A smaller economy is likely to be forced into painful guns-versus-butter trade-offs in which domestic audiences may prioritize internal spending over spending on foreign commitments, while economic turmoil is likely to prompt domestic audiences to seek relief.[81]

To be sure, material constraints are by no means fully determinate of political constraints. Policymakers can insulate themselves from domestic accountability by financing war through borrowing and deficit spending rather than taxation, as well as by relying on volunteer forces, airpower, or unmanned capabilities.[82] Nevertheless, domestic support for retrenchment is likely to be correlated with the material factors that constrain the patron's resources and impose costs in blood and treasure, as described above.

Resource constraints also increase the likelihood that a patron will succeed in securing allied burden-sharing. The patron's threat of abandonment is inherently more credible when its capacity to uphold its commitments is diminished. In addition, the patron's resource constraints are likely to manifest in behaviors that raise allies' fears of abandonment. These include cuts to military readiness, reductions in its foreign-deployed military forces, efforts to seek détente with or accommodate adversaries in order to avoid overextension and reduce the risk of conflict, and a reluctance to use force and become entangled in conflicts on allies' behalf.[83] In terms of political constraints, domestic pressure to retrench and avoid armed conflict raises the possibility that domestic actors will force policymakers to renege on their commitments.[84] As I describe in chapters 2 to 4, these forces were on full display in the foreign policy of Richard Nixon, whose presidency saw the United States reducing defense spending, withdrawing some forces from abroad, and pursuing rapprochement with China and the Soviet Union.

Each of these dynamics is likely to make allies doubt the reliability of their patron's commitment to defend them. Shortages in manpower and equip-

28

ment, of course, raise questions about the patron's ability to meet allies' security concerns. A patron's efforts to seek détente with adversaries during a period of weakness are likely to generate fears that it might strike a bargain with those adversaries at the expense of allies.[85] And the patron's hesitancy to be involved in foreign conflicts and its desire to cut costs may provoke uncertainty among allies about the amount of assistance it would provide to them in the event that they were attacked—if it actually came to their defense at all. In the case of South Korea, for example, the United States proved reluctant to respond to a series of North Korean provocations during the late 1960s, including an assassination attempt on the South Korean president and the shooting down of a US aircraft. This was in large part because the Vietnam War constrained the United States' ability and willingness to escalate tensions on the Korean Peninsula for fear of becoming involved in yet another conflict in the region—a development that unnerved the South Korean government.[86] Yet, precisely because of these fears of abandonment, a patron is more likely to succeed in getting allies to enhance their own military capabilities. Pressure from Congress to withdraw US forces from Europe during the late 1960s and early 1970s, for instance, gave US officials leverage to encourage NATO allies to increase their defense spending.[87]

The discussion above leads to the following hypothesis:

> **Hypothesis 3.** A patron is more likely to encourage allies to shoulder more responsibility for their own defense, and more likely to succeed in doing so, when it faces constraints on the resources it can devote to its foreign commitments.

Alternative Explanations

In testing my hypotheses, I pit them against three families of competing explanations: the logic of public goods; the effects of US signals of support, especially US troop deployments; and allies' domestic politics.

PUBLIC GOODS THEORY AND THE LOGIC OF ASYMMETRIC ALLIANCES

One family of explanations expects alliance burden-sharing to be directly proportional to allies' relative power. Mancur Olson and Richard Zeckhauser's economic theory of alliances, for example, argues that larger allies devote disproportionately more of their resources to the alliance, as alliance deterrence is akin to a public good from which the larger members derive the most benefit and to which they are capable of making decisive contributions.[88] Similarly, James Morrow's theory of asymmetric alliances argues that alliances between great powers and smaller powers are defined by an

CHAPTER 1

asymmetric exchange of goods; the more unequal the power balance, the more asymmetric the relationship.[89] Stronger allies need less security from the alliance, provide more security for the alliance, and give up less autonomy, whereas weaker allies need more security, provide little security themselves, and forfeit a large amount of autonomy.

My theory, by contrast, predicts a nonlinear relationship between allies' latent military power and their burden-sharing expectations. Larger allies will face less burden-sharing pressure and spend less on defense than the abovementioned theories suggest, since patrons may suppress allies' capacity to provide for their own security for the sake of forestalling their ability to reclaim foreign policy autonomy. In other words, because allies with greater latent military power are more capable of becoming self-reliant, patrons are likely to seek to constrain their independence.

US SIGNALS OF SUPPORT

A number of scholars argue that signals of support encourage allies to undercontribute to their own defense.[90] By this logic, US allies contribute less to alliances when they are recipients of US signals of support, particularly foreign deployments of US military forces, which have long been considered among the strongest signals of commitment because of the lives they put at risk and the combat power they make available on allies' behalf.[91] My theory, however, suggests that the United States is in some cases willing and able to make its protection conditional on allied burden-sharing regardless of how many troops it has deployed to an ally's territory. Signals of support like troop deployments are not fixed determinants of burden-sharing; rather, the United States can use the threat of withdrawing them for coercive leverage.[92] The credibility of its threats is shaped by ex ante factors, which, in my theory, are allies' perception of threat and constraints on US resources.

ALLIED DOMESTIC POLITICS

Allies' domestic politics may create conditions that are more or less favorable for burden-sharing. There are several generalizable factors that merit particularly close attention. The first is allies' economic conditions. Allies facing economic hardship, such as a recession or budgetary crisis, may be less capable of devoting resources to defense and less susceptible to US burden-sharing pressure. The second is the personal characteristics of allied state leaders. As Matthew Fuhrmann argues, leaders with significant prior executive-level business experience might be less likely to burden-share owing to their greater tendency toward self-interested behavior, concern for material costs and benefits, and feelings of power and control over events in their own lives.[93] The third factor is the political ideology of allies' governing parties and coalitions. A great deal of research suggests that left-wing parties have more dovish foreign policy preferences than right-wing parties. Thus, allies that have left-wing governments may be more likely to make concessions to adversaries while also spending less on defense and, as such, may be less likely to contribute less to burden-sharing.[94]

One might expect the impact of allies' political ideology to have been particularly significant during the Cold War. During this period, left-wing governments would presumably have been more prone to seeking détente with the Soviet Union due to their comparatively more compatible governing ideologies, as well as more broadly skeptical of the need for allying with Washington. Left-wing governments might also have perceived a lower degree of threat from the Communist bloc, and so have been less dependent on the United States and less opposed to rapprochement with the Soviet Union.[95] Consequently, one might expect that the United States would have been more likely to avoid seeking burden-sharing from allies with left-wing governments owing to the greater risk of alienating them. Those governments would also have been less likely to give in to US pressure.[96]

A final example of how allied domestic politics may affect the use and success of US burden-sharing pressure is unique to Germany and Japan. Constructivist scholars have argued that Germany and Japan developed cultures of antimilitarism due to their experiences in World War II. In this telling, both countries have been reluctant to rearm and use their military forces for anything but self-defense, out of fear of granting their militaries influence in domestic politics and out of a desire to avoid repeating the mistakes of the past and antagonizing their neighbors.[97] This line of argument would thus predict that Germany and Japan would be relatively impervious to US burden-sharing pressure due to their inherent reluctance to develop larger military establishments and use force.

Testing the Argument

I evaluate my theory using several qualitative case studies drawn from the history of US alliances. Qualitative evidence is especially valuable for understanding the use and success or failure of US burden-sharing pressure, since quantitative indicators of allied contributions do not prove whether and to what extent the United States actually approached allies on the subject of alliance burden-sharing. I investigate the causal mechanisms behind my hypotheses by process-tracing the decision-making calculus driving both the level of US burden-sharing pressure and allies' willingness to contribute more or less. Drawing on declassified US government documents as well as secondary historical and contemporary observer texts, I examine US burden-sharing pressure on the FRG, Japan, and South Korea from the mid-1960s through the mid-1970s, as well as Iceland during the 1950s.

CHAPTER 1

These cases are ideal for tracing the effects of my theory's key independent variables, because the within- and between-case comparisons show significant variations in these independent variables.[98] West Germany and Japan were two of the United States' most powerful allies, consistently ranking in the top three of US allies in terms of GDP, surplus domestic product, and population for much of the 1960s and 1970s. Thus they posed comparatively more credible threats to exit the alliance, and I would expect to see evidence that the United States feared empowering them to go their own way.

South Korea ranked near the middle in terms of population but toward the bottom in terms of GDP and surplus domestic product. It was also among the poorest states in the world by GDP per capita during the early 1960s, though its rapid economic growth during the 1960s and 1970s brought its surplus domestic product closer to the world average (see figure 1.2). I would expect South Korea and West Germany to have been comparatively more vulnerable to US burden-sharing pressure than Japan because of their direct contiguity to North Korea and the Soviet Union, respectively.

In the language of my theory, West Germany and Japan represent Cautious Success (high latent military power, less benign threat environment) and Grudging Cheap-Riding (high latent military power, more benign threat environment) cases, respectively, whereas South Korea shifted from a Cost Imposition (low latent military power, less benign threat environment) to a Favorable Bargaining (moderate latent military power, less benign threat environment) case between the early 1960s and the late 1970s. On net, then, I would expect to see among these three cases the greatest level of burden-sharing pressure directed toward South Korea (during the 1970s) and the least toward Japan, with West Germany in between them.

These cases additionally feature within-case variation on US resource constraints. The costs of the Vietnam War strained US military resources and led to increasing retrenchment pressure from the US Congress, exemplified in the amendments and resolutions sponsored by Senate Majority Leader Mike Mansfield. The result was increased uncertainty about the credibility of the US commitment, and policymakers used congressional pressure as a lever to extract allied burden-sharing.

Iceland stands apart from the other three cases because as a Benign Neglect case (low latent military power, more benign threat environment), it is effectively a "null" case, where I would predict little US burden-sharing pressure coupled with Iceland being reluctant to make any contributions. Iceland ranked last or near-last among US allies in population, SDP, and GDP. Thus, it provided no military contributions beyond base access, which it offered somewhat grudgingly owing to its comparatively low perception of threat. While there is little variation over time to explain, I include it as a short case study to illustrate the challenges the United States faced in securing access to its base at Iceland's Keflavik Airport.

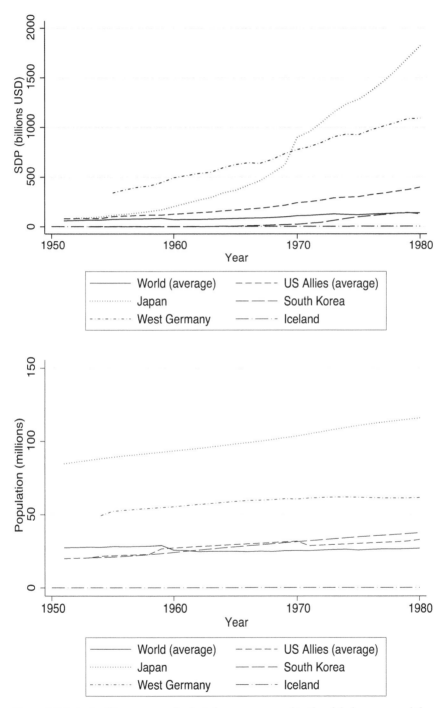

Figure 1.2. Latent military power of selected cases compared to the global average and the average of US allies. Data are from Gleditsch 2002.

CHAPTER 1

These cases also attempt to hold some important factors constant. All four countries hosted a substantial US troop presence, with West Germany, Japan, and South Korea hosting the most US foreign deployed forces among US allies and Iceland having the most on a per capita basis (with the other three cases ranking second through fourth). This similarity allows me to demonstrate that US willingness and ability to encourage burden-sharing varied enormously across these cases despite all of them hosting a substantial US troop presence. All four countries are also located near geostrategically valuable waterways.[99] Furthermore, by comparing cases that took place during a period of bipolarity over a similar time period, I am able to roughly hold the overall threat environment constant in terms of the aggregate balance of power. While the threat environments of allies in East Asia and Europe differed insofar as they were proximate to different Soviet allies—NATO contended with the Warsaw Pact, Japan and South Korea with China and North Korea—the common denominator was the Soviet Union, which, as one of two superpowers, loomed large as the ultimate source of threat in both regions.[100] Thus, although local conditions in each region shaped perceptions of threat, both regions faced a common overarching adversary.[101]

Finally, these cases also feature extreme values on many of my independent variables. Such cases are useful for tracing the logic of my hypotheses because they are the cases in which one would expect the theory's causal mechanisms to operate the most strongly.[102] West Germany and Japan had large economies and populations, and thus greater capacity for self-help, while Iceland had little military capacity by virtue of its extremely small size. West Germany and South Korea also have extreme values for external threat by virtue of their land border with the Communist bloc. Moreover, because the costs of the Vietnam War generated such intense pressure on the United States' ability to sustain its commitments and deep domestic divisions over its role in the world, the Vietnam War period is ideal for investigating the effects of resource constraints and domestic retrenchment pressure on US burden-sharing pressure.

Each of the following four chapters presents one of the case studies described above. I begin with West Germany, then proceed through Japan, South Korea, and finally Iceland. My conclusion discusses how the explanatory power of this book's predictions compares with those of alternative explanations, as well as the findings' generalizability, avenues for future research, and theoretical and policy implications.

34

CHAPTER 2

"A Legitimate Role in the Defense of the Alliance, but on a Leash"

West German Burden-Sharing, 1961–1974

West Germany's position was among the most precarious of any US ally throughout the Cold War.[1] The FRG not only was on the front line of the NATO border with the Warsaw Pact, but also was a country divided, with a quarter of the German population residing in the Soviet satellite state of East Germany. What made the status of Germany even more sensitive to its neighbors and to the United States was both the history of German militarism in the twentieth century and the reality of latent German power. West Germany had the largest population in NATO outside the United States, and by 1960 its per capita GDP had effectively caught up with Britain's.[2]

Thus, US officials were faced with a set of dilemmas. On the one hand, NATO officials recognized that the defense of Western Europe required a strong, willing partner that could make real contributions to its own security and that of NATO. The US embassy in Bonn described the FRG as "the fulcrum of the European balance of power," while the National Security Council's 1953 policy statement on West Germany (NSC 160/1) similarly argued that as "potentially the strongest continental European power west of the USSR . . . its reliable cooperation with other free European nations is indispensable for a strong and stable Europe," and recommended harnessing German power for NATO.[3] But on the other hand, Washington and the rest of NATO feared letting German power loose and allowing the FRG to become independent of the alliance. There was little guarantee that a strong, assertive West Germany would be a dependable and accommodating US ally, or even that it would not become a menace to the Continent. NATO, then, offered a route to redirecting German power away from expansionism; as a National Intelligence Estimate (NIE) put it in 1969: "The Alliance provides security for West Germany against the USSR, while relieving the anxieties Western Europe would have about independent German military power."[4]

CHAPTER 2

Within this context, Washington, NATO, and Bonn played a delicate balancing act when it came to German burden-sharing. By the early 1950s, the reality of the Cold War was such that the NATO alliance could no longer afford to exclude its potentially second-most powerful member. Thus, the NATO members grudgingly accepted the creation of the West German Bundeswehr, ended their occupation of the FRG, and welcomed it into NATO in 1954. Nevertheless, West Germany faced limits on the size of its forces and the types of weapons it could produce and possess, and its military units were integrated into NATO command.[5] Moreover, Washington stationed more than 200,000 US forces on West German territory, with large troop presences from other NATO members as well to reassure the FRG that the alliance would defend it.

In the decades that followed, the contours of FRG burden-sharing varied, but the basic policy objective—simultaneously harnessing German power yet constraining it—remained ever present. During the 1960s, burden-sharing debates with the United States were dominated by the completion of German rearmament and the costs of the US military presence in Europe, with Washington requesting that Bonn purchase US military equipment to offset the balance of payments deficit that was depleting US gold reserves. Nevertheless, although the United States favored increasing West German burden-sharing to reduce its own costs—and indeed often accomplished it—its enthusiasm was tempered by the fear that a more powerful, self-reliant West Germany would be more difficult to control. The early 1970s saw a relaxation of tensions with the Soviet Union, but temporary reduction in threat perception was offset by pressure from the United States, which sought to encourage greater allied self-reliance in the wake of the Vietnam War and a sustained congressional effort to force US troop withdrawals from Europe. As a result, West German military spending increased markedly as Bonn sought to mollify US criticism and reduce pressure for troop withdrawals.

Empirical Predictions

As a case of Cautious Success, my theory would predict fairly high levels of FRG burden- sharing (see table 2.1). Although US officials had good reason to be wary of West Germany becoming too self-reliant, this fear should have been partially offset by the need for collective defense against the Soviet Union. Moreover, the FRG's proximity to the center of Soviet military power should have also given the United States a significant amount of leverage over it. During the late 1960s and early 1970s, in turn, I would expect to see evidence that the United States promoted burden-sharing due to the costs of the Vietnam War, its diminishing economic position, and accompanying domestic isolationism. Correspondingly, I would expect these efforts to have

36

"A LEGITIMATE ROLE IN THE DEFENSE OF THE ALLIANCE"

Table 2.1 West Germany's scores on the independent variables

Latent military potential	External threat	US resource constraints	Prediction
High	High	High in late 1960s and early 1970s due to the Vietnam War	Fairly high interest in FRG conventional force improvements throughout, especially in the early 1960s and early 1970s. US desire for burden-sharing partially offset by desire to constrain FRG freedom of action. US burden-sharing pressure achieves a good deal of success.

been relatively successful, facilitated as they were by congressional pressure within the United States calling for reducing the US footprint in Europe and forcing allies to increase their share of the alliance's defense burden.

Evidence from the case largely bears these predictions out, while rival theories' expectations are partially supported, at best. Despite hosting the largest number of foreign-based US military forces of any ally, the FRG spent a sizable amount on defense as a percentage of GDP. While this is in principle consistent with the economic theory of alliances—which expects larger allies to contribute more because they can decisively impact the balance of power—the evidence instead shows that FRG burden-sharing was more the product of US coercion coupled with FRG perceptions of threat. Moreover, the period of maximal left-wing influence in West German politics— Willy Brandt's tenure as chancellor from 1969 to 1974—was also one in which FRG defense spending rose sharply in response to US pressure and its fear of abandonment, contrary to the expectations of domestical political explanations.

Strategic Context

The primary strategic challenge facing NATO, and particularly the FRG owing to its geographic position, was the threat of Soviet military power in both conventional forces, where Soviet bloc capabilities were believed to exceed those of NATO, and nuclear weapons, where the United States started with a significant advantage that eroded over time. Throughout the 1960s and early 1970s, the Soviet Union maintained around 3 to 3.5 million armed forces. This included an army of around two million, of which about two-thirds were stationed in Europe (see table 2.2).

Disagreements over the proper balance between emphasizing conventional and nuclear forces, in turn, were a perpetual source of tension between

CHAPTER 2

Table 2.2 Soviet military power, 1963–1975

Year	Total manpower	Total ground forces	Divisions in Eastern Europe	Divisions in European USSR
1963	3.3 million	2–2.3 million (150 divisions)	75	26
1965	3.15 million	2 million (140 divisions)	75	26
1968	3.2 million	2 million (140 divisions)	63	26
1970	3.3 million	2 million (157 divisions)	60	31
1973	3.4 million	2 million (164 divisions)	60	31
1975	3.6 million	1.8 million (166 divisions)	63	31

Source: International Institute for Strategic Studies, *The Military Balance*, vols. 1963, 1965, 1968, 1970, 1973, 1975, 1980.

the United States and European NATO members. European officials regarded a conventional defense of Europe as expensive and likely to be ultimately fruitless. Moreover, they feared that a conventional military buildup would simply make it easier for the United States to avoid using its nuclear weapons on their behalf, signal to the Soviet Union that NATO was reluctant to use nuclear weapons in the first place, and ultimately increase the likelihood of a destructive war that would be fought on their territory.[6] As a result, they preferred to rely on the threat of nuclear retaliation, and many of them sought a nuclear option of their own. Britain and France obtained their own nuclear arsenals in the late 1950s and early 1960s, and West Germany explored a similar option while also seeking to establish a NATO nuclear stockpile that it could access.[7]

Initially, US assessments did not radically depart from this prevailing European view. During the 1950s, the overwhelming US nuclear advantage made relying on the threat of nuclear retaliation attractive, as exemplified in President Dwight Eisenhower's "New Look" approach to defense that viewed nuclear weapons as a source of deterrence cheaper than conventional forces. But the United States was still reluctant to abandon conventional options, as US officials regarded conventional forces as important for deterring limited provocations and quick land grabs and delaying a Soviet invasion long enough for the threat of nuclear escalation to end a conflict.[8] In particular, Eisenhower wanted Europe to assume responsibility for the alliance's conventional defense so that Washington could withdraw the bulk of its forces from the Continent.[9] Eisenhower used the threat of troop with-

38

drawals to (unsuccessfully) encourage the creation of a European Defense Community, and he and his predecessor Harry Truman made West German rearmament a precondition for the US troop presence in Europe.[10] By the late 1950s, the Soviet Union had developed thermonuclear weapons and appeared capable of inflicting unacceptable damage on the United States even after absorbing a nuclear first strike. As a result, Eisenhower and his successors began putting more emphasis on the importance of conventional forces to raise the threshold at which nuclear use would be required and thus spare the United States from devastation. Correspondingly, they put enormous pressure on Europe to increase their conventional forces in the late 1950s and early 1960s.[11]

This disagreement about the desirability of conventional buildups meant that if Washington wanted its allies to expand their conventional forces, it had to pressure them—and, indeed, it did so repeatedly. This is not to suggest that European NATO members were uninterested in conventional forces. West Germany, in particular, because it was so exposed geographically, saw conventional forces as important to blunting a Soviet attack and reducing the speed at which German territory would be lost—especially since the use of nuclear weapons on the battlefield was likely to decimate the German population.[12] But European desires for conventional capabilities were nevertheless exceeded by Washington's. Many European policymakers, including in West Germany, favored having access to nuclear weapons to avoid both being left at the mercy of the US arsenal and having to fight a devastating, expensive conventional war.[13]

West German burden-sharing posed special challenges. President Harry Truman cautioned that permitting German rearmament might repeat the post–World War I mistake of allowing Germany to keep an independent military. The Korean War had transformed US and allied perceptions of the threat posed by the Soviet Union, which in turn shifted the US consensus in favor of encouraging a German military contribution. Nevertheless, US officials were unwilling to accept an independent, maximally sized and equipped West German military that could, as Truman's secretary of state Dean Acheson put it, "act as the balance of power in Europe," playing the Soviet Union and United States against each other and acting as a power center in its own right.[14] Instead, the Truman and Eisenhower administrations pressed for the creation of a unified European force in which German units would be embedded without an independent command structure of their own.[15] West German leadership held out on accepting the arrangement in an attempt to bargain for the formal end to Allied occupation and equal political status for the other members of NATO, and the proposed European Defense Community ultimately foundered on opposition from France. Nevertheless, the allies settled on a similar solution through NATO, with German forces being assigned to integrated NATO command.[16]

CHAPTER 2

Dilemmas of German Rearmament, 1961–1963

When the Kennedy administration assumed office, NATO had fallen short of the goals set in the previous decade for a conventional force, having only twenty-two full divisions (including Washington's six) in Germany out of a planned thirty. The only bright spot in this disappointing trend was West Germany, which accounted for the majority of European divisions in the country.[17] The initial German plan was to create a 500,000-soldier military, which would be larger than those of Belgium and the Netherlands, similar in size to Italy's, and smaller than Britain's and France's—and on the low end of all of those as a percentage of population.[18] Progress in German rearmament had stalled, in part because of FRG officials' misgivings about a purely conventional defense for the country and their efforts to procure "dual-use" military technologies (e.g., bombers, artillery, missiles) that could allow them to make use of a NATO nuclear stockpile.[19] By 1960, less than 300,000 of the original manpower target had been met.[20] Nevertheless, West Germany's contributions dwarfed those of other members during the period. Britain, for one, actively cut both its overall conventional forces and those stationed in Central Europe, while France diverted large numbers of forces to North Africa, and Belgium and the Netherlands downsized their forces in Central Europe.[21] The end result was that Germany was an outlier not in terms of its military's size, but in terms of its actual contribution to NATO, as all of its forces were committed to frontline defense. By contrast, those of other Western European partners were often further afield— especially in the cases of allies like France, Portugal, and the United Kingdom, which maintained sizable overseas empires.

As part of their broader effort to move NATO in the direction of a "flexible response" posture that would lean less on nuclear weapons and more on conventional forces, Kennedy and his advisers were determined to persuade European members to increase their military contributions.[22] Several factors motivated the Kennedy administration's emphasis on conventional forces. The first was the continuing threat posed by the Soviet Union, especially in light of the extended Berlin Crisis of 1958 to 1962. Over the course of several years, Premier Nikita Khrushchev made a series of ultimatums that NATO members would have to withdraw their presence from West Berlin, and he threatened to close off access to the city, culminating in attempts to block Western access and the construction of the Berlin Wall beginning in 1961. The crisis convinced Kennedy of the need for greater conventional options to resist Soviet aggression, and his administration allocated funds to increase its presence in Europe (albeit temporarily) and called on European NATO members to do the same.[23]

Second, the United States faced a balance of payments deficit that threatened to undermine the US dollar and cause a currency crisis. Under the Bret-

40

ton Woods monetary system established in 1944, the US dollar served as the reserve currency for much of the global banking system and was directly convertible to gold at $35/ounce. The expenses Washington incurred as a result of its large overseas presence, however, produced an outflow of dollars from the United States that threatened its ability to continue backing up the dollar with gold. This deficit was tolerable only as long as those who held dollar reserves did not create a "run" on gold by cashing in their holdings, at which point confidence in the dollar, and in turn its value, would plummet.[24] Owing in large part to their restrictions on US imports and the massive US military presence on the Continent, the European members of NATO were responsible for a substantial share of the US balance of payments deficit. By the time Kennedy took office, this deficit had reached a point where foreign dollar holders were beginning to exchange their reserves for gold because of the sheer amount of dollars in foreign hands, putting pressure on US gold stocks.[25] His administration, as well as that of his successor Lyndon Johnson, made reducing this deficit a top priority, which meant that a NATO conventional buildup would have to come from Europe, not Washington.

Third, impending nuclear parity with the Soviet Union meant that nuclear weapons would almost surely devastate US territory, which weakened the deterrent value of threatening nuclear retaliation. Indeed, even the use of smaller-yield nuclear weapons on the battlefield became less attractive as the Soviets developed their own tactical nuclear options. The Kennedy administration thus sought more conventional options—not so much to develop capabilities that could outright win a conventional war, but rather to guard against limited provocations and delay a Soviet advance so that diplomacy could prevail, and thus avoid either making empty threats of massive nuclear retaliation or inviting a nuclear strike on the US homeland.[26]

PREDICTIONS

While the Kennedy administration did not have to contend with a costly foreign war or economic turmoil at home, it did face a continuing and even elevated level of threat from the Soviet Union, along with a mounting balance of payments deficit that put pressure on US force commitments abroad. During the early 1960s, then, I would expect US policymakers to have solicited a moderate-to-high level of FRG force improvements, and that this pressure would have been fairly successful due to West Germany's vulnerability to the Warsaw Pact. However, I would also expect to see evidence that US officials did so with some reluctance due to the fear of resurgent German military power, and that they sought to channel West Germany's contributions in directions that constrained its freedom of action. As table 2.3 notes, these predictions are largely borne out. The Kennedy administration successfully pushed the FRG closer to its proposed rearmament. However, it

CHAPTER 2

Table 2.3 Predictions for US burden-sharing pressure toward West Germany, 1961–1963

Latent military potential	External threat	US resource constraints	Prediction	Outcome
High	High	Lower	Fairly high interest in FRG conventional force improvements, but also interest in burden-sharing schemes that limit FRG freedom of action. US burden-sharing pressure achieves a good deal of success.	US pressure focused on persuading the FRG to purchase US military equipment to rearm, with substantial success.

attempted to balance its need for German contributions and balance of payments relief with its desire for political control by offering assurances about US troop levels, keeping the Bundeswehr under NATO command, and compelling the FRG to purchase US military equipment, further binding Bonn to Washington.

US BURDEN-SHARING PRESSURE: BALANCING CONTROL
AND COST-SHARING

US burden-sharing pressure, in turn, had two prongs. The first focused on compelling the FRG to continue its rearmament. In this regard, the Kennedy administration achieved a good deal of success. In response to US pressure, the FRG proceeded with a massive military buildup in the early 1960s, with the West German military rising from 300,000 service members to nearly 450,000 between 1960 and 1964, and its military spending increasing by almost a full percentage point of GDP during this same period (see figures 2.1 and 2.2). Its buildup vastly exceeded that of other NATO allies over the same period. Britain, for one, effectively ignored US pressure, while France openly criticized US ambitions for conventional force levels, refused to make more forces available for the defense of Germany, and ended universal military training for French citizens.[27]

At the same time, US policymakers were careful to avoid pushing the West Germans too far. In the words of an adviser, Kennedy "was very conscious of the possibility that given a few turns or twists of events, you could be headed back into another situation where Germany could again become a menace," while the US secretary-general of NATO Dirk Stikker pointed out in 1962 that "there was clearly a sense of the growing military strength of the Federal Republic and the beginnings of a wave of nationalism," noting warily that "even Chancellor Adenauer, the most European of the Germans, had recently re-

42

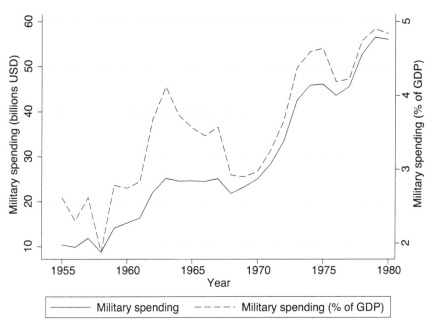

Figure 2.1. West German military spending (constant 2005 US dollars), 1955–1980. Military spending data are from Version 5.0 of the Correlates of War's National Material Capabilities Dataset (Singer 1987) and GDP data (purchasing power parity) are from Gleditsch 2002. Figure adapted from Blankenship 2021 with permission from *Security Studies*.

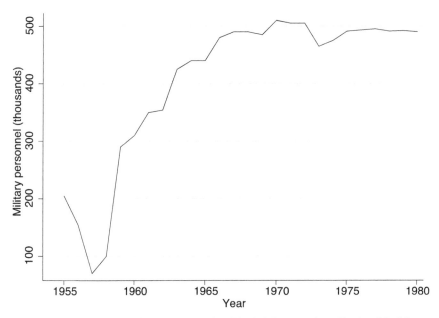

Figure 2.2. West German military personnel, 1955–1980. Data are from Version 5.0 of the Correlates of War's National Material Capabilities Dataset (Singer 1987).

CHAPTER 2

ferred with evident pride to Germany as the second strongest member of NATO."[28] The State Department similarly concluded that the FRG's latent military power meant that it had the "capacity to embark on a potentially disastrous independence in foreign policy."[29] US officials who opposed troop withdrawals from Europe did so on the grounds that the US presence tied the Germans to NATO, and that reducing troop levels would encourage the FRG to pursue a more independent course that leaned more heavily on France and toward unilateral rapprochement with the Soviet Union, and it might even be tempted to seek a grand bargain in which German officials traded away NATO membership in exchange for German unification.[30]

Additionally, US policymakers feared that overly emphasizing conventional weapons and seeking a drastically expanded FRG military contribution would encourage it to seek self-reliance on its own terms—including by obtaining nuclear weapons. For this reason, US officials paired their conventional burden-sharing pressure with nuclear assurances.[31] Because the growing Soviet nuclear arsenal called into question the credibility of US extended deterrence, many members of NATO—with the FRG front of the line—clamored for a nuclear-sharing scheme that could give Europe a say in the use of the nuclear weapons that were so central to their fates. As a result, the FRG was the primary audience of a years-long US and NATO campaign to create a nuclear-sharing scheme for the alliance. Most notably, Kennedy proposed a Multilateral Force (MLF), first floated in the closing days of Dwight Eisenhower's presidency, in which the NATO alliance would have access to a collective pool of sea-based nuclear weapons on vessels controlled by multinational crews; at the same time, he stressed that the MLF would be a complement to, not a substitute for, conventional forces.[32] The primary motivation for the MLF was to discourage other NATO allies—and especially the FRG—from obtaining independent nuclear arsenals.[33] While the MLF ultimately never came to fruition, owing in part to opposition from the Soviet Union, Britain, and France, it was replaced with the NATO Nuclear Planning Group, which instead of providing nuclear weapons to the alliance offered members input into NATO nuclear strategy.[34]

These concerns fed into the second prong of US burden-sharing in regard to the FRG. As the largest host of US forces by far, the FRG was a major drain on US balance of payments. To counteract its deficit, the United States negotiated a series of biannual "offset" agreements, beginning in 1961, in which the FRG agreed to purchase upward of $1 billion in US military equipment to staunch the outflow of US dollars. These offset agreements served to build up the West German military, but with US-manufactured arms to bind it to the United States and NATO more closely by making it dependent on US hardware. West German policymakers recognized this consequence and resented it.[35] From the US perspective, offset allowed for more FRG burden-sharing but limited domestic arms production and, critically, reduced the need for West German manpower by making the US presence more sustain-

44

able. Moreover, the West German military was tightly integrated into NATO to reduce the dangers of FRG burden-sharing. All of its military forces were under NATO command, and the country lacked an independent general staff that would have allowed it to operate independently outside NATO.[36]

US pressure was frequently accompanied by threats of troop withdrawals. Kennedy administration officials made it clear to FRG leaders that the continued presence of US forces would be strongly influenced by West German burden-sharing.[37] On several occasions, West German officials indicated they faced difficulties in meeting the full agreed offset values, and each time, their pleas were met with a firm line. In late 1962, for example, Kennedy warned Adenauer of "disastrous consequences" if the FRG did not follow through on its offset pledges.[38] Early the following year, in response to signals that the FRG was hesitant to sign another offset agreement, Kennedy and his advisers pursued a campaign of burden-sharing pressure on the FRG and the rest of NATO that included threats of troop withdrawals.[39] While the sincerity of Kennedy's threats cannot be taken for granted, they were consistent with internal discussions. Kennedy directed that "we should get ready with actions to squeeze Europe." He argued that "we should be prepared to reduce quickly, if we so decided, our military forces in Germany" in order to cut costs and put pressure on the Europeans to do more for themselves, remarking, "We cannot continue to pay for the military protection of Europe while the NATO states are not paying their fair share and [are] living off the 'fat of the land.'"[40] Kennedy's secretary of defense Robert McNamara was the most consistent proponent of troop withdrawals. Throughout his tenure, McNamara repeatedly made it clear to West German officials that the US troop presence was contingent on offset purchases.[41] During a conversation with the FRG defense minister Kai Uwe von Hassel in the lead-up to the second offset agreement in 1963, McNamara bluntly stated that "America cannot carry this burden [of defense] if it couldn't reduce this deficit" via offset payments, warning that maintaining troop levels would be "simply impossible" otherwise.[42]

The success of US pressure had a great deal to do with West Germany's geography. Although FRG officials were skeptical that the defense of NATO could be based on anything but the threat of nuclear escalation, by virtue of the country's vulnerability and their desire to defend as far forward as possible to blunt a potential Soviet attack, they found it difficult to ignore US pressure and threats of troop withdrawals.[43] "The geographic position of the Federal Republic," as Defense Minister Franz Josef Strauss put it, made it "unthinkable" to ignore US pressure the way France did.[44] Indeed, Chancellor Konrad Adenauer and his successors explicitly pursued rearmament not only to hedge against the possibility of abandonment but also to curry favor with the United States and demonstrate the FRG's value as a loyal ally and thus discourage troop withdrawals.[45]

US policymakers recognized and were willing to exploit the FRG's vulnerable position. Secretary of State Dean Rusk, for example, cautioned the

CHAPTER 2

German ambassador in January 1963 that geography made it very dangerous for the FRG to risk defying the United States. That month, France effectively rose up in open revolt against the United States within NATO, vetoing Britain's admission into the European Economic Community and proposing a treaty of friendship with West Germany, which the Kennedy administration feared could be the precursor to an independent Franco-German bloc within NATO that might include nuclear cooperation. As a result, while internally admitting that the geography meant that "there's not much we can do about France," Kennedy intensely and successfully pressured the FRG to back away from the French partnership and insert a preamble into the treaty reaffirming the country's loyalty to NATO, wielding the threat that the FRG would have to choose "between its relationship with France and its ties with the rest of Europe and the US."[46] Moreover, the Berlin Crisis served as a reminder of the reality of the Soviet threat, rendering West German officials more amenable to conventional force improvements. Adenauer was loath to make concessions on access to the city, which was nominally the FRG's capital, but he nevertheless balked at the prospect of actually going to nuclear war over it. The FRG's dependence on US protection and Adenauer's fear that the United States might be willing to make concessions on Berlin, along with recognition of the need for conventional options as a first line of defense against limited provocations and faits accompli like those that occurred during the Berlin Crisis, contributed to a conventional buildup that exceeded those of other NATO members in the early 1960s.[47]

Kennedy's approach to FRG burden-sharing exemplifies the ambivalence that one would expect given the conflicting incentives it presented. On the one hand, Kennedy feared the implications of a fully remilitarized Germany, especially one armed with nuclear weapons. As a result, he and his administration reassured West German officials of their intentions to maintain US troop levels in Germany and their willingness to use nuclear weapons on behalf of Europe.[48] On the other hand, however, Kennedy used the threat of troop withdrawals to encourage the FRG to complete its rearmament plan, with a heavy reliance on procuring US military equipment to equip the Bundeswehr. Indeed, at around $500 million each year during the first half of the 1960s, offset purchases constituted nearly a quarter of the FRG defense budget.[49] Kennedy thus attempted to thread the needle in pursuit of what Undersecretary of State George Ball referred to as the goal of "giving the Germans a legitimate role in the defense of the Alliance, but 'on a leash.'"[50]

Rising Resource and Domestic Constraints, 1964–1968

Kennedy's assassination in November 1963, coupled with improved Soviet-US relations after the Cuban Missile Crisis in October 1962, slowed the pressure for NATO conventional force improvements.[51] After the end of the

46

Berlin Crisis and the physical separation of East and West Berlin, the Soviets would never severely threaten the status of West Berlin again, and the two superpowers cooperated on the issue of nuclear nonproliferation—largely in an effort to prevent West Germany's acquisition of nuclear weapons.[52] With the brief exception of the invasion of Czechoslovakia in 1968, there would be a nearly sixteen-year lull in NATO-Warsaw Pact hostilities.[53] As a result, most NATO members—including the FRG and United States—took an interest in pursuing détente with the Soviets, both to reduce the chances of war and to pursue areas of mutual gain like arms reductions and trade.[54]

Instead of coming from external threat, the primary sources of tension over burden-sharing during the Lyndon Johnson administration came from within the alliance. From 1965 to 1968 Washington's deteriorating balance of payments position, which was worsened by its dramatically increased military presence in Vietnam, put the US troop presence in Europe at risk and made West German burden-sharing—and especially its offset purchases— as important than ever. Mounting US costs in Vietnam, the general improvements in East-West relations, and resentment that NATO allies—who had long since recovered from World War II and now enjoyed high standards of living—were not assuming more of a role for their own defense led to sustained pressure from a large portion of Congress to withdraw US forces from Europe. At the same time, an economic slowdown in the FRG led the country to weigh defense cuts and seek an end to offset agreements. These pressures culminated in a nearly year-long crisis during 1966 and 1967, resulting in the dissolution of West German chancellor Ludwig Erhard's governing coalition over offset payments and a trilateral offset agreement between Britain, the United States, and West Germany.

PREDICTIONS

Because it faced a somewhat more benign threat environment owing to the end of the Berlin Crisis and the emergence of détente, I would expect the Johnson administration's interest in seeking FRG force improvements to be high but slightly less intense than the Kennedy administration's. This should have proved short lived, however, owing to the rising costs of the Vietnam War. Moreover, I would expect the Johnson administration to continue to emphasize offset agreements as a means to both arm the FRG and combat the United States' growing balance of payments deficit (see table 2.4).

VIETNAM AND CONGRESSIONAL PRESSURE
FOR TROOP WITHDRAWALS

The Vietnam War was fought in East Asia, but its ripple effects carried profound implications for Western Europe. The costs of Vietnam served to further increase the US balance of payments deficit and put pressure on US

CHAPTER 2

Table 2.4 Predictions for US burden-sharing pressure toward West Germany, 1964–1968

Latent military potential	External threat	US resource constraints	Prediction	Outcome
High	High, but lower than 1961–1963	Rising due to Vietnam War	Slightly lower interest in FRG conventional force improvements initially but increasing over time. Continued US interest in burden-sharing schemes that limit FRG freedom of action. US burden-sharing pressure achieves a good deal of success.	FRG rearmament completed, and purchases of US military equipment continued. FRG defense spending and offset purchases during 1966–1967 were less than hoped for due to economic and budgetary woes, but US pressure succeeded in preventing defense cuts.

gold stocks.[55] The war strained military manpower, and coupled with sluggish economic growth, rising inflation, and the mounting balance of payments deficit, it provided further impetus for troop withdrawals as a cost-saving measure to stem the outflow of US dollars.[56]

The war undermined congressional support for the US presence in Europe as well. The year 1966 saw the first major congressional resolution by Senate Majority Leader Mike Mansfield to cut US forces in Europe, which was followed by similar resolutions in 1967, 1969, and 1974, as well as by the Mansfield Amendments in 1971, 1973, and 1974.[57] Mansfield and other proponents of troop withdrawals, including Senate Foreign Relations Committee Chair William Fulbright, argued that the demands of Vietnam made stationing hundreds of thousands of troops in Europe unsustainable, and that the United States was no longer as economically preeminent as it had been following World War II, while US allies had grown rich under its protection. They sought to rein in the costs of US commitments and avoid another military entanglement and favored prioritizing domestic spending.[58]

As a result, NATO allies—including the FRG—increasingly doubted the reliability of US protection. West German officials feared that US commitments in East Asia put pressure on the resources it could devote to Europe and also gave it incentive to pursue accommodation with the Soviet Union. FRG policymakers likewise expressed alarm at the rising tide of pro-retrenchment, "neo-isolationist" sentiment in the US Congress.[59]

This posed challenges for US policymakers, who feared that the FRG might consider alternatives to relying on US protection—including closer relations with France and the Soviet Union, as well as unfettered rearmament that could include nuclear weapons acquisition. Reliance on France had always been a distant second-best option, as it could not offer the kind of protection the United States could.[60] But with the US commitment in doubt, the FRG's other options became increasingly attractive.[61] More generally, the Johnson administration feared that French behavior, particularly its withdrawal from NATO's military command in 1966, could represent a model that other NATO allies might follow.[62] The State Department cautioned that US withdrawal would likely push the Germans into the arms of the Soviet Union, which could ultimately deprive NATO of its second-most powerful member, and other policymakers began to increasingly come to the same conclusion.[63] Ambassador George McGhee, for one, worried that if the United States seemed on the verge of withdrawing troops, West Germany "would be forced to reorient its basic security policy," which "could take the form of . . . a 'go-it-alone' nationalism or efforts to accommodate itself to the Soviets."[64]

US fears became more pronounced as evidence mounted that the FRG was, in fact, "reexamining [its] relations to the United States and to NATO."[65] During a visit to Washington in September 1966, both Chancellor Ludwig Erhard and his foreign minister Gerhard Schroeder warned that the Americans might soon be facing a less friendly government that might reorient its foreign policy away from the United States if troop withdrawals appeared imminent and US officials pushed too hard on offset arrangements.[66] Schroeder told Rusk, "What was needed were some long-term assurances (like no reductions by 1970 or so) about maintaining levels."[67] Indeed, West German politicians skeptical of relying on Washington and more in favor an independent foreign policy—most notably the Gaullist faction within the Christian Democratic Party, as well as the Social Democrats—became more influential, and the governments that succeeded Erhard's in the late 1960s and 1970s explored outside options.[68] After Erhard's government fell in late 1966, the Social Democrats increased their share of power under Chancellor Kurt Kiesinger's "Grand Coalition" government in 1967, with Social Democrat Willy Brandt as foreign minister.[69] Many US officials feared that the FRG would shift its foreign policy under the new government, and Kiesinger's cabinet was indeed interested in exploring closer relations with France and rapprochement with the Eastern bloc.[70] Ambassador McGhee wrote to Rusk in November 1966 warning, "There is reason to think that Germany has reached a watershed in its postwar political development. In retrospect, it may well appear that the Erhard govt was the last [government] of the postwar era."[71]

US officials also feared that the FRG might be tempted to pursue a dramatically expanded campaign of military self-reliance. US policymakers continued to recoil at the prospect of a fully rearmed FRG and were wary of asking too much of it. Although Johnson was in favor of greater FRG burden-sharing, he expressed horror at the implications of Mansfield's push for massive withdrawals, remarking that it could lead the FRG toward the

CHAPTER 2

path of "complete rearmament," and he openly worried about the prospects of a return to German militarism.[72] Similarly, although West Germany did not pursue nuclear weapons acquisition during this period, FRG leaders—like Adenauer before them—implicitly linked potential nuclearization with concerns about US credibility, particularly as congressional pressure escalated, and used their concern about US reliability and the future of NATO to justify dragging their feet on signing the NPT.[73]

US BURDEN-SHARING PRESSURE AND THE BALANCE OF PAYMENTS CRISIS

The Johnson administration, then, faced a new iteration of a perennial problem: encouraging West German contributions while ensuring that the FRG remained attached to, and dependent on, the NATO alliance. As a result, US officials attempted to thread the needle by simultaneously assuring West Germany that Washington would not withdraw forces while also making these assurances conditional on West German burden-sharing, and especially on offset purchases. Johnson administration officials sought to mollify West German officials' fear that withdrawals were imminent "no matter what the Germans offered," assuring the FRG that there would be no unilateral withdrawal of US forces from Europe so long as offset payments continued.[74] Moreover, the United States increased military maneuvers in Central Europe and rotated two mechanized infantry brigades into West Germany.[75] The year 1969 saw the first of what became the annual Return of Forces to Germany (REFORGER) exercise, in which the United States surged two divisions into West Germany. The exercise served both a military function—training for an actual contingency in which rapid reinforcement would be necessary—and a political one: mitigating doubts about both Washington's ability to come to West Germany's defense as well as the seriousness with which it took this commitment.[76]

At the same time, US policymakers wielded threats of troop withdrawals to secure West German burden-sharing. The combination of reduced tensions with the Soviet Union, the mounting balance of payments deficit, and fear of a dramatically expanded Bundeswehr meant that the bulk of this pressure focused on offset purchases.[77] Briefing papers for Johnson's December 1963 meeting with Chancellor Ludwig Erhard stressed that it should be made clear that if the United States was to maintain its troop presence, it was an "absolute necessity" for the FRG to provide offset, and National Security Adviser McGeorge Bundy advised Johnson that the FRG "should be left in no doubt" that the continuation of US deployments in Germany was contingent on offset.[78] McNamara similarly told Erhard and Hassel in May 1964, during the negotiations over the 1965 to 1967 offset agreement, that the United States "just cannot continue to maintain forces in Germany without full offset payments"; in a subsequent meeting in May 1966 he again

50

threatened that forces would be withdrawn unless the full offset payments were received.[79] As a result, despite delays and foot-dragging, West Germany always delivered—albeit under duress.[80]

The domestic pressure US officials faced only bolstered their threats. Johnson pointed to voices in Congress and the public calling for reduced US presence and more allied burden-sharing in Europe, and he sought to use offset as a way to quell them.[81] He presented allied burden-sharing as a means of appeasing Congress, and his administration made it clear to FRG officials that without adequate cost-sharing, troop withdrawals were likely.[82]

In late 1966, the offset arrangement between Washington and Bonn came under enormous strain due to domestic pressure from both sides. The Johnson administration faced increasing pressure from Congress to reduce the costs of US overseas deployments, and the Vietnam War strained US manpower and spending. The FRG, meanwhile, faced its first recession in over a decade and a budgetary crisis that forced the Erhard government into painful fiscal trade-offs.[83] As a result, by late 1965 the FRG was behind in its offset payments, and Erhard's government made desperate appeals for a reprieve, culminating in his visit to Washington in September 1966 to plead his case. Johnson refused to give way, however; he continued to insist on offset as a condition for maintaining US troop levels and asked for plans to withdraw US forces from Europe.[84] Defense Secretary McNamara drew up plans to cover any shortfall in offset payments by withdrawing an estimated 50,000 US troops from Germany.[85] Others in the administration, such as Ambassador McGhee, opposed troop withdrawals on the grounds that it would lead the FRG to distance itself from the United States, undermine deterrence, and weaken the rest of NATO's confidence in the United States.[86] Johnson likewise had little inherent desire to withdraw troops, but in light of the pressure from Mansfield he saw little choice but to wield that threat.[87] In a phone conversation with McNamara that month, Johnson indicated his desire to put pressure on Erhard: "Looks like to me, we ought to take advantage of this opportunity to make him tell us that he cannot afford to have our troops there."[88] As a result, Erhard left empty-handed, pledging that the FRG would "do its best" to fulfill its offset agreement.[89] His government ultimately collapsed due to the budgetary shortfall and embarrassment following his failed visit.

In the months that followed Erhard's fall, the debate over the best course of action continued. Some, especially McNamara, favored making good on the threat of troop withdrawals. Others, especially officials in the State Department, cautioned that doing so would undermine faith in the United States and could result in the unraveling of NATO.[90] Johnson was caught in a dilemma; he recognized the risks that troop withdrawals entailed, but Congress forced his hand. In the end, Johnson stayed the course of insisting on offset and spurning major troop withdrawals, but he turned to creative solutions for how the West Germans could make their payments.

Johnson told his representative to offset negotiations, John McCloy, in early 1967 that "in the absence of a financial solution . . . Congressional and public opinion would be intense, and the Germans should recognize that the situation might get out of hand," and Rostow remarked that "the final decision on US forces will inevitably depend in part on how much money McCloy can get out of the Germans."[91] When McCloy asked whether Johnson could "hold the line" against withdrawals if the FRG agreed to offset, he replied: "Perhaps, but you have to go over there and find out what they will do."[92] In his own meeting with Chancellor Kiesinger, Johnson stressed that although "he wanted to be friends with Germany," voices in Congress were asking, "Why should we keep on maintaining our troops there?"[93]

As a result, Johnson succeeded in securing another offset agreement in 1967. But it was unorthodox in three ways. First, the trilateral agreement involved Britain as well, as it faced a similar balance of payments deficit and was on the verge of massive force withdrawals from Germany. Second, rather than relying exclusively on purchases of US military equipment, the West German central bank agreed to buy huge volumes of US treasury bonds, and its president promised to hold US dollars rather than convert them to gold. This served to both stem the outflow of US dollars and also reduce the risk of a massive run on US gold stocks. Notably, the officially autonomous Bundesbank undertook this drastic step—which its president later expressed regrets about—under pressure from the West German government.[94] Third, the FRG fell short of full offset, which forced Johnson to make two painful adjustments. The first was that the United States covered Britain's shortfall to prevent reductions in British forces, while the second was that Washington withdrew a small portion of its forces (around 30,000).[95]

The Johnson administration similarly oversaw the completion of West German rearmament. By the time he left office in early 1969, the FRG had effectively met its 500,000 manpower target and continued to bolster its stock of equipment and weaponry with purchases from the United States.[96] Erhard proved more amenable to US ambitions for greater conventional options in defending NATO, in no small part because he viewed a larger West German contribution as a means to appease US pressure and stave off US troop withdrawals. Indeed, virtually all of the increase in European NATO conventional capabilities during the Johnson years stemmed from the FRG's efforts.[97] While many NATO allies saw US partial withdrawals in the wake of the 1967 offset agreement as an excuse to draw down their own forces, only Germany—under US pressure, including direct appeals from Senator Mansfield—reversed its own plans to do so.[98] Moreover, US negotiators used the trilateral negotiations as an opportunity to pressure the FRG to formally accept a greater role for conventional weapons in NATO's defense in responding to limited provocations, which served as the precursor to the alliance's formal adoption and codification of flexible response in late 1967.[99] As in previous years, Erhard and his successors' willingness to yield to US pressure stemmed from the FRG's position of vulnerability. As a State Department memorandum put it in July 1967: "The Germans know their security depends on the US umbrella."[100] A 1969 report on German-US relations similarly argued that the FRG's bargaining power was restricted by its "geographic position—an exposed country, with a contiguous border with the Soviet bloc."[101]

Outside of purely military contributions, the FRG provided considerable foreign aid to US partners, especially South Vietnam. Erhard caved under great personal pressure from Johnson in early 1966, and as a result, South Vietnam received an annual average of $7.5 million from the FRG for several years.[102] The end result was that Bonn became the second-largest source of aid to Saigon, after Washington.[103] Similarly, Washington looked to Bonn as a source of economic assistance for Greece, and the FRG served both as a major source of foreign aid and as the primary market for Greek exports.[104] Nonmilitary contributions like these allowed Washington to harness German resources for the purpose of resisting Communist expansion without encouraging and enabling the FRG to become more independent.

When the Soviet Union invaded Czechoslovakia in August 1968, the United States put additional pressure on its NATO partners to enhance their conventional capabilities. But US efforts were partially undercut because heightened concern about the Soviet threat also led Mansfield to pause his efforts in Congress to force US troop withdrawals.[105] In turn, most allies did little to increase their conventional contributions; Germany and Greece were among the few to increase their spending, whereas other NATO members either did nothing or, like Belgium and Canada, simply delayed previously planned reductions.[106] The following year, after Richard Nixon had assumed the presidency, his secretary of defense Melvin Laird complained that "frankly, many people in Congress had expected a bigger European response to the Czechoslovakian invasion than we got. So far as dollars and cents are concerned, there has not been that much of a response."[107]

US officials realized that the post-Czechoslovakia relief from pressure for troop withdrawals would be temporary. In November 1968, at a meeting of the North Atlantic Council, Secretary of State Rusk gave a prescient warning to NATO leaders:

> What the Europeans decide to do will largely dictate what the US does. Europe is in the presence of a miracle that it may not understand. The US has 650,000 men in Southeast Asia but continues to maintain its forces in Europe. There is already considerable pressure in Congress to eliminate these forces and any US Administration must be able to say that NATO friends take the issues seriously and that we are working together in comradely common effort where each pulls his own weight. If the Mansfield resolution had been voted by the Senate in June, it would have had a majority. The Soviets saved us; this pressure has been postponed but probably not indefinitely.[108]

CHAPTER 2

The later years of the Johnson administration, then, were marked by considerable ambivalence on the part of US policymakers, who carefully attempted to combine their burden-sharing pressure—given new impetus by the constraints imposed by Vietnam, the balance of payments deficit, and Congress—with assurances that significant changes in troop levels would not occur in the presence of sufficient offset payments. As a result, Washington was ultimately able to forestall a massive withdrawal of US forces thanks to West German offset purchases, as well as avoid major cuts to German conventional forces despite economic conditions in the FRG. Indeed, although West German defense spending effectively flatlined during the Johnson administration, the FRG nevertheless expanded the forces under its command to within reach of its long-promised 500,000 and armed them with US-produced equipment.

The Era of Diminished Resources, 1969–1974

The trends that began shaking the NATO alliance in the last years of the Johnson administration continued and even accelerated during Richard Nixon's presidency. By the time Nixon took office, tens of thousands of Americans had died in Vietnam, with tens of billions of dollars invested, all with little progress to show for it. Public and congressional opposition to the war continued to intensify, and the war's constraints on military manpower had led Johnson to withdraw two divisions from Europe in 1968.[109]

In addition, the United States was bogged down in a period of economic malaise that contrasted with the impressive growth in much of the rest of the world, including among US allies. The competitiveness of the US economy—which had been unrivaled in the years following the destruction of World War II—began to erode as competitors regained their strength in Europe and Asia, US productivity gains slowed, and the United States' trade deficit increased dramatically. All of this, in turn, further contributed to the United States' mounting balance of payments deficit. These trends were accompanied by rising unemployment and inflation ("stagflation") during the late 1960s and into the 1970s.[110] (The levels of unemployment and inflation are shown in figure A.2 in the appendix.) The month prior to Nixon's inauguration, the outgoing national security adviser Walt Rostow wrote to his successor Henry Kissinger that the rising tide of stagflation was "a domestic issue with the greatest significance for our foreign policy since a lack of wage-price discipline is more likely to erode our world position than any other single factor."[111] The net result, then, was that US economic preeminence had diminished, the US economy itself was stagnant, and the Vietnam War further drained US resources.

As shown in table 2.5, my theory would expect the Nixon administration to have faced pressure to reduce the costs of its overseas commitments due

Table 2.5 Predictions for US burden-sharing pressure toward West Germany, 1969–1974

Latent military potential	External threat	US resource constraints	Prediction	Outcome
High	High	High	High interest in FRG conventional force improvements. US burden-sharing pressure achieves a good deal of success.	Under pressure from the Nixon administration and the US Congress, the FRG substantially increased defense spending and continued to offset US balance of payments deficit.

to the mounting costs of the Vietnam War, US economic difficulties, and the continuing balance of payments crisis. As a result, it should have put even greater emphasis on FRG force improvements than the Johnson administration did. Furthermore, I would predict that US pressure would be highly successful, as the US threat of abandonment was both inherently credible, due to the pressure to retrench, and inherently salient, due to West Germany's geographic vulnerability.

DOMESTIC PRESSURE FOR RETRENCHMENT INTENSIFIES

The Vietnam War, political turmoil at home, and the United States' diminished economic position constrained US freedom of action. In a statement to Congress in early 1970, for example, Nixon declared that "the postwar period in international relations has ended," contrasting the current situation to that of twenty years prior, when "we were the only great power whose society and economy had escaped World War II's massive destruction."[112] This reckoning resulted in a reorientation of US foreign policy that aimed to cut costs, avoid foreign entanglements, seek détente with the Communist powers, and encourage cost-sharing by US allies.[113] Nixon began withdrawing US forces from Vietnam, and in 1971 he suspended the $35/ounce convertibility of dollars to gold. This ultimately led to the end of the fixed exchange rate system that had been established in 1944 and its replacement with a system of free-floating currencies.

More broadly, Nixon pursued arms control agreements with the Soviet Union, rapprochement with China, and limited troop withdrawals from Europe and Northeast Asia to reduce the risk of the United States becoming involved in conflicts and conserve economic and military resources.[114] These efforts were in no small part motivated by the costs of Vietnam and the United States' intractable economic situation, which made reducing tensions more attractive as a means of decreasing the probability of war and containing the

CHAPTER 2

arms race attractive as a means of cutting costs, and by domestic constraints within the United States.[115] Nixon viewed the United States as dangerously overextended and saw limited retrenchment, détente, and burden-sharing as the keys to allowing the United States to regroup and fight another day.[116]

This reorientation was reflected in congressional efforts to withdraw US forces from abroad and encourage allied burden-sharing as well. Rather than proposing nonbinding resolutions, as he had in previous years, Senate Majority Leader Mansfield for the first time introduced in 1971 binding legislation mandating troop reductions, and he did so again in 1973 and 1974. His efforts were accompanied by other congressional resolutions and bills aiming to withdraw troops and demand that West Germany and NATO make greater contributions, along with the National Commitments Resolution of 1969 and the War Powers Act of 1973, which limited the president's ability to deploy US forces abroad without congressional approval.[117] More generally, Congress forced defense cuts while simultaneously increasing domestic spending.[118]

Predictably, these developments alarmed German leaders. The Social Democrats' rise to power in 1969 manifested this dissatisfaction with the United States, as Willy Brandt, now chancellor, made rapprochement with the Soviets and normalizing relations with East Germany—a policy shift termed *Ostpolitik*—a priority.[119] Brandt linked US domestic pressure to doubts about US reliability and warned that troop withdrawals would destroy Europe's faith in the United States.[120] In a meeting with Defense Secretary Melvin Laird in 1970, the West German defense minister Helmut Schmidt "made a strong plea for maintaining a substantial US troop presence in Europe" and warned that "if the US cuts its troop level, Germany and other European countries would inevitably begin to accommodate with the East."[121] The following year, in response to the Mansfield Amendment, Brandt publicly proclaimed doubt in the viability of the US commitment to NATO.[122] Similarly, an NIE in 1972 reported that "disillusion with the US as a social, economic, and foreign policy model, together with what some perceive as a decline in US power, doubtless has reduced the deference once paid to American views."[123]

What also raised concerns about US unreliability was the US effort toward détente with the Soviet Union, which included the Strategic Arms Limitations Treaties in 1972 and 1979 (SALT I and II, respectively), as well as efforts toward Mutual and Balanced Force Reductions (MBFR) with Europe. US allies feared that the result could be a US-Soviet bargain in which allied interests were sold out to make the superpowers more secure.[124] The US-Soviet Agreement on the Prevention of Nuclear War (1973), for example, raised concerns about US willingness to use nuclear weapons, which was core to the defense of NATO.[125] The West Germans also resented the concerted US-Soviet push for a nonproliferation treaty, which they saw as discriminatory and as evidence that the United States attached more importance to its relations with its adversary than to the well-being of its allies.[126] Such concerns were not unreasonable; Mansfield, for example, cited the comparatively less tense relations that had prevailed since the Cuban Missile Crisis (the 1968 invasion of Czechoslovakia aside) as evidence that Soviet intentions no longer demanded a massive US presence in Europe.[127]

Like his predecessors, Nixon was deeply preoccupied with ensuring that the FRG remained tightly bound to NATO, remarking in 1971 that "as a freshman Congressman he saw three reasons for NATO: the threat from the Soviet Union, the weakness of Western Europe and the need for a home for the Germans," arguing that "one could perhaps debate the first two of the original reasons for NATO, but the third still existed."[128] Nixon and other members of his administration internally expressed fears that West Germany—as well as the other members of NATO—were likely to undertake "increasing accommodation to the Russians on political and economic issues" in response to perceptions of US unreliability.[129] They worried that this process could incite a trend toward either "Finlandization," with allies distancing themselves from the United States and becoming increasingly willing to defer to Soviet interests, or nuclearization.[130] Reports that FRG officials were concerned that US troop withdrawals were inevitable and resented US strong-arm tactics over conventional burden-sharing and nuclear nonproliferation reawakened old fears, dating back to the Eisenhower administration, that the FRG might be willing to exit NATO and accept neutrality in exchange for reunification with East Germany.[131]

As a result, Nixon sought to allay West German fears of imminent US withdrawal, and he vigorously opposed Mansfield's efforts. Nixon claimed in his 1970 report on foreign policy that the United States would no sooner withdraw from Europe than from Alaska, and he made his first visit as president in February to March 1969 to Europe, where he attempted to reassure NATO capitals.[132] He visited again the following year, strongly reaffirming the United States' commitment to defend NATO and promising that the United States would not make any unilateral withdrawals.[133] Nixon declared the NATO security guarantee to be "unique" and "irreplaceable" and proclaimed that "the United States will, under no circumstances, reduce, unilaterally, its commitment to NATO."[134] The administration further stressed that it would consult and inform the NATO allies on bilateral US-Soviet negotiations on arms control and other issues.[135]

Internally, Nixon argued against troop withdrawals on the grounds that "the key to what we do is what effect does it have on Germany. . . . Some Europeans would think to move toward the Russians because they are uneasy about more US reductions," and his advisers—including Secretary Rogers, the supreme Allied commander Europe, and the NATO ambassador—agreed that "reductions would push [the FRG] toward the Russians."[136] Nixon further posited that "the effect [of withdrawals] would be catastrophic" on Germany,

CHAPTER 2

potentially setting off a chain of events in which "the Germans left the fold and the umbilical cord [was] cut."[137]

Additionally, the threat from the Soviet Union remained, though whether it had on net increased was uncertain. In terms of capabilities, the Soviets spent a great deal modernizing their military forces starting in the mid-1960s, and after Czechoslovakia stationed five divisions in the country, in addition to those already present in the other Soviet satellites in Eastern Europe.[138] By the time Nixon assumed office, the Soviets had also effectively reached nuclear parity with the United States, making the prospect of an US first strike in the event of a Soviet invasion of Europe even less attractive.[139] Growing Soviet military power was one of the core reasons that US and NATO officials gave for the need to invest more in defense.[140]

Perceptions of Soviet intentions were more varied. In both the United States and in West Germany, policymakers were under no illusions that Soviet ambitions to dominate Europe had vanished. But after nearly a decade of reduced tensions following the Cuban Missile Crisis, the risk of war in the short term seemed less likely.[141] European publics and policymakers were eager to take advantage of the thaw in relations to further relax tensions and shift resources away from defense, running the risk that "NATO could put itself out of business" as members rushed to embrace détente.[142] Brandt's government in particular saw an opening for rapprochement with the Soviet Union, regarding it as effectively accepting of the status quo in Europe and more concerned with economic stagnation at home.[143] This served as one of the motivations for *Ostpolitik*, as Brandt hoped that by building bridges with the Soviet bloc and increasing cultural and economic contact, the risk of war could be reduced and the status quo kept intact until Soviet satellites could be wedged away.[144] The result was the normalization of West and East German relations, the Treaty of Moscow with the Soviet Union in which both sides accepted the territorial status quo, and expanded interbloc trade.

US PRESSURE INTENSIFIES, FRG MILITARY SPENDING RISES

Although Nixon put great emphasis on reassuring the FRG and was wary of German self-reliance, he sought to reorient the distribution of burdens in US foreign policy by cutting US costs while encouraging allies to increase their own capabilities. US military spending declined throughout much of the decade, and the Nixon Doctrine (often referred to as the "Guam Doctrine" after Nixon's speech on the island in 1969), while originally targeted at Asia, stressed that allies everywhere would increasingly have primary responsibility for defending themselves.[145] Nixon asserted that "the American people have grown somewhat weary . . . of international burdens" and argued that "the Nixon Doctrine will enable us to remain committed in ways that we can sustain."[146]

58

The United States still frequently had to drag NATO—including West Germany—along the path to conventional force improvements. This was partly because, as in the past two decades, European NATO members were skeptical that a conventional defense of Europe was either possible in light of Soviet conventional superiority, desirable given its costs, or necessary because of nuclear deterrence coupled with the push toward East-West détente, which seemed to reduce the prospect of war in the short term.[147] Additionally, the Nixon administration's push for NATO conventional burden-sharing was undercut by its simultaneous efforts to negotiate MBFR with the Soviet Union in an effort to limit the risk of war and reduce defense costs. European officials questioned the need for force improvements if Soviet forces were to be withdrawn, and they feared that increasing their own force levels would simply give the Americans an excuse to reduce their own. Indeed, MBFR was born of the Nixon administration's fear of the Soviets' potential to quickly overwhelm Europe before NATO could mobilize, and the administration strongly opposed unilateral withdrawals, which would reduce the Soviets' incentives to make any concessions of their own.[148] The West Germans were in effect holding out for the possibility that détente would allow a general reduction in armaments.[149]

The result was a familiar quandary. On the one hand, the United States' concern about the conventional balance in Europe undercut its threat to drawn down US forces. But on the other hand, if the conventional balance improved, a true European military buildup would become less necessary. This challenge was reinforced by European doubts about the viability of a truly conventional defense for NATO, coupled with concerns that their efforts would simply encourage US withdrawals. As a result, despite its reluctance to withdraw US forces from Europe unilaterally, the Nixon administration had to lean on the implicit threat of withdrawals—made more credible by congressional activism—paired with promises of maintaining US troop levels if NATO complied.

Even as US officials reassured the FRG and the rest of NATO, the consensus within the Nixon administration was that these assurances should be coupled with veiled—or sometimes not so veiled—threats of abandonment. Defense Secretary Laird wrote to Nixon in 1969 that "I would judge the need to be for a nice balance between (i) reassurances about the American commitment to NATO, which are clearly in order, and (ii) polite reservations in response to any invitations to 'stabilize' (i.e., freeze) US force levels in Europe, which might pose serious Congressional and policy problems," thus allowing the United States to effectively balance threats and assurances. He further advised Nixon that although "the Europeans will be watching closely for any sign from you that their worries are over," US officials "should not suggest, even by silence, that these are our views. To do so would, in my judgment, risk dissipating what little momentum there now is in the European improvement effort, and complicate our forthcoming dialogue with

CHAPTER 2

Congress."[150] A 1971 NSC paper similarly prescribed that US policymakers "reaffirm our intention to maintain and improve US forces in Europe, *if the Europeans do their share in improving their forces.*"[151] A subsequent State Department memo likewise pointed to the importance of combining threats and assurances as a means of obtaining this allied burden-sharing: "Steps to share a greater proportion of the common defense burden are a tangible earnest [signal] of European intent to meet the terms of the President's 1970 pledge, repeated at this NATO meeting, and warmly welcomed, that the US would maintain and improve its forces in Europe, *provided the Allies do likewise.*"[152] This consensus became formal US policy, as two National Security Decision Memoranda (NSDMs) in 1971 made clear the conditional nature of US assurances of support and the emphasis Nixon put on allied burden-sharing. NSDM 133 in September 1971 stated that "given a similar approach by our allies, the US will improve its combat forces in Europe and not reduce them except in the context of a mutual and balanced force reduction with the Warsaw Pact," a position restated in NSDM 142 that December.[153]

Compared to his predecessors, Nixon was more interested in allied force improvements relative to offset. This reflected a realization that despite the risks of encouraging FRG burden-sharing, the alliance required greater cost-sharing if it was to maintain an adequate deterrent posture despite constraints on the resources Washington could commit. While acknowledging the reality of the Soviet military buildup, Nixon did not believe the conventional gap was insurmountable, given the size of European NATO's economies and populations.[154] At a meeting with NATO commanders, Nixon "stressed the firmness of the US policy of non-isolationism," claiming that "although there are many voices heard in the United States the policy is established by the President and the Europeans can be assured there will be no unilateral withdrawal." At the same time, however, Nixon attempted to dispel the "impression in the European press that the US wishes to obtain from NATO countries some financial arrangement whereby the NATO countries would assume the burden or a substantial part of the burden for supporting US forces." Instead, he argued, "rather than having members of the NATO Alliance in effect subsidize US forces in Europe, he would welcome having the funds used to shore up and build up the local strength of the member countries' armed forces."[155] On a number of occasions, Nixon and his advisers internally compared relying strictly on offset and European payments to putting US forces in the position of being "mercenaries."[156]

Domestic pressure from Congress gave Nixon's threats more weight. His administration continually emphasized the US domestic political situation, with Nixon warning at a meeting with NATO foreign and defense ministers in April 1969 that "it would be very popular . . . to announce a reduction of the US defense program, or to announce the withdrawal of divisions from Europe."[157] The following year, Nixon likewise told NATO officials that "were the NATO partners to do more in their own defense, that would be

60

quite decisive in firming up US support for making our present contribution to the Alliance."[158] Internally, Nixon expressed his worries to other US officials, stressing that NATO leaders had "just got to believe that the situation is serious. A Mansfield resolution will surely pass if they don't make a bigger effort."[159] On a number of occasions, Nixon struck a similar tone with Brandt personally, warning that unless the FRG did more both in terms of contributing to NATO's defense capabilities and in offsetting the US balance of payments deficit, Congress would force troop withdrawals.[160] Indeed, the Jackson-Nunn Amendment in Congress in 1973 effectively mandated troop withdrawals without offset.[161] In the run-up to offset negotiations in 1974, Nixon made a speech in which he argued that the Europeans "will find it almost impossible to get Congressional support for continued American presence at present levels" if the Europeans did not increase their efforts and pursued economic integration that excluded the United States.[162] In effect, then, policymakers attempted to play the role of a "good cop," allowing the pressure from their domestic audiences to play the "bad cop" who would push allies to contribute more to the common defense—in terms of both offset and defense investments.[163] Implicit in US assurances was the threat that if allies did not increase their efforts, the United States would have difficulty avoiding troop withdrawals.

Other members of the administration employed similar pressure, with numerous US officials making statements to the effect that while the United States intended to maintain its troop levels, this was conditional on allies' willingness to share in the burden.[164] The US ambassador to West Germany made clear to Brandt "the administration's intent to maintain substantial US forces in Europe, although at the same time pointing to heavy pressures in certain quarters in the US for reduction. To counter these latter pressures, it was vitally important that Germany and other European countries do everything possible to improve their own defense contribution."[165]

Henry Kissinger likewise told Brandt in September 1973 that although "we are trying to stem" congressional pressure, "the more offset we can get, the more it will help," and he warned the Italian ambassador to Washington that keeping the lid on congressional pressure "is made more complex when the Europeans do not do enough."[166] Kissinger recommended taking a firm line on offset internally as well, stressing that "we will face renewed Congressional pressure . . . if we do not get a substantially better offset than the previous Administration."[167] During the buildup to the 1972 to 1973 offset negotiations, Kissinger's close confidant on the NSC, Helmut Sonnenfeldt, recommended to him that the United States use the Mansfield Amendment to put pressure on the Germans, but with the caveat that "we have no intention whatsoever of a repetition of the Erhard crisis."[168] US pressure continued into the "Year of Europe" initiative in 1973, in which the administration attempted to create a new Atlantic Charter and strike a grand bargain with allies on the issues of trade and defense burden-sharing. Throughout the year, US officials

CHAPTER 2

repeatedly emphasized that it was in the Europeans' interest to make concessions, lest they empower domestic proponents of troop withdrawals in the United States.[169]

The result of US pressure was increased offset payments of $1.5 billion in 1969 and over $2 billion in 1971 and 1973. These agreements included a combination of FRG military purchases, purchases of US government securities, direct payments, financing of improvements in facilities and infrastructure used by US forces, and Bundesbank loans on which the FRG paid the interest. The FRG and other NATO other allies likewise sought to defuse US pressure by increasing their defense spending and making contributions to collective defense.[170] As was typical of the preceding two decades, the FRG was more responsive to US pressure than other NATO members. West German military spending nearly doubled between 1970 and 1975, from around $25 billion to more than $45 billion, and as figure 2.1 shows, FRG defense spending as a percent of GDP increased more than 1.5 percentage points over this period, compared to less than 1 percentage point for the rest of NATO. More broadly, the newly formed Eurogroup, comprised of most European NATO members and designed to coordinate military investments, developed the European Defense Improvement Program (EDIP) in December 1970. After the Mansfield Amendment the following year, the EDIP earmarked around a billion dollars for common defense investments over five years, in the hope that it would forestall US withdrawals. EDIP included funding for both collective NATO military infrastructure and national force improvements. In addition, West Germany was asked to provide $80 million in transportation aircraft to Turkey, and it was one of the standout countries in terms of funds allocated to force improvements, including $50 million to procure heavy lift helicopters. The following year, the Eurogroup agreed to an additional collective defense budget increase of $1 billion for 1972—as part of the Alliance Defense for the Seventies (AD-70) initiative—which included a double-digit percentage increase in German defense spending and FRG efforts to procure more than a hundred F-4 fighter aircraft. Over the next few years, the FRG added several more armored brigades as well, and by the end of the decade, it was US and West German force improvements that accounted for the modest increase in NATO forces deployed in Central Europe relative to the early 1970s.[171]

The continued threat of the Soviet Union was ultimately what made the prospect of US abandonment intolerable. As was typical, the West Germans were the most sensitive to US pressure, given that a Soviet surprise attack could quickly seize large swaths of German territory. Nevertheless, given the relaxation of tensions during the 1970s—a period defined by US-Soviet détente but also by Brandt's efforts to pursue warmer ties with the Soviet Union and East Germany—it was not so much changes in the external threat that motivated increases in German defense spending but rather US pressure and the credibility of its threats of abandonment.[172]

Indeed, the evidence overwhelmingly suggests that the FRG and other NATO members took domestic constraints in the United States very seriously. Their defense efforts were designed in large part to stave off US withdrawals and satiate Washington, and they were otherwise reluctant to bolster their capabilities, hoping instead that détente would allow for general military reductions.[173] One US official noted in 1969 that the Europeans saw "their defense requirements primarily in terms of what they need to provide to keep the Americans committed," while the West German ambassador reported that the war in Vietnam and the "neo-isolationist trend" made major troop withdrawals quite possible.[174] The following year, the West Germans requested "an indication . . . of the minimum European defense contribution we will need . . . in order to constrain budgetary and congressional pressures."[175] Whereas in October 1970 the Germans had taken a somewhat hard line on burden-sharing, expressing surprise at US ambitions for substantially larger NATO defense budgets and full offsets, they became far more amenable the following year, after Mansfield introduced his first piece of binding legislation to cut US troops in Europe by 50 percent, in the form of an amendment to that year's Selective Service bill in the Senate. The result was concrete German commitments under EDIP and AD-70, including substantial increases in defense spending and procurement.[176] Similarly, while Brandt attempted to hold out for an agreement that would offset less than half of US costs in 1973 to 1974, the real possibility of troop withdrawals mandated by the Jackson-Nunn Amendment forced the FRG to move closer to US demands, resulting in an agreement that covered effectively all US costs just days after Nixon delivered a March 1974 speech warning about potential troop withdrawals.[177]

The evidence in this chapter shows that although the FRG received an enormous number of reassurance measures from the United States—in the form of US troop deployments, steps toward nuclear sharing, and countless public and private promises—the FRG's geographic vulnerability and US resource constraints facilitated US officials' ability to pressure West Germany into accepting high levels of burden-sharing. The FRG spent billions of dollars on offset payments to the United States throughout the 1960s and 1970s, and US officials were often quite blunt in their threats of troop withdrawals. Because of its vulnerability, West Germany was consistently more responsive to US pressure than most other NATO members that could free-ride on the defense of Germany.

Changes in perceived Soviet capabilities and intentions shaped FRG defense contributions inconsistently. While the Berlin Crisis of 1961 to 1962 drove both US pressure and German burden-sharing, improvements in the threat environment after the crisis did not halt the success of US pressure efforts. This was in part because even as the short-term prospect of Soviet invasion diminished (though by no means disappeared), the prospect of US

CHAPTER 2

disengagement from Europe appeared to grow more likely, due to a combination of the US balance of payments deficit, the Vietnam War, an anemic US economy, and ultimately, congressional pressure to withdraw US forces from Europe. During the early 1970s, German defense efforts increased even as improvements in East-West relations seemed to make the threat environment more benign. Although their efforts were motivated in part by a Soviet military buildup, the evidence suggests that what the West Germans sought instead was the lowest possible contribution that would allow them to satisfy US pressure while they pursued rapprochement with the Soviet bloc in hope of cementing a peaceful coexistence.

The seemingly erratic relationship between changes in Soviet capabilities and behavior and FRG burden-sharing arose in large part because the changes affected both US and FRG threat perceptions in ways that often canceled each other out. This is consistent with my expectation, discussed in chapter 1, that geography would be a more consistent predictor of contributions. The invasion of Czechoslovakia in 1968, for example, did not yield much in the way of new military commitments, in part because it temporarily derailed the efforts of troop withdrawal proponents in the United States. Meanwhile, the general climate of détente seemed to strengthen the arguments of troop withdrawal proponents like Mansfield. Moreover, while Soviet capabilities did increase, they did not alter the fundamental dynamics of deterrence in the NATO alliance. The conventional balance had long tilted in favor of the Warsaw Pact, and European NATO members—including the FRG—had long viewed an entirely conventional defense of Europe as out of reach. As in previous periods, West German policymakers viewed conventional force improvements as a bargaining chip to influence US policy toward Europe at least as much as a cornerstone of NATO deterrence.

Additionally, the case of the FRG illustrates the trade-off between control and cost-sharing. US officials recognized the dangers of encouraging German burden-sharing, particularly insofar as it entailed threats of US troop withdrawals, even as they pressured West Germany to boost its force levels and enhance its capabilities—often with US-purchased equipment. Nevertheless, escalating constraints on US resources—owing both to the balance of payments deficit and, later, the Vietnam War—coupled with the massive Soviet conventional military presence near the German border meant that US officials had to overcome their misgivings. The United States needed an armed West Germany on the front line with the Warsaw Pact, and so it put pressure on it to spend more on defense—fairly successfully, as the FRG was highly vulnerable to attack.

However, US officials were mindful to ensure that the FRG did not become *too* self-reliant. US officials took great pains to reassure the West Germans of Washington's commitment to defend them, and they emphasized forms of burden-sharing that bound the FRG to NATO. These included the purchase of US arms through offset arrangements that made the FRG dependent on US-produced arms while simultaneously compensating the United States for the costs it incurred by stationing troops in Germany; the integration of West German military forces into NATO command; and non-military forms of burden-sharing like foreign aid.

The case of West Germany, then, was one in which the burden-sharing dilemma pushed US policymakers in opposite directions simultaneously. Few allies' military contributions would have been as useful—or as dangerous—as those of the FRG. US officials could not optimize burden-sharing without undermining their political control over West Germany, or vice versa. The result was an interminable balancing act.

CHAPTER 3

"Between Scylla and Charybdis"

Japanese Burden-Sharing, 1964–1976

After the end of World War II, the United States sought to ensure that Japan would not threaten its neighbors again, while simultaneously trying to keep Japan from aligning with the Communist bloc.[1] It did so initially through occupation, which lasted until 1952, when the two countries signed the Mutual Security Treaty (MST), which they later revised in 1960. In addition to formalizing their commitment in the MST, the United States also stationed tens of thousands of forces on Japanese territory, in large part to reassure the Japanese of US protection. Secretary of State Dean Rusk argued in favor of the US presence in Japan because "even relatively small" withdrawals "might severely undermine the confidence of Japan in our determination to maintain strong defenses in the Far East, and thus weaken its desire to maintain its Free World alignment."[2] The US presence also provided additional forces that could be deployed elsewhere in the event of conflict on the Asian mainland.

Japanese burden-sharing, however, was very limited. Japan's constitution did not allow it to maintain military forces for purposes other than self-defense, and its defense spending was always at a very low level of its GDP. Indeed, under the MST, the United States was obligated to protect Japan, but Japan was responsible only for the defense of its own home territory.[3] This relatively low level of burden-sharing was facilitated by Japan's secure position, as it was separated from mainland Asia by the Sea of Japan.

This situation appeared to be on the verge of change during the late 1960s and 1970s, as Japan's meteoric economic growth rendered it increasingly capable of assuming the burden for its own defense, and the costs of the Vietnam War put pressure on the United States to retrench and devolve more responsibility to its allies. In 1969, President Richard Nixon began large-scale withdrawals of US troops from Vietnam and announced the Guam Doctrine, which proclaimed that allies would be responsible for shouldering more of the burden for their own defense. As a result, Japan moderately in-

66

creased its defense spending and contemplated a more far-reaching shift toward autonomous defense, potentially even including nuclear weapons acquisition. Nevertheless, despite Japan's objectively large capacity for burden-sharing, US officials refrained from soliciting significantly greater efforts for fear it would push Japan to move closer to the Soviet Union and even potentially revive Japanese militarism. The United States reassured Japan that the Guam Doctrine would not mean a reduction in the US commitment to Japan's (or East Asia's) defense, and that the US détente with the Soviet Union and more amicable ties with China would not involve sacrificing Japanese interests. Ultimately, the Japanese neutralism that US policymakers feared never came to fruition.

Empirical Predictions

Competing explanations make mixed predictions about Japanese burden-sharing. The logic of public goods theory and alliance asymmetry would expect fairly high Japanese burden-sharing due to the country's enormous latent military power, while one would predict modest Japanese burden-sharing on the basis of the US troop presence it hosted. Japan's domestic politics, meanwhile, would point to fairly low burden-sharing due to Japan's culture of anti-militarism, particularly when left-wing parties had more influence.

There is a good deal these theories cannot explain, however. Japanese defense spending was much smaller than one would predict on the basis of its size. Moreover, the evidence shows that despite the substantial US troop presence, Japanese officials feared US abandonment, in large part because of US resource and domestic political constraints in the wake of the Vietnam War. Finally, while Japanese domestic politics can partially explain why Japan was so resistant to assuming greater defense responsibilities, they cannot explain why Japan contemplated a greater military role in the early 1970s and increased defense spending (albeit modestly) in response to US pressure. The evidence also suggests that Japanese officials saw little need for burden-sharing mainly because their perception of threat was relatively modest.

Alliance control theory's predictions, by contrast, receive strong support. Japan represents a case of Grudging Cheap-Riding. The country was insulated from US burden-sharing pressure, both because it was far safer from attack than contiguous allies such as South Korea and because US policymakers feared that a more capable, self-reliant Japan would be less cooperative. As a result, Japan faced relatively light US burden-sharing pressure, which its margin of security allowed it to deflect (see table 3.1). Nevertheless, constraints on US resources due to the costs of Vietnam enhanced the US threat of abandonment and made encouraging Japanese self-reliance more attractive to US policymakers, which in turn led to moderate increases in Japanese military spending.

CHAPTER 3

Table 3.1 Japan's scores on the independent variables

Latent military potential	External threat	US resource constraints	Prediction
High	Low	High in late 1960s and 1970s due to the Vietnam War	Low-to-moderate interest in Japanese conventional force improvements throughout, but increasing interest in the late 1960s and early 1970s. US burden-sharing pressure achieves little success, but its success increases modestly during the late 1960s and 1970s.

Strategic Context

Japan's primary security challenges stemmed from the two giants of the Communist bloc: the Soviet Union and China. Nevertheless, because Japan was separated from the Asian mainland by water and distant from the center of Soviet military power in Eastern Europe, and because Soviet and Chinese capabilities for projecting power in the region were still limited, the Japanese regarded the likelihood of invasion as quite low.[4] Throughout much of the late 1950s and early 1960s, many Japanese observers did not see an immediate threat to their security, due to both their favorable geography and the buffer provided by US forces in South Korea and South Vietnam.[5] The Japanese public, as well as the left-wing parties—the Social Democratic Party of Japan (JSP) and the Japanese Communist Party (JCP)—saw little need for a US military presence, and the JSP even questioned the need for armed forces at all.[6] Even the ruling conservative Liberal Democratic Party (LDP) tended to be more sanguine about Japan's security environment when compared to US assessments.[7]

Japanese policymakers were hesitant to assume a major military role in East Asia after the experience of World War II, and the Japanese constitution forbade war as an instrument of policy and instructed against possessing armed forces. Indeed, Japanese officials viewed the US alliance as a means to realize their ambition to divert resources to growth and development rather than defense. This culminated in the 1951 Yoshida Doctrine, named after Prime Minister Shigeru Yoshida, which guided Japanese policy for decades and emphasized that Japan would rely on the United States for defense and focus its efforts on economic tools of statecraft and growth at home.[8] Yoshida resisted US pressure to rearm and participate in the regional defense of East Asia during the early and mid-1950s, acquiescing only to the creation of the modest-sized Self-Defense Forces (SDF) in 1954, which were to be equipped mainly thanks to Washington's military assistance.[9]

For the United States, Japan was strategically vital, and its alignment with Washington could not be taken for granted. With a population of over 90 million and an economy comparable in size to West Germany's (and which would become much larger by the 1970s), combined with its proximity to China, North Korea, the Soviet Union, and the Soya, Tsushima, and Tsugaru Straits that hemmed in the Soviet Pacific Fleet, Japan's size and position made it the cornerstone of the US posture in East Asia.[10] As a Department of State guidelines paper put it in March 1962: "The long-term goal of US policy toward Japan is the development of Japan as a major power center in Asia acting in concert with US and Free World interests."[11] Since the 1950s, US policymakers had seen the security guarantee to Japan as a way to discourage it from becoming either a neutral competitor or a nuclear-armed state. Japan's latent military strength, in addition to its history of expansion, contributed greatly to fears in both the United States and the other countries of East Asia that left to their own devices, the Japanese might pursue their security unilaterally in a way that might not serve US interests and might threaten the region. These fears included Japan obtaining nuclear weapons, charting a neutral course by moving closer to the Communist powers, and pursuing independent, unilateral conventional arming.[12] The US ambassador to Japan pointed to these concerns directly in July 1965 when he emphasized the importance of ensuring that "Japanese industrial potential does not drift to the Communist side or into a position of neutrality."[13]

Each of these factors—Japan's strategic importance, economic and latent military power, relative position of safety, and history and pacifist constitution, as well as US policymakers' concerns about Japan's continued pro-US alignment—in turn informed how the United States approached the subject of Japanese burden-sharing. US officials realized that US protection— even if it discouraged Japanese self-reliance—was a key factor in keeping Japan from shifting toward neutralism, acquiring nuclear weapons, or simply becoming sufficiently self-reliant that neither of these could be ruled out. As a result, even the Eisenhower administration's more ambitious requests for Japanese rearmament during the 1950s would have involved a force of only around 300,000, substantially lower than those of West Germany, France, and Britain, despite Japan having nearly twice their populations.[14]

The Emerging Giant, 1964–1968

During the mid-1960s, Japan's enormous latent military power, coupled with its comparatively permissive threat environment, should have rendered US policymakers reluctant to wholeheartedly embrace Japanese self-reliance in defense. As shown in table 3.2, I would expect there to have been modest and ambivalent US efforts to encourage Japanese defense burden-sharing, along with attempts to solicit economic contributions instead. Because Japan was

CHAPTER 3

Table 3.2 Predictions for US burden-sharing pressure toward Japan, 1964–1968

Latent military potential	External threat	US resource constraints	Prediction	Outcome
High	Low	Rising	Low-to-moderate US interest in Japanese force improvements, counterbalanced by concerns about Japanese freedom of action.	US policymakers were ambivalent about Japanese burden-sharing, and instead sought to cultivate economic contributions from Japan, with limited success.

relatively insulated from attack, US efforts to stimulate Japanese burden-sharing should have had limited success.

RELUCTANT US BURDEN-SHARING PRESSURE

By the time Johnson assumed office in November 1963, Japan had emerged from its postwar recovery and was growing rapidly (see table 3.3). As a result, some US officials—particularly in the Treasury and Defense Departments—saw the moment as ripe to begin asking Japan to assume more of the burden for its own defense. In January 1964, as Secretary of State Dean Rusk prepared to visit Japan, both Secretary of Defense Robert McNamara and Secretary of the Treasury Douglas Dillon pleaded with him to ask the Japanese to increase their military arming.[15] McNamara made similar overtures during a visit from the director general of the Japan Defense Agency that June, and the Joint Chiefs of Staff concurred with the view that Japan should ramp up its defense capabilities.[16]

The State Department, however, was more circumspect. Despite agreeing on the value of greater Japanese burden-sharing, a number of officials—most notably the US ambassador to Japan Edward Reischauer and Assistant Secretary of State for Far Eastern Affairs William Bundy—were reluctant to press the matter too far because they feared that doing so would both encourage and empower Japan to go its own way.[17] In August 1964, writing on challenges in US-Japan trade, Reischauer wrote that the "gradual growth of defense consciousness in Japan and willingness [to] consider [a] larger role in Asian affairs is inevitably being accompanied by revival of some degree of Japanese nationalism," adding that "it is essential . . . to recognize that irritations aroused by international economic issues could help deflect this nationalism into less desirable channels."[18] Reischauer described in December 1964 the "basic long-term goal of US policy toward Japan" as being "the development of Japan as a major power center in Asia acting in concert with US and Free World objectives." But he noted that "it must also

70

"BETWEEN SCYLLA AND CHARYBDIS"

Table 3.3 Japan's GDP and GDP per capita in constant 2005 US dollars (purchasing power parity), 1965–1975, including as a percentage of Soviet and Chinese GDP

GDP (billions USD)	GDPpc (USD)	GDP (% of USSR)	GDP (% of China)	Year
472.96	4,812.30	41.5	79.8	1965
1,013.67	9,774.09	62.9	130.0	1970
1,404.05	12,670.99	65.6	143.2	1975

Source: Data are from Gleditsch's (2002) Expanded Trade and GDP Dataset.

be realized that the two parts of our long-term goal are not necessarily complementary in all regards," and further pointed out that "Japan has become potentially a major power center, but it is only slowly beginning to exercise its potential powers in international affairs. As it increasingly does so . . . a greater divergence could arise between Japanese and US objectives." Reischauer cautioned that "with the growth of Japan's power, our direct leverage on troublesome issues has lessened," pointing in particular to the issue of trade ties with the Communist bloc, on which the Japanese were more eager and the Americans more circumspect.[19]

Reischauer's doubts were shared by Bundy, who wrote to Secretary of State Rusk in January 1965, "We must insure that the US-Japan military partnership remains more attractive to Japan than the alternatives of military non-alignment or independent defense measures."[20] In a lengthy memo in August of that year, Bundy warned that "any [Japanese] government which proposed a sharp expansion of defense expenditures would risk its early replacement, in all probability by a more neutralist government less likely to ensure Japan's continued, effective Free World alignment," noting that the "US interest in Japan's remaining an active political and economic Free World associate is far greater than our interest in the contribution expanded Japanese forces might make to Free World military strength." He further added that "we cannot exclude the possibility that we would live to regret the re-establishment of powerful Japanese forces at home and overseas. . . . Nor should we overlook the fact that, seeking the most efficient and economic means to achieve powerful forces, a growing number of Japanese might be tempted by the nuclear route."[21] But Bundy recognized that there was an even more fundamental dilemma: a self-reliant Japan was a less pliant Japan. His argument is worth quoting at length:

> There is another reason why we should consider carefully before pressing the Japanese to accelerate their defense effort. It may not be in our interest that the Japanese become exclusively and completely responsible for home defense, leaving the US with no defense role in Japan. Retention of a real defense role for our Japan-based forces is important in justifying the US-Japan security relationship to Japanese skeptics, in maintaining the credibility of our strategic

CHAPTER 3

commitment to Japan, in providing cover for the counter-offensive, intelligence and other activities our Japan-based forces fulfill, and in preserving our influence in Japanese defense planning now that Japan MAP [Military Assistance Program] has been terminated.[22]

Bundy concluded that the United States should communicate that although it welcomed qualitative improvements in Japanese capabilities, "we consider the size and composition of Japanese forces a matter for Japanese decision free of any form of US pressure."[23]

As a result, US policy toward Japan was one of gesturing at the importance of burden-sharing, but without serious pressure behind it.[24] An NIE in November 1965 concluded that "while some qualitative improvement is in prospect, there is little chance that [Japanese prime minister] Sato will press for any major increases in Japan's own defense forces over the next two or three years." A memo from Secretary of State Rusk to President Johnson in November 1967 similarly concluded, "Fundamentally, we want Japan as a partner—not as a rival—in Asia, but as [a] partner sharing the political and economic burdens of regional responsibility. While we do not now seek a greater Japanese military role, other than in its own defense, Japan's actions should contribute to—and not detract from—effective fulfillment of our military and security commitments to Asia."[25] A telegram from the US embassy in Japan the following year similarly noted that the "Japan[ese] consensus might come to tolerate something more than very gradual acceleration of buildup in Japan's own defense which has been case over last few years, but any value to US of such a trend would be offset by probability that it would be accompanied by assertive nationalist overtones and aggressive demands for phase down of US bases."[26] US officials, then, recognized the delicate balancing act of trying to keep Japan tied to the United States while also assuming more responsibility for its own defense, and as a result, their efforts to encourage Japanese burden-sharing were relatively subdued and were not accompanied by the same intense threats of abandonment as in the cases of West Germany (chapter 2) and South Korea (chapter 4). As a partial substitute, US officials sought to instead encourage economic burden-sharing by Japan, in the form of Japanese development assistance to non-Communist states in the region through the Asian Development Bank, and to South Vietnam in particular.[27]

For similar reasons, US officials were judicious in reassuring Japan about the credibility of the US commitment. The assistant secretary of state for Far Eastern affairs wrote to Secretary of State Dean Rusk in January 1965, "We must insure that the US-Japan military partnership remains more attractive to Japan than the alternatives of military non-alignment or independent defense measures."[28] China's acquisition of nuclear weapons in late 1964 provided new impetus for reassuring the Japanese to discourage them from considering nuclear weapons themselves. Indeed, Japanese policymakers began both internally discussing the merits of obtaining nuclear weapons and seeking external reassurance from the United States that it would protect East Asia—including Vietnam, South Korea, and Taiwan—using its nuclear weapons. To this end, Japanese officials floated the prospect of Japanese proliferation in the absence of a US willingness to use nuclear weapons on its behalf. Japanese officials were deliberately ambiguous in their representations to US officials about Japan's nuclear intentions despite making a joint communiqué in 1965 affirming Japan's non-nuclear status.[29] In July 1966, for example, in a conversation with Secretary of State Rusk, the Japanese prime minister, Eisaku Sato, pointed out that "now that Communist China has a nuclear capability . . . arguments have appeared in Japan that Japan would need nuclear weapons for its own defense."[30] Sato also used the threat of nuclearization to put pressure on the United States to relinquish sovereign control of the Ryukyu Islands—including Okinawa, home to key US military installations—back to Japan.[31]

The ambassador had concluded in December 1964: "We must . . . be very watchful of any tendencies in Japan to doubt the firmness of US defense commitments or the value of our nuclear deterrent in defense of Free World positions in Asia and in particular Japan. In this regard we must be alert to any weakening of Japan's current position and stance in the face of [Chinese Communist] nuclear-weapon rattling."[32] After Chinese nuclearization in 1964, Johnson administration officials reassured Japan of the credibility of the US commitment, including its commitment to use US nuclear weapons to defend Japan in the case of a nuclear attack. President Lyndon Johnson himself remarked in January 1965 that "if Japan needs our nuclear deterrent for its defense, the United States would stand by its commitments and provide that defense," and that "Japan need not give even a second thought to the dependability of its American ally. If Japan is attacked, the United States will contribute to its defense."[33] When Johnson visited Japan in January 1965, he and Prime Minister Sato issued a joint communiqué that publicly reaffirmed the US commitment to defend Japan, which Johnson subsequently reinforced during Sato's visit to Washington two years later.[34]

LIMITED JAPANESE BURDEN-SHARING

Given US reluctance to take a hard line on the issue of Japanese military power, it is not surprising that Japan invested relatively little of its resources into self-defense. Between 1964 and 1968, Japanese military spending averaged under 0.9 percent of its GDP (see figure 3.1). Because of its geographic position, Japan was relatively insulated from US burden-sharing pressure. Chinese power projection capabilities were minimal, and the Soviet Union did not have substantial air and naval forces in the Far East until later in the 1970s and 1980s.[35] Besides, Japanese officials saw the two Communist powers as preoccupied with each other.[36] Many in Japanese politics and the

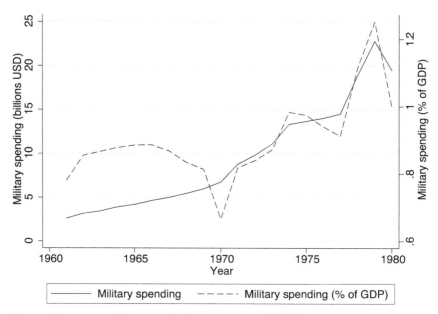

Figure 3.1. Japanese military spending in constant 2005 US dollars, 1961–1980. Military spending data are from Version 5.0 of the Correlates of War's National Material Capabilities Dataset (Singer 1987), and GDP data (in purchasing power parity) are from Gleditsch 2002. Figure adapted from Blankenship 2021 with permission from *Security Studies*.

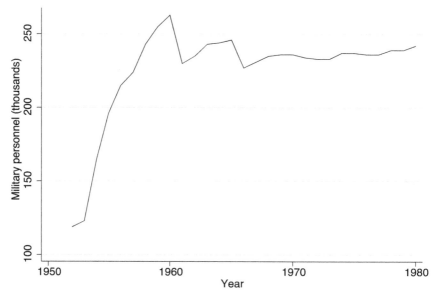

Figure 3.2. Japanese military personnel, 1952–1980. Data are from Version 5.0 of the Correlates of War's National Material Capabilities Dataset (Singer 1987).

public perceived little threat to their security and were ambivalent about the need for a US troop presence at all—particularly ground forces.[37] Indeed, Bundy noted that Japan's reluctance to ramp up military readiness were "mainly governed by (a) lingering antimilitary sentiments growing out of Japan's disastrous war experiences; (b) doubt of the practical value of large Japanese forces—in view of the lack of any clear threat to Japanese territory, US treaty commitments to Japan, and the desire to build friendly relations with neighboring, formerly occupied countries; and (c) reluctance to accept the cost of sizeable forces."[38] Bundy viewed Japan's reluctance to assume more responsibility for its own defense as yet another reason to be skeptical of pressuring it do so. He reasoned, "There is little evidence that absence of US pressure would significantly reduce the pace of the Japanese defense buildup, which over the years has proceeded at its own rate, influenced much more by domestic Japanese political considerations than by our urgings." He concluded: "The fact that our pressure is likely to become less rather than more effective as Japanese national independence and self-determination grow is added reason for not attempting to exert it."[39]

US policymakers likewise had mixed success encouraging Japanese economic burden-sharing, which they viewed as a potential substitute for strictly military contributions. US officials were consistently frustrated at Japan's foreign assistance contributions.[40] And they were unsuccessful in encouraging Japan to purchase US exports to offset the foreign exchange costs the United States incurred by virtue of its defense spending in Japan. Much to the frustration of US policymakers in the Kennedy and Johnson administrations, the Japanese preferred to put their defense spending toward domestic production of arms and equipment rather than purchases of US materiel, which would have stemmed the outflow of dollars from the United States.[41] In 1963, Deputy Secretary of Defense Roswell Gilpatric argued that of the more than $300 million in costs the United States incurred by having its forces stationed in Japan, "realistic military sales/cooperative logistics goals for offset would be $50 million for FY 64, $100 million for FY 65, and $150 million for FY 66."[42] By late 1967, the gap between Japanese offsets and US expenditures was around 65 percent.[43] In contrast, in the FRG, US officials successfully pressured West German officials to fully offset US defense costs throughout much of the 1960s—often through direct threats of troop withdrawals (see chapter 2). But Japan did provide modest direct financial support for the costs of basing US forces in Japan. After somewhat bitter initial negotiations in 1955, Japan arranged for host-nation support (HNS) that accounted for roughly 15 percent of Japanese defense spending.[44] HNS was an attractive avenue for burden-sharing insofar as it allowed Japanese policymakers wary of acquiring more military power and US policymakers uneasy about Japanese self-reliance to pursue burden-sharing arrangements without increasing the pace of Japanese rearmament.[45] These arrangements proved short-lived, however, and HNS did not become a permanent institution until 1978.[46]

CHAPTER 3

The Era of the Guam Doctrine, 1969–1976

Events during the late 1960s and early 1970s prompted decision makers in both the United States and Japan to reevaluate the terms of their relationship. As discussed in chapter 2, the two most significant developments were the enduring costs of the Vietnam War, which drained US resources and created a sizable constituency within the United States for retrenchment abroad and defense budget cuts at home, and a stagnant US economy that had lost its postwar position of dominance, faced increasingly stiff competition from Europe and Japan, and suffered from high unemployment and inflation (stagflation) simultaneously (see figures A.1 and A.2 in the appendix).[47]

My theory would thus predict increased emphasis on Japanese defense burden-sharing during the early 1970s as a result of political and resource constraints within the United States (see table 3.4). But US policymakers should have carefully weighed the risks of Japanese burden-sharing and ultimately rejected the option of fully leaving the defense of Japan to the Japanese. Japan, fearing abandonment in the 1970s more than it had during the 1960s, should have responded to US pressure with modest efforts toward military self-reliance.

JAPANESE FEARS OF ABANDONMENT

Japanese policymakers viewed developing political and economic conditions in the United States as a portent of US retrenchment from its other mil-

Table 3.4 Predictions for US burden-sharing pressure toward Japan, 1969–1976

Latent military potential	External threat	US resource constraints	Prediction	Outcome
High	Low	High	Moderate US interest in Japanese force improvements, counterbalanced by concerns about Japanese freedom of action	US policymakers weighed the desirability of encouraging substantial Japanese military self-reliance at great length, but settled on encouraging only moderate, qualitative improvements in Japanese capabilities. Fearing the possibility of abandonment, Japanese policymakers increased defense spending but did not dramatically increase the size of the SDF.

76

itary commitments in East Asia, leading some to favor "a more independent foreign policy" that would "loosen" Japan from the United States.[48] The State Department's country director for Japan noted in April 1968 that the US failure to secure victory in the Vietnam War, the turmoil in US domestic politics, and Johnson's decision not to run for re-election "are all cited as evidences of American weakness" in Japan, and that the Japanese were concerned that US foreign policy "is constantly swinging with the whims of public opinion."[49] A telegram from the US embassy in May similarly suggested that domestic volatility within the United States might create in Japan a momentum to more seriously consider both nuclear weapons and "more than very gradual acceleration of buildup in Japan's own defense which has been [the] case over [the] last few years," which could "be accompanied by assertive nationalist overtones and aggressive demands for phase down of US bases."[50] When National Security Adviser Henry Kissinger visited Japan in June 1972, the Japanese foreign minister, Takeo Fukuda, raised concerns that "the economic strength of the US is somewhat distorted," as "the arms race and the Vietnam war are eroding the US economic position in the world," and advised that the United States conserve its resources so that it could sustain its overseas presence.[51]

A number of additional factors—which were largely products of the costs of Vietnam, the United States' diminished position, and accompanying domestic retrenchment pressure—intensified Japanese fears of abandonment. The first of these was President Nixon's announcement of the Guam Doctrine in July 1969, which proclaimed that allies—particularly in East Asia—would be expected to do more for their own self-defense.[52] Nixon and Kissinger viewed the international system as increasingly "multipolar," as US preeminence had diminished while its allies' strength had increased.[53] As a result, they sought to pass on more of the costs of regional defense to allies and reduce US involvement in future conflicts.[54] As Nixon put it in Guam, "Asia is for Asians. . . . We must avoid the kind of policy that will make countries in Asia so dependent upon us that we are dragged into conflicts such as the one we have in Vietnam."[55] The following year, the United States began to withdraw tens of thousands of troops from Japan and South Korea, further alarming the Japanese. In response, Japan and South Korea issued a joint communiqué in July 1970 in which they asserted that "US military presence is a key factor in safeguarding the security of the Far East."[56] Japan's doubts about US credibility were further exacerbated when South Vietnam fell to an invasion from North Vietnam in 1975.[57]

What also caused great consternation was the United States' rapprochement with the Communist bloc. Nixon regarded détente with the Communist bloc as a means to mitigate the risk of conflict while also reducing the costs of the military arms race, and thus an essential component of his effort to bring the costs of US commitments in line with the resources that could be used to support them. Most notable was Nixon's opening of relations

CHAPTER 3

with China, which marked the beginning of US efforts to exploit the rift between China and the Soviet Union and force the latter to split its attention and resources.[58]

Japan, meanwhile, feared that improved relations between the United States and the Communist powers might be the precursor to a larger withdrawal of US forces from the region, and even to a superpower fait accompli in which Japanese interests were sold out by US policymakers seeking to reduce the possibility of war for the United States.[59] As Johnson's special assistant Walt Rostow put it, Japan did not "want us buddying up too close to either Communist China or the USSR."[60] US-Soviet arms control agreements such as the Strategic Arms Limitation Treaties (SALT I and II), which aimed to limit the nuclear arms race, and the US-Soviet Prevention of Nuclear War Agreement, which provided for great power consultation in situations of elevated risk of nuclear war, raised suspicions about a great power condominium and questions about US willingness to go to war on its allies' behalf.[61] The State Department's director of policy planning, Winston Lord, noted that the Japanese had "apprehensions that understandings between the US and USSR may reduce the danger of Great Power confrontations without removing the possibilities of local conflict."[62] The opening to China in particular shocked the Japanese because they were not consulted and were barely notified prior to Nixon's public announcement of his upcoming visit to Beijing. Conservatives in the LDP felt particularly betrayed in light of their loyalty to the United States, with Sato claiming the Americans "let me down."[63]

As a result of concerns about a decoupling of US and Japanese security interests, many in Japan began to consider pursuing a more independent foreign policy, one less dependent on the United States. For one thing, Japan pursued better relations with China and the Soviet Union.[64] Even some Japanese conservatives in the LDP, traditionally characterized by intense anti-communism and strong support for the US alliance, shifted to favoring rapprochement with the Communist bloc.[65] As one NSC paper put it in August 1971, Nixon's surprise overtures to China "inspired speculation in Japan about the future of the US/Japan relationship, demands for a more 'independent' foreign policy, and fears and recriminations about Japan's own China policy."[66] This ultimately led to the September 1972 restoration of diplomatic ties between Japan and China, as well as numerous high-level visits between Soviet and Japanese officials.[67] Japanese threat perceptions, in turn, diminished due to the improvement in its own relations with the Communist bloc.[68] Additionally, Japan's search for alliance alternatives included increased consideration of pursuing nuclear weapons, with Japan launching an initially covert centrifuge program—though not an overt nuclear weapons program—and refusing to ratify the NPT until June 1976.[69]

These developments were not lost on US officials in the Nixon and Ford administrations. The State Department warned that "alternative foreign policy orientations may become more attractive to Japan," including "non-alignment, independent nationalism, or close political ties with China or the Soviet Union," and it argued that the United States needed to "reassure" Japan in order to discourage it from "acting independently."[70] The scenario that US officials most feared was the emergence of a more independent, neutrally oriented Japanese foreign policy. In a conversation with Kissinger, Undersecretary of State Alexis Johnson remarked, "I don't see a Japan-China axis developing. . . . I do see, however, a neutral Japan—a Japan taking an independent position. If, for example, they lost confidence in our nuclear umbrella, they could renounce the Security Treaty in order to avoid domestic problems. This could be tempting for them."[71] US officials believed historical animosity with China made a Sino-Japanese partnership unlikely, but they did not rule out a negotiated détente in which Japan restricted US access to bases on Japanese territory—especially for use in conflicts over Taiwan or even South Korea—in exchange for normalized relations.[72] Indeed, Japanese officials articulated these possibilities directly, with the Japanese ambassador arguing that the US opening to China would cause problems for Japan's ruling LDP party, and that "a fundamental policy objective of Peking was to split Japan off from the US and 'neutralize' it."[73]

A related worry was the prospect of Japanese-Soviet alignment. An NSC memo to Kissinger argued, "We would do well to realize that the Soviets have much to offer to Japan, including an implied guarantee of security against China. Despite the traditional Japanese distrust and antipathy toward Russia . . . the role of the USSR cannot be discounted in Japanese calculations."[74] The need to reduce Japan's incentives for unilateral military arming or for reaching out to the Soviet Union was a key justification US officials gave to the Chinese for the US alliance with and continued presence in Japan.[75]

Finally, US policymakers were also preoccupied with fears of Japanese nuclearization, stoked not only by Japan's reluctance to ratify the NPT and awareness of Japanese concerns about US reliability, but also by Japan's economic and industrial capacity.[76] An NIE in early 1969 argued that Japanese desire for "'armed neutrality' . . . would be accelerated if faith in the US alliance were somehow shaken."[77]

AMBIVALENT US BURDEN-SHARING PRESSURE

These competing pressures—constraints on US resources, on the one hand, and fear of Japan's outside options, on the other—molded the Nixon and Ford administrations' policy toward Japan, which attempted to balance the need for greater burden-sharing with the need to not push it too far. US policymakers throughout the 1970s sought to encourage Japan to bear a somewhat greater defense burden. Indeed, greater allied self-reliance was the hallmark of the Guam Doctrine, and this pressure for increased Japanese burden-sharing continued into the Ford administration.[78] Much of the impetus for the pressure came from Congress, and US officials used it to

CHAPTER 3

their advantage, making frequent reference to how Congress might react if Japan did not step up.[79] The US ambassador to Japan told Japanese policymakers in August 1968 that "if our future relationship was going to develop in a constructive manner, it was important that the American people get a sense that Japan was bearing a responsibility commensurate with its growing power."[80] Nixon's defense secretary Melvin Laird similarly told Prime Minister Sato in July 1971 that "the US Congress consistently pressed the Administration on whether there was true partnership in our security relations. There was Congressional reference to the 7 percent, or more, of Gross National Product (GNP) the US devoted to national security as opposed to the 1 percent or less provided by Japan."[81]

However, among US officials there was nevertheless a great deal of ambivalence about burden-sharing pressure on Japan, and about the steps Japan was taking to boost its defense effort. US policymakers recognized that the United States could not continue to shoulder the burden as it had previously.[82] Kissinger remarked in June 1970 to a former Japanese foreign minister that "Japan could and should carry a greater burden of its own defense. It was not a healthy situation for the US to carry the whole burden, especially when other countries could contribute."[83] Nixon similarly told Japanese prime minister Kakuei Tanaka in May 1973 that "an economic giant cannot remain a political pygmy."[84] This view was particularly strong among officials in the US Treasury Department, who were primarily concerned with the balance of payments deficit that Washington incurred by having forces in Japan, but Defense Secretary Laird also argued in favor of higher Japanese defense spending.[85]

But US officials feared that encouraging too much self-reliance would produce a neutral, potentially nuclear-armed Japan.[86] Japan's meteoric growth was rapidly turning it into an economic and potential military powerhouse; between 1965 and 1970, Japan's GDP more than doubled, surpassing that of West Germany and the United Kingdom. US policymakers saw Japan as a potential dominant power and competitor in East Asia, and as such, they sought to avoid unleashing Japan by encouraging it to remilitarize.[87] Secretary of State Rogers wrote to Nixon in 1970 regarding US troop withdrawals from Korea that "while some concern on the part of the Japanese is healthy," it was essential "not to cross over the line that would cause the Japanese to have such doubts about our deterrent capabilities and intentions with respect to Japan and the rest of the area."[88]

Indeed, US policymakers were explicit in their emphasis on the dangers of Japanese burden-sharing. In August 1971, the NSC Interdepartmental Group for East Asia drafted National Security Study Memorandum (NSSM) 122, which laid out four options for burden-sharing in the relationship, ranging from the status quo to "actively encourag[ing] Japan to assume some or all the present US security role in East Asia." The downsides of shifting more burdens onto Japan, the paper argued, included:

"BETWEEN SCYLLA AND CHARYBDIS"

- Stimulat[ing] Japanese competition with US economically and politically in other areas
- Mak[ing] Japan less amenable to US influence
- Arous[ing] Chinese fears of Japanese militarism and suspicions of US intentions; endangers détente
- Increas[ing] risks that Japan may embark on road to complete military independence and nuclear rearmament[89]

The NSC group subsequently met twice that month to discuss the paper and the future course of the United States-Japan alliance. The discussions that took place reflected a clear recognition of the dilemma posed by Japanese burden-sharing. During the first meeting, those present raised concerns about asking Japan to take more responsibility for its own defense. Undersecretary of State Johnson argued that "Japan can be a maverick, and the pendulum can swing wildly from one extreme to the other. We are afraid we might get the Japanese to move too much," while Kissinger asked, "Can we stop the pendulum from swinging back to the other extreme?" and did not receive a clear answer.[90] Deputy Defense Secretary David Packard noted, "We want the Japanese to play a larger role than they have been playing, but at the same time we don't want them to play too large a role."[91]

The participants agreed to meet again later that month, at which time Kissinger noted that they had previously agreed that "we were not eager to see Japan's economic power translated into military and political power." Undersecretary of State Johnson expressed a similar sentiment, submitting that "I'm not so sure Japan is getting a free ride. We have to ask ourselves if a heavily armed, nuclear Japan is in our interest. I don't think this is necessarily so."[92] Their worry was that an autonomous Japan would be less willing to defer to US policy preferences. Johnson argued that if Japan became more autonomous, "there will be less association with the US in the UN on the [Taiwan] issue," and further noted that "in spite of demonstrations and some anti-US outbursts, the Japanese Government has had good relations with us on all issues. Their instinct has also been to help us in the Vietnam War. In the future, they will probably be less cooperative."[93] Another possibility raised by Kissinger was that a withdrawal of the US presence in the region could "lead to a Finnish-type neutrality," in which rather than pursuing military arming, the Japanese instead attempted to retreat from the Cold War contest and accommodated the Soviet Union.[94] Ultimately, the tension between these US goals—of maintaining influence over Japanese foreign policy while also sharing the burden of defense—was summarized well by Kissinger:

> We want to maintain close ties with Japan. Nobody disagrees with that. What do we want Japan to do? We want Japan to: (1) continue to provide the bases and facilities essential to our Pacific security posture; (2) spend more for a conventional defense; (3) play a more constructive role in the economic

CHAPTER 3

development of Southeast Asia; (4) continue to seek great power status through nonmilitary means and without nuclear weapons. At the same time, we say that Japan will be more autonomous, and this means they will not follow us as much as they have in the past. I am not objecting to these goals, if we can get them. But is it likely?[95]

US policymakers never decisively resolved this tension in either direction. In March 1972 the outgoing ambassador to Japan Armin Meyer summed up the prevailing ambivalence when he wrote to Nixon on the issue of United States-Japan relations and the sharing of burdens in the relationship: "My own tendency has been to steer the course between Scylla and Charybdis. Tough we should and must be. Also essential is the maintenance of a political regime in Japan cooperating fruitfully with America."[96]

Instead, the administration outwardly chose an incremental approach consistent with its internal ambivalence. Nixon elected to seek "moderate increases and qualitative improvements in Japan's defense efforts, while avoiding any pressure on her to develop substantially larger forces or to play a larger national security role," a policy that was laid out in NSDM 13 in May 1969 and remained the Nixon and Ford administrations' overarching position.[97] During Kissinger's visit in June 1972, he spoke to the question of burden-sharing, declaring to the Japan-US Economic Council, "We are not trying to push Japan into anything. We believe that what the Japanese do will be in terms of their own judgment of their national interests."[98] He struck the same tone in private, telling Minister of Foreign Affairs Takeo Fukuda that "we are not pushing Japan into rearmament," and that the United States did not "have any intention of pushing Japan into a military role."[99] Subsequent analysis and discussion within the Nixon administration throughout 1973 and 1974 similarly stalemated on the question of Japanese burden-sharing, with US officials wary that pressing Japan to dramatically bolster its capabilities and assume a greater regional role would not only alarm its neighbors but also further push it toward greater independence from Washington. Thus, NSSM 172 ultimately concluded that the status quo was acceptable.[100]

This approach continued under Gerald Ford's presidency (1974–1976).[101] US policymakers continued to hope that Japan would increase its air and maritime (especially antisubmarine) capabilities, but had as Kissinger put it, there was "no interest in stimulating substantial increases in the size of Japan's armed forces or their assumption of overseas security responsibilities."[102] Officials continued to recognize the trade-off inherent in Japanese burden-sharing, with one analyst for the NSC remarking in October 1974: "A fundamental dilemma must be noted at the outset. The US still wishes to keep very close ties to Japan. Or it may decide consciously to 'cut Japan loose,' however gradually. . . . We seem to be following a confusing and perhaps unavoidable pattern of ambiguity: of urging Japan toward a more active role while keeping some policy considerations off limits."[103] The following month,

82

two other NSC staff members similarly wrote that "the dilemma is how, on the one hand, we can get Japan to take a broader approach and to play a more active political role on global multilateral problems and to more greater equality and reciprocity in our alliance relationship, while, on the other hand, we do not put intolerable strains in our relationship with Japan or on the LDP's domestic political base, do not push Japan toward regionally destabilizing roles, and do recognize both the current Japanese preference for a low-profile role and the risks in Japan's moving beyond this role too rapidly."[104]

At the same time, US officials went to great lengths to reassure Japan that the Guam Doctrine and the emergence of a "multipolar" era in which the United States would expect more from its allies did not mean that US protection would diminish.[105] One prong to the US reassurance effort was to communicate that US rapprochement with China would not involve "secret deals" between China and the United States that affected Japanese interests.[106] Kissinger told the Japanese ambassador shortly after Nixon announced his visit to China in July 1971 that "we really considered our relationship with Japan as the center of our policy in the Pacific" and that "we are not replacing Japan with China," while Nixon wrote to Sato that "my visit to China will not be at the expense of old friends."[107] In December 1971, Acting Secretary of State Alexis Johnson wrote to Nixon that Nixon's upcoming meeting with the Japanese prime minister "will be a success if Sato leaves reassured that we understand and will protect Japan's concerns in dealing with Peking, and that there will be future opportunities for similar consultations."[108] Kissinger struck a similar tone during his subsequent trip to Japan in June.[109] Indeed, before Nixon's visit with Prime Minister Tanaka in August that same year, Kissinger wrote to him that among the core objectives of the visit was "to reaffirm the US-Japan alliance . . . as a relationship which requires concrete contributions by both sides to keep it going. E.g., while we furnish nuclear protection, the Japanese must make it possible for us to use Japanese bases," and he noted that this took on particular urgency in light of "Tanaka's Peking visit and Japan's opening of peace treaty negotiations with the Soviet Union."[110]

The United States' reassurances were in no small part to secure Japan's ratification of the NPT.[111] In a 1971 meeting with Prime Minister Sato, Defense Secretary Laird "assured Sato the US would maintain a proper and sufficient nuclear deterrent vis-à-vis the USSR."[112] Kissinger likewise stressed the importance that the United States placed on Japanese NPT ratification and reassured Japanese officials of the US commitment during his June 1972 trip. Prior to the visit, Undersecretary of State Johnson had argued that "it would therefore be helpful if in connection with reconfirming the US desire to have Japan ratify the NPT, you could assure the Japanese that the US-Japan Security Treaty remains the key to regional stability in Asia and continues to be an essential element in the relationship between Japan and the US."[113] In a conversation with the Japanese foreign minister in May 1974,

CHAPTER 3

Nixon claimed that although the United States opposed proliferation, "I would not indicate what Japan should do." The United States' relatively light pressure was not the result of ambivalence about the goal of nonproliferation; Kissinger's talking points for his own meeting with the Japanese foreign minister included reaffirming that "US interest in Japanese ratification [of the NPT] remains high." Rather, it reflected the relatively limited leverage the United States had due to Japan's relatively larger margin of security, in contrast to cases of more vulnerable allies such as South Korea, where the United States wielded blunt threats of abandonment to discourage proliferation (see chapter 4).[114]

MODEST JAPANESE BURDEN-SHARING

In response to concerns about the US commitment in the wake of the Guam Doctrine, shifting US domestic opinion in favor of retrenchment, and the fall of South Vietnam, coupled with pressure from their US counterparts, Japanese officials made modest efforts toward greater self-reliance. A number of Japanese policymakers, most notably the Defense Agency director general Yasuhiro Nakasone, came to view a push toward more "autonomous self-defense" as an essential response to the Nixon Doctrine and a hedge against the possibility of US abandonment.[115] But mainstream LDP opinion, including in the cabinets of Sato, Tanaka, and Miki, was more skeptical of the need for radically expanding the SDF, given the still relatively permissive threat environment, and instead favored a more incremental approach.[116] The result of this back and forth was Japan's first-ever Defense Agency white paper in October 1970, which argued that US protection should "complement" rather than "substitute" for Japanese defense and proposed upgrading the SDF by pursing qualitative improvements, as well as its first-ever attempt to lay out a defense strategy that codified the size and structure of the SDF, in the form of the 1976 National Defense Program Outline (NDPO).[117] The 1976 NDPO reflected Defense Agency senior official Takuya Kubo's concept of "Fundamental Defense Capability," developed over the previous several years, which called for a "small but high quality" SDF.[118] All the while, the country increased its defense spending; between 1969 and 1976, the Japanese defense budget nearly tripled, from $5 billion to nearly $15 billion in constant 2005 dollars, and it topped $20 billion by the end of the decade (see figure 3.1). Following the 1970 white paper, this spending targeted technology, research, and development, as well as domestic production of its own planes, ships, and other equipment, rather than enlarging the SDF, with the goal of obtaining a small but capable force that could handle limited contingencies and deter faits accomplis.[119] Nevertheless, Japanese defense expenditures as a percentage of GDP rose only slightly, peaking around 1 percent of GDP, and its armed forces did not grow in overall size (see figure 3.2). Instead, the SDF upgraded its older, often US-made equipment with newer, domestic-produced equipment and expanded its ground-to-air defense systems.[120]

Ultimately, US fears of renewed Japanese militarism did not materialize, mostly because of a combination of limited Japanese perceptions of threat and the United States' reluctance to press too much for self-reliance.[121] US policy was to encourage "Japan to continue to improve gradually its conventional military capability for the defense of its territory, but to avoid any regional security role."[122] As Kissinger put it in 1971, "Our experience along this line with the Europeans indicates that they will only spend more on defense if they are convinced their own security is at stake and that we will not spend more to provide their security," adding, "We know Japan's tendency to extremes. Now they are non-militarists, but if we convince them otherwise, can we stop the pendulum from swinging back to the other extreme?"[123] Moreover, Japanese perceptions of threat were quite low as a result of the country's separation from the Asian mainland.[124] Undersecretary of State Johnson remarked that the Japanese "do not perceive the threat—unlike the Germans or the Koreans. They do not see a threat coming from the Soviet Union—unless there is a nuclear conflict involving the entire world. They do not see for a generation at least a conventional threat coming from China"; later he remarked that the Japanese "perceive no sense of threat."[125] While the Soviet Union had begun building up its forces in the Far East, it was not until later in the 1970s and 1980s that growing Soviet strength in the region—including a large naval force—became an increasingly serious concern for the Japanese.[126] Moreover, Japanese threat perceptions were further curbed by the climate of détente that prevailed in the aftermath of normalized relations with China and relaxation of tensions with the Soviet Union, coupled with the reality that the Sino-Soviet split forced the Soviets and Chinese to devote substantial resources against each other.[127]

As my theory expects, US burden-sharing pressure toward Japan was relatively light during the 1960s and 1970s. Not only was Japan insulated from US pressure by virtue of its margin of security, but US officials balked at the prospect of encouraging Japan to substantially increase its military capabilities out of fear that it would embolden the Japanese to leave the alliance or obtain nuclear weapons and make it easier for them to do so. Their reluctance waned somewhat during the 1970s as the costs of the Vietnam War and pro-retrenchment sentiment at home constrained the United States' ability to meet its foreign commitments. These same constraints likewise increased Japanese fears of abandonment, and as a result, Japan increased its defense spending, despite the climate of détente that prevailed for much of the 1970s. Nevertheless, because US policymakers continued to fear that Japanese rearmament would lead to a more assertive, independent Japan that would be less willing to align its foreign policy with that of Washington—fears that

CHAPTER 3

were magnified as Japan explored outside options such as closer relations with China and the Soviet Union and nuclear weapons—their efforts to encourage Japanese burden-sharing were half-hearted and marked by ambivalence. Thus, the United States' ability to coerce Japan into making a higher defense effort was undercut by its concern that too much burden-sharing would lead Japan to go its own way, as well as by Japan's relatively secure geographic position, which led many Japanese citizens and policymakers to perceive a lower level of threat.

The case of Japan provides a particularly clear example of how the trade-off between control and cost-sharing shapes alliance policy—and in particular, how concerns about too much allied independence can act as a straitjacket, limiting great powers' ability to relieve their defense burdens by assigning responsibilities to local partners. US officials were consistently ambivalent on the subject of Japanese burden-sharing, in some cases suggesting that Japan should do more while in other cases expressing serious reservations about a potentially resurgent Japan. Their calculus shifted somewhat in favor of seeking greater Japanese contributions during the period of the Nixon Doctrine in the early 1970s, when US resources were severely constrained by the Vietnam War and economic and political conditions at home. But despite the Nixon administration's professed desire for allies to rely primarily on their own efforts for self-defense, it is striking just how little pressure US officials put on Japan—arguably, the prime case of an ally that could have taken up the mantle of regional defense in Washington's stead.

CHAPTER 4

"They Live at Our Sufferance"

South Korean Burden-Sharing, 1964–1980

The Republic of Korea (ROK) constituted a central front in the Cold War. As one of the only US allies in East Asia that shared a land border with the Communist bloc, South Korea existed under the shadow of the threat of attack, and the United States regarded it as a bulwark against further Communist expansion. As a result, after signing the Mutual Defense Treaty (MDT) in 1953 and negotiating a cease-fire in the Korean War, Washington left some 60,000 US forces in the country to deter future North Korean attacks.

Its vulnerability also forced Washington and Seoul to concern themselves with South Korea's own defensive capabilities. With a GDP per capita of less than $200 in 1955, Seoul's ability to provide for itself was limited, and the country depended heavily on US military and economic assistance.[1] Nevertheless, the country's meteoric growth in the 1960s and 1970s bolstered the country's ability to assume more responsibility for its own defense, and as a result it came under increasing US pressure to increase its defense spending and wean itself off US assistance. Washington's enthusiasm for South Korean burden-sharing was magnified by the Vietnam War, which strained not only US economic and human resources but also domestic tolerance for foreign entanglements.

The United States-South Korea alliance, then, was defined by the ROK's vulnerability. South Korea's small size relative to its neighbors meant that it had no realistic potential for exiting the alliance. Moreover, its geography rendered South Korea prone to fears of abandonment. As a result, the country faced very high levels of US burden-sharing pressure, especially during the 1970s, and this pressure was quite successful. By the mid-1970s, the country's own military spending accounted for almost all of its on defense outlays, whereas in the 1950s and 1960s US assistance had furnished the lion's share of South Korea's capabilities.

CHAPTER 4

Empirical Predictions

In the language of the typology presented in chapter 1, South Korea was initially on the borderline between being a Cost Imposition and Favorable Bargaining case, and over time it shifted firmly into the latter category. South Korea's capacity for self-reliance was inherently limited by its modest size, and it had a severe threat environment owing to the proximity of North Korea, China, and the Soviet Union. Alliance control theory would thus expect US policymakers to be quite willing to seek greater burden-sharing by the ROK, especially during the 1970s as South Korea's economic growth began gradually pulling the country out of poverty; between 1963 and 1980 the country averaged double-digit annual GDP growth rates, and by the end of the 1980s what was once among the poorest US allies had become one of the wealthier. Additionally, the costs of the Vietnam War, the United States' diminishing economic position, and congressional pressure to retrench should have put pressure on the United States to place more of the defense burden on South Korea and do less itself, while also pursuing rapprochement with its adversaries. Throughout, US burden-sharing pressure should have been quite successful owing to South Korea's vulnerability to attack from North Korea. In sum, I would predict rising levels of burden-sharing throughout, with a dramatic increase in the 1970s (see table 4.1).

These predictions are ultimately borne out, while competing theories—public goods logic, US signals of support, and South Korean domestic politics—have difficulty explaining South Korean burden-sharing. Despite its modest size and hosting upward of 40,000 US forces, by the late 1970s South Korea was devoting a substantial portion of its economy to defense, rivaling that of any other US ally. Additionally, South Korean domestic politics cannot explain changes in its burden-sharing over time. Instead, the evidence shows that South Korean burden-sharing was in large part a response to US pressure, strengthened as it was by the intensity of South Korean threat perceptions and by the credibility of US threats of abandonment resulting from resource and domestic political constraints during the late 1960s and 1970s.

Table 4.1 South Korea's scores on the independent variables

Latent military potential	External threat	US resource constraints	Prediction
Initially low, but increasing to moderate by mid-1970s	High	High in late 1960s and 1970s due to the Vietnam War	Modest initial interest in South Korean conventional force improvements gives way to intense interest during the 1970s. US burden-sharing pressure achieves a good deal of success.

88

Strategic Context

The primary collective defense challenge facing the United States-South Korea alliance was deterring another invasion from North Korea like the one that had occurred in 1950. The size of South Korea's population and economy exceeded that of its neighbor, but North Korea received material backing from China and the Soviet Union, which, coupled with North Korea's substantial military spending-to-GDP ratio, put South Korea at a disadvantage in terms of equipment even as it maintained rough parity in manpower. And, of course, there was the possibility that China would directly support such an attack. In addition, South Korea was geographically exposed and lacked strategic depth because its capital, Seoul, was only fifty kilometers from the demilitarized zone with North Korea. North Korean forces repeatedly infiltrated South Korea, and the two sides regularly exchanged fire in the demilitarized zone.[2]

Although the United States had initially marked South Korea as outside of its "defensive perimeter," the Korean War dramatically altered US perceptions of the threat of Communist expansion in Asia and elsewhere. US officials came to view defending South Korea as strategically important for blocking the Communist bloc's expansion by both land and sea.[3] Indeed, the Japanese had long regarded the Korean Peninsula as a steppingstone to invading their home islands—as a "dagger pointed at the heart" of Japan.[4]

ROK Participation in the Vietnam War, 1964–1968

When Lyndon Johnson assumed office in late 1963, South Korea was still in the early stages of what would be decades of rapid growth, and the country

Table 4.2 North Korean military power, 1963–1980

Year	Total manpower	Total ground forces
1963	338,000	308,000
1965	353,000	325,000
1968	384,000	345,000
1970	413,000	370,000
1973	470,000	408,000
1975	467,000	410,000
1978	512,000	440,000
1980	678,000	600,000

Source: International Institute for Strategic Studies, The Military Balance, vols. 1963, 1965, 1968, 1970, 1973, 1975, 1980.

CHAPTER 4

Table 4.3 Predictions for US burden-sharing pressure toward South Korea, 1964–1968

Latent military potential	External threat	US resource constraints	Prediction	Outcome
Low	High	Rising	Moderate US interest in South Korean force improvements, and high South Korean susceptibility to US pressure	US policymakers sought some South Korean force improvements but mostly focused on soliciting South Korean contributions to the Vietnam War, with a good deal success.

was still highly dependent on external assistance. I would thus expect relatively limited US interest in South Korean conventional military self-reliance, as indicated in table 4.3. South Korea was lacking not manpower—its population was more than double that of North Korea—but rather the ability to equip and supply its soldiers. As a result, while South Korea provided the vast majority of military personnel on the Korean Peninsula, the United States shouldered a huge portion of the ROK's defense costs, with US military aid accounting for upward of 80 percent of the South Korean defense budget throughout the 1950s and most of the 1960s.[5] US officials perceived South Korea as (at least temporarily) incapable of fending for itself without considerable economic and military assistance. The deputy assistant secretary of state for Far Eastern affairs argued in October 1964 that "the Korean Government cannot at present increase its share of the burden," and that "pressure on the Korean defense budget has made it necessary to maintain pay and allowances at a detrimentally low level" such that if US assistance was cut, ROK forces would by necessity be cut as well.[6] US policymakers treated US assistance as key to ensuring that South Korea was able to maintain sufficient military readiness, pay civil servants and the armed forces enough to keep them satisfied with the current government, and focus on economic growth so that it could maintain popular legitimacy and eventually be able to stand on its own.[7] Indeed, US officials regarded defense procurement spending as a means of injecting funds into the South Korean economy to foster economic growth, and likewise provided surplus US agricultural products to improve the South Korean armed forces' standard of living.[8]

The one area where the ROK made an outsize contribution was in sending troops to fight in South Vietnam. As the United States began to escalate its military involvement in Vietnam during the mid-1960s, it sought support from other US allies in the Asia-Pacific region, as well as from Europe. But outside of small deployments from Australia, New Zealand, the Philippines, and Thailand, very little help was on offer. US policymakers were initially reluctant to seek South Korean support, given the threat from North Korea, but the paucity of contributions from other allies forced their hand. Moreover, because South Korea suffered not so much from manpower constraints as from financial constraints—while the reverse was true of Washington, given its presence throughout Western Europe and East Asia—deploying Korean soldiers for combat in Vietnam was attractive insofar as it allowed the United States to avoid troop withdrawals elsewhere. In turn, Washington was responsible for the financial costs of equipping and supplying Korean forces in Vietnam. The first US requests for South Korean participation in the Vietnam War came in May and December 1964, and South Korea responded by sending just over 2,000 noncombat troops. Then, in early 1965, South Korea agreed to send one combat division.[9]

South Korean president Park Chung Hee—who assumed power in 1963 and whose rule would become increasingly more authoritarian until his assassination in 1979—saw involvement in Vietnam as a way to gain clout with the United States as a loyal ally in the hope of securing other favors. In light of the continuing threat from North Korea, Park sought assurances that US forces would not be withdrawn, additional military and economic assistance to help the country bridge the equipment gap with North Korea, and a revision to the MDT that would include language closer to that in the NATO treaty, promising that "an attack on Korea would be regarded as an attack on the United States."[10] In an effort to satisfy Park's requests and ease ROK perceptions of vulnerability such that he felt sufficiently reassured to deploy forces to Vietnam, the United States defrayed the costs of keeping South Korean forces in Vietnam, increased its military aid to South Korea, and promised not to withdraw troops from South Korea without prior consultation.[11] However, US officials refused to entertain one of the ROK's most sought-after concessions—revising the MDT to guarantee that US assistance would be automatically forthcoming in the event of an attack on South Korea—and pointed to the US Constitution's bar on the president's ability to unilaterally alter treaties.[12] As the situation in Vietnam deteriorated in 1966, the United States requested and secured the deployment of another division of South Korean forces to Vietnam, in exchange for more economic and military assistance. But the Johnson administration again refused to revisit the MDT, instead dispatching Vice President Hubert Humphrey to privately assure Park that US assistance would be automatic in the event of a North Korean attack.[13]

This was the limit of South Korea's bargaining power. US policymakers made it very clear that the United States "could not make any commitment to keep any specific number of troops in any specific locality for any specific period of time," nor "give assurance of the maintenance of any specific level of military assistance."[14] Instead, they promised only that "our commitment to their defense is absolute under the 1954 Mutual Defense Treaty, and that we would certainly consult with them on any changes in force levels which might be dictated by our regional and global requirements."[15]

CHAPTER 4

Moreover, US officials threatened to withdraw US troops from Korea in the absence of ROK participation in South Vietnam.[16] US envoy Cyrus Vance told Park during his early 1968 trip to Seoul that "were they even to consider removing troops from South Vietnam we would pull ours out of Korea."[17] While the sincerity of US threats cannot be taken for granted, they were consistent with the administration's internal discussions. In April 1968, Johnson's special assistant Walt Rostow noted in a letter to Johnson, "We have told them many times that we have no plan to reduce the general level of our ground forces [in South Korea]—by implication as long as they have forces in Viet-Nam. Suggest you repeat that we have no plan to reduce our ground forces under present circumstances, but avoid going further than promising full consultation . . . on any later plan concerning ground forces."[18]

The strains on the ROK presence in Vietnam mounted due in large part to a spike in provocations from North Korea. Beginning in 1966, South Korea experienced an uptick in lethal attacks by North Korean infiltrators, which Park feared could force him to redirect resources away from frontline defense.[19] The most significant of these occurred in January 1968, when North Korean infiltrators attempted to assassinate Park at the Blue House, and then a few days later abducted the spy ship USS *Pueblo*. In response, the United States started bilateral negotiations without South Korean representation for the return of the *Pueblo* and, much to Park's chagrin, put serious pressure on the ROK to refrain from any kind of retaliation.[20] As a result, Park canceled plans to expand the South Korean presence in the Vietnam and instead devoted manpower to increasing the size of the ROK's military reserves and investing in the country's domestic weapons production.[21]

US Retrenchment and Détente, 1969–1974

By the time Richard Nixon came to office in 1969, nearly 40,000 Americans had died in the Vietnam War, tens of thousands more had been wounded, and billions of dollars had been spent, with no clear end in sight.[22] Moreover, Nixon inherited a US economy that had diminished from its post–World War II peak (see figure A.1 in the appendix). This was partly the result of the meteoric growth of other economies—particularly in Western Europe and Japan—whose exports could now compete with those of the United States. But the US economy itself was in dire straits too, with unemployment and inflation rising in tandem (see figure A.2 in the appendix) due to a combination of increased government spending on the Vietnam War and Johnson's Great Society domestic programs, a rising trade deficit, and massive numbers of US troops in Europe, Vietnam, Korea, and Japan, which led to a huge increase in the amount of dollars in foreign hands.[23] Because the dollar was directly convertible into gold at $35/ounce, US gold stocks slowly depleted over the course of the 1960s as dollar holders sought to di-

92

"THEY LIVE AT OUR SUFFERANCE"

vest themselves of what they feared was an overvalued currency that could not be backed up with gold as promised.[24]

In light of the United States' broader competition with the Soviet Union—which entailed hundreds of thousands of forces deployed in Europe, Japan, and South Korea, and the financial toll of the nuclear arms race—the cost of the Vietnam War not only became unsustainable in its own right, but also brought into question Washington's willingness and ability to meet its other commitments. Public opinion and the US Congress put pressure on the Nixon administration to reduce the United States' overseas footprint, cut defense spending, and avoid future entanglements.[25] As discussed in chapter 2, much of the focus was on Europe, but members of Congress eyed cuts in Korea as well.[26] US military spending dropped each year between 1969 and 1976 except 1974, and Nixon gradually withdrew US forces from Vietnam. In addition, Nixon sought ways to cut the US trade deficit, delinked the dollar from $35/ounce convertibility to gold in 1971, and reduced US force levels in South Korea.[27]

During the first half of the 1970s, I would expect intense US pressure to increase South Korea's military capabilities for two reasons (see table 4.4). The first is South Korea's rapid economic growth, which made the country increasingly capable of assuming more responsibility for its own defense. The second is the constraints on US resources due to the Vietnam War and economic troubles at home. And I would expect US pressure to be quite successful. South Korean fears of US abandonment dated to Secretary of State Dean Acheson's 1950 speech that seemed to put the ROK outside the US "defensive perimeter," and they had structural roots in the country's vulnerability to attack from North Korea. Doubts about US reliability in the wake of Vietnam should have intensified these fears. In the remainder of this section, I discuss the ways in which Nixon and his successors were able to use South Korean fears of abandonment to secure a sizable increase in the ROK's efforts toward self-reliance.

US MOVES TOWARD RETRENCHMENT

In the wake of Vietnam and amid an ailing economy, Nixon attempted to rein in the costs of US foreign commitments in two ways. The first was pulling

Table 4.4 Predictions for US burden-sharing pressure toward South Korea, 1969–1974

Latent military potential	External threat	US resource constraints	Prediction	Outcome
Low, but rising	High	High	High US interest in South Korean force improvements, and high South Korean susceptibility to US pressure	US policymakers sought substantial South Korean force improvements and were highly successful.

CHAPTER 4

back some of its forward-deployed military forces and encouraging its allies to assume more responsibility for their own defense. Nixon famously articulated this approach in a July 1969 speech on the island of Guam, in which he promised that the United States would assist its allies in Asia if they were attacked but reserved the right to decide how much assistance would be forthcoming, as well as what form that assistance would take. In any case, most of the burden would fall to US allies to defend themselves. The goal of the Guam Doctrine was to rein in the costs of US commitments and to reduce the probability of entanglement in future conflicts, and its hallmark was a reduced US overseas military footprint.[28]

Consistent with the Guam Doctrine, Nixon announced in March 1970 that the US Seventh Infantry Division deployed in South Korea would be withdrawn, having made the decision to withdraw the previous November in order to cut costs, appease Congress, and shift more of the burden of defending South Korea onto the ROK.[29] By 1972, the US presence on the peninsula had fallen from around 60,000 personnel to just over 40,000, with most positioned away from the demilitarized zone (see table 4.5).[30] This served to reduce both the risk of US entanglement and the number of forces tied down in Korea, both of which had given rise to long-standing complaints among US officials.[31] Hand in hand with the Guam Doctrine, the second shift in US policy was détente with the Communist bloc. In addition to pursuing friendlier relations with the USSR through arms control and limited expansions of trade, the United States sought reduced tensions on the Korean Peninsula and rapprochement with China, culminating in Nixon's visit to Beijing in 1972. Détente in East Asia served a number of functions, including reducing the likelihood of conflict in the region, thus facilitating the US military drawdown in the region and decreasing the chances it would have to intervene militarily in light of budgetary, manpower, and domestic constraints.[32] Additionally, Nixon hoped that "flipping" China would help contain the Soviet Union during a period of US weakness, while improved relations with both Communist powers might make them more amenable to pressuring North Vietnam into a peace settlement. In the wake of détente, the United States shifted to a strategy of preparing to fight one major war (in Europe) and one limited war (in Asia), rather than two major wars (one in Europe and one in Asia) and one limited war. In turn, this facilitated the United States' efforts to withdraw troops from South Korea, as US foreign policy in East Asia no longer centered around "the containment of the Soviet Union and China" simultaneously, as Nixon put it in his 1972 foreign policy report.[33]

ENCOURAGING SOUTH KOREAN SELF-RELIANCE

Thanks to near-double-digit annual growth between 1961 and 1969, US officials increasingly believed that South Korea had become capable of assuming more responsibility for its own defense, though they knew the US role would have to diminish gradually rather than all at once due to the continuing North Korean threat.[34] As a result, and in keeping with the stated goals of the Guam Doctrine, Nixon made achieving parity between South and North Korean forces a central priority.[35] During a meeting with Park in August 1969, Nixon encouraged him to continue down the road to self-reliance. When Park later protested the Seventh Infantry Division's withdrawal, Nixon wrote to him that "as the strengths and capabilities of our Allies increase it is reasonable to expect them to assume more of the responsibility for their own defense and specifically to provide the bulk of the manpower required for that purpose"; Defense Secretary Melvin Laird similarly encouraged South Korea to seek greater capacity for domestic arms production.[36] To help South Korea stand on its own, Nixon committed the United States to provide a burst of military assistance, set out in September 1971's NSDM 129 as a $1.5 billion program, with upward of $200 million annually to modernize the ROK's military forces using a combination of grant military aid, credit for purchases of US Foreign Military Sales (FMS), and excess US equipment.[37] Internally, policymakers discussed US military assistance as a way to support the ROK in bridging the gap between relying entirely on US assistance to becoming more self-sufficient.[38]

To cushion the blow of troop withdrawals, officials in the Nixon administration did reassure the ROK that the United States remained committed to ensuring South Korea's security. This entailed a delicate balancing act—affirming that the United States would come to the ROK's defense if its security was jeopardized, yet trying to reduce and delay the scope, size, and timing of its intervention. Nixon personally reaffirmed the US commitment to South Korean security both during an in-person meeting in August 1969 and in subsequent letters to Park throughout 1970.[39] US ambassador Porter similarly told Park in 1970 that increased US military assistance was the "result of [US government] desire to reassure [ROK government] and people of our continuing concern for their safety, even though we are withdrawing some troops."[40] July 1971 saw the first of what would become annual defense minister–level Security Consultative Meetings to assuage ROK fears about not being consulted on US policy on the peninsula.[41] In addition, US officials reassured the South Koreans that the opening to China did not mean South Korea had become less important, and that it refused to negotiate with China on the US-ROK alliance.[42] The Nixon administration also launched two new military exercises with South Korea in 1969 and 1971 to demonstrate US ability to project power on the Korean Peninsula.[43]

Despite this—and although Nixon did not remove any additional forces from Korea after 1971—the prospect of future withdrawals was always on the horizon. Internally, the administration continually weighed the prospects for further reducing the US presence. Nixon made it clear early in his presidency that a large US presence on the peninsula was not a permanent solution, remarking to Kissinger in December 1969 that "I want a plan

CHAPTER 4

developed *now* to bring about the ROK take over. US to provide a trip wire and air and sea support only."[44] Nixon sought to maintain flexibility in his decisions on force levels in Korea, making them on a short-term basis.[45] In March 1970, NSDM 48 proposed that "the feasibility and timing of further reductions in the US military presence in Korea should be thoroughly evaluated," and in mid-1971, Nixon decided to maintain one division in South Korea through 1973.[46] Over the next several years, US officials continued to debate the merits of withdrawing more forces. Secretary of State Rogers expressed a willingness to withdraw more forces a year or two after the Seventh Infantry Division's removal, while Defense Secretaries Melvin Laird and James Schlesinger indicated their openness to doing so as well; Schlesinger even proposed to make US forces in South Korea part of a "mobile reserve" based outside of Korea that could be used elsewhere in the region.[47]

To the South Koreans, US officials gave ambiguous assurances on troop levels. Even Kissinger, who internally opposed plans for further withdrawals in the absence of a peace agreement on the Korean Peninsula, told the ROK prime minister in December 1970 that "in principle he could see the possibility of a Korean withdrawal, for example in the case of a peace settlement."[48] The vice president and secretary of defense took a similar tack during their own visits to Seoul.[49] When US officials did make assurances, they were typically short-term. A joint agreed minutes in October 1970 stated that "the United States confirms that, based on present conditions, it does not plan or intend to reduce the number its troops stationed in Korea."[50] Kissinger and Nixon made similar promises throughout the early 1970s to the effect that the United States did not currently have plans to withdraw, or that the United States would not change troop levels through 1973 or 1974.[51] Encouraging progress toward a peace agreement between North and South Korea in mid-1972 and into 1973 led Nixon to temporarily put the brakes on further troop withdrawals.[52] Kissinger told the ROK foreign minister in February 1973 that troop levels "might fluctuate a few thousand one way or another, but would remain essentially the same."[53] US assurances on troop levels nevertheless continued to pertain only to the very short-term. Kissinger, for example, told the ROK foreign minister in early 1974, "We plan no substantial changes in US force levels at least in the near-term."[54] Ambassador Habib similarly noted in May 1974 that "the ROKG had been informed that there will be no change in the level of US forces in Korea through FY75. It was pointed out that the ROK Government expects at least a one-year notice of any future changes in our force levels."[55]

US officials deliberately played on the ROK's uncertainty about future force levels to push them toward self-reliance. NSDM 48, for example, both outlined US troop withdrawals and directed that the United States would aim to provide the ROK with military and economic aid "provided that the ROK assumes, to the extent feasible, a larger defense burden."[56] In his

May 1970 response to Park following the announcement of the Seventh Infantry Division's withdrawal, Nixon gestured at offering economic aid "provided your Government assumes a larger defense burden."[57]

Frequently, the Nixon administration coupled its pressure with the implicit threat that Congress might cut US force levels or military assistance if the ROK did not make a greater effort. In his May 1970 letter to Park, Nixon noted that "an initiative from you showing that Korea is ready to assume more of the burden of its own defense will add to Korea's image and to Congressional and public support" for the military assistance program.[58] Defense Secretary Melvin Laird similarly pointed out to Park in January that "pressures for reduction of our forces in Korea are increasing."[59] Shortly before the Seventh Infantry Division's withdrawal was announced, during an NSC meeting, members of the administration debated the pace of future troop withdrawals, with Secretary of State Rogers voicing his support for a withdrawal of 20,000 forces initially and "adding that Congress will move in the face of such a reduction and the savings that would result."[60] The following year, in a meeting with Park, Laird argued that "the ROKs can make additional major constructive steps toward self-reliance in weapons production," stressing that "positive Congressional concurrence was not assured. Already, I told Pak, the Armed Services' Committee conference had specified a 50,000-man reduction for US ground forces. . . . We would have to allocate that reduction in the least harmful way possible."[61]

US officials recognized the degree of South Korea's dependence on US protection and used it as leverage. A paper by the State Department's policy planning staff put the matter quite directly in June 1968: "ROK leaders will be unhappy over the withdrawal of the two US divisions and the prospect that other forces would eventually follow, but in time they would realize that they had no rational alternative but to go along. we can probably continue to rely on ROK dependence on US logistic support to inhibit any rash adventures."[62] There was little concern that South Korea might try to realign by seeking alternative partners, because by and large, it continued to see the Communist countries as highly threatening and détente as dangerous. A December 1970 NIE noted that while the ROK was "edging cautiously toward a different relationship with neutralist and even communist states," this development was "likely to remain a matter of very small steps, far behind those of most other non-communist states," because of the high level of threat South Korea still faced.[63] Nixon put the matter even more bluntly in April 1971, remarking that the South Koreans "live at our sufferance."[64] Ambassador Porter made the same point when discussing the troop withdrawals with Kissinger in March 1970, arguing that "we could swing the option which we wanted. The ROKs would go into their usual banging tactics, but could be held."[65] Again in December 1971, as Park was seeking domestic emergency powers, the next ambassador, Philip Habib, argued that Park "is perceptive enough to see that we can accelerate the American disengagement that he fears, and we can play

CHAPTER 4

Table 4.5 Number of US military personnel present in South Korea, 1965–1975

US military personnel	Year
58,636	1965
47,076	1966
55,057	1967
62,263	1968
66,531	1969
52,197	1970
40,740	1971
41,600	1972
41,864	1973
40,387	1974
40,204	1975

Source: Data are from Kane 2006.

on that fear. He should therefore understand if he uses powers granted to him under other than clearest evidence of serious emergency, no assurance can be given that US people, Congress, and administration will continue to provide him with moral and material support."[66]

ROK FEARS OF REDUCED US PROTECTION

ROK officials reacted with alarm to these developments. Park regarded the Guam Doctrine and withdrawal of the Seventh Infantry Division as signs of reduced US commitment. He resented that he had not been consulted, writing to Nixon of his "profound shock" at the withdrawal.[67] More generally, Park saw dwindling US support for South Vietnam—and, later, Taiwan—as potential harbingers of his own country's future.[68]

What also raised fears of abandonment in South Korea was the combination of rising North Korean provocations coupled with perceived US softness toward North Korea, China, and the Soviet Union. The Nixon administration was loathe to respond to regional provocations in a way that would increase the risk of yet another war in Asia.[69] At the same time, the late 1960s and early 1970s saw both a North Korean military buildup and an uptick in North Korean provocations, including an attempted assassination of President Park and the shooting down of a US EC-121 reconnaissance aircraft in early 1969, causing tensions to run high in the ROK. The United States' responses to these provocations—restraint coupled with private, bilateral negotiations—unnerved the South Koreans. In 1968, ROK officials were shaken by what they

98

saw as the United States' focus on securing the return of the USS *Pueblo* at the expense of safeguarding Park from future assassination attempts.[70] Ambassador Porter reported that "Park doubted both the resolve of the United States and her commitment in Korea, partially because of US involvement in [Southeast Asia] and partially because of alleged delays in providing military equipment to ROK military forces and in modernizing those forces," and that Park "objected to the bilateral discussions . . . between US and North Korean representatives."[71]

The US opening to China similarly contributed to ROK insecurity. Reduced Sino-American tensions fostered a fear of abandonment among US allies, as they seemed to diminish the value of US alliances by removing the United States' primary adversary in East Asia.[72] According to a US Senate fact-finding group, Park saw "the new US policy to China" as a sign that "US interest in Asia . . . was decreasing."[73] The ROK's fear was that the United States would be lured into a false sense of security that would lead it to reduce its military commitment to South Korea, or that it would be tempted to deliberately sell out South Korean interests in broader negotiations with China.[74] In particular, ROK officials expected that China might ask the United States to remove its forces from the Korean Peninsula.[75]

The cumulative effect of US behavior was to shake Park's faith in the US commitment to the ROK. He believed that further withdrawals were only a matter of time and viewed self-reliance as the only surefire way to safeguard South Korean security. In December 1971, several months after Nixon had announced his trip to China, Park declared a state of emergency and sought emergency presidential powers. Ambassador Habib described the situation that month: "They knew there would be no further withdrawal of US forces from Korea in 1972. Beyond that, however, they could not be sure of what would happen." He likewise remarked that "President Park believed ROK needed to be prepared for any contingency."[76] The next several years did little to mollify Park's fears. His security concerns were manifested in South Korean domestic politics as well, with Park escalating internal repression in 1972 as he instituted the Yushin Constitution (which concentrated power in the president), eliminated the National Assembly, and cracked down on dissent. Habib remarked in early January 1974 that "the Koreans, including President Pak, have already assumed that we are going to reduce forces beginning about '75."[77]

INCREASING SOUTH KOREAN BURDEN-SHARING

The early 1970s marked the beginning of a decade-long push for South Korean military self-reliance. Indeed, Park was quite explicit in linking his desire for self-sufficiency to US pressure and his doubts about US protection. In July 1971, he told Defense Secretary Laird that "the ROKs are trying to develop self-reliance, and thereby relieve the burden on the US," and he

CHAPTER 4

attempted to use ROK self-reliance efforts to justify delaying withdrawals in the interim. Park asserted that he had "no intent of asking US troops to stay in the Republic of Korea indefinitely" and that he "hoped the US would retain its capability in South Korea until the ROKs did attain self-sufficiency."[78] Ambassador Habib reported in December the following year that

> President Park is determined to move toward a policy of greater "self-reliance," diplomatically, economically and militarily. Concern over the great powers, including the US, is a clear theme in Park's justification for his domestic political actions as well as the South-North dialogue. However, Park's view of self-reliance, paradoxically, includes a desire and an expressed need for the US presence and assistance to continue—at least in the short run. His concern that we will reduce our aid program, withdraw our troops sooner than he would like, and his doubt over the firmness of our treaty commitment, come to the surface from time to time. Generally speaking, he wishes to hold on to these elements of strength for as long as he can, expecting they will diminish as time goes on.[79]

By the time Nixon left office in 1974, the results of Park's push for self-reliance were beginning to become evident. The ROK built up a reserve force of 2.5 million soldiers and pursued a five-year military modernization in 1971 to 1975. In addition, the country withdrew its forces from South Vietnam and returned them to the Korean Peninsula.[80] South Korean military spending more than tripled, from around $0.5 billion in 1961 to 1965 to more than $1.5 billion in 1974 (see figure 4.2). While ROK military spending as a percentage of GDP was relatively flat in the early 1970s, this was largely a function of South Korea's extraordinary growth, as the country's GDP doubled between 1970 and 1974, as well as the final US military assistance program, which injected a substantial amount of aid between 1970 and 1973 and briefly relieved the burden on the South Korean defense budget.[81] By 1975, the growth in South Korean military spending had accelerated such that it began keeping pace with the country's double-digit economic growth, and it was on track to reach 4 percent of GDP (up from 1%) by the end of the decade. Whereas US military assistance accounted for roughly two-thirds of total South Korean defense outlays during much of the 1960s, by 1974 the ROK was paying for more than three-quarters of its defense capabilities.[82]

On reviewing the progress of the military assistance program in 1973, an interagency report concluded that the South Korean military had made enormous strides—so much so that US policymakers concluded that South Korea was approaching military parity with the North. They argued that "our objectives should include having the Koreans agree to increase their defense spending sufficiently to assume a greater share of their own defense responsibilities in a move toward increasing their military self-sufficiency."[83] Kissinger and Nixon concurred, and in July 1973 Kissinger approved NSDM

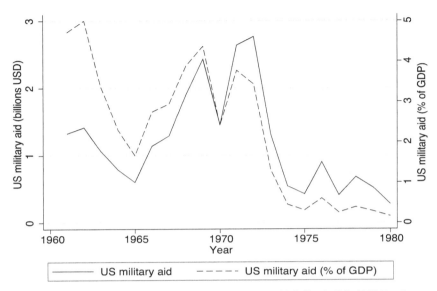

Figure 4.1. US military aid to South Korea (constant 2005 US dollars), 1961–1980. Foreign aid data are from the US Agency for International Development's "Greenbook," and GDP data (purchasing power parity) are from Gleditsch 2002.

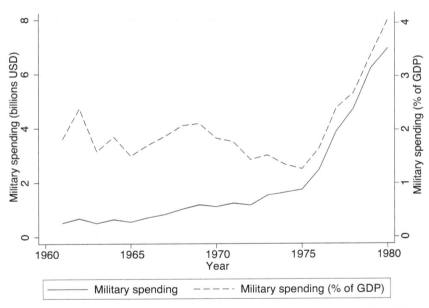

Figure 4.2. South Korean military spending (constant 2005 US dollars), 1961–1980. Military spending data are from Version 5.0 of the Correlates of War's National Material Capabilities Dataset (Singer 1987), and GDP data (purchasing power parity) are from Gleditsch 2002.

CHAPTER 4

227, which reaffirmed the US military modernization program, and noted that future military assistance should focus on South Korean air defenses over its land forces.[84] The following year, studies by both the Central Intelligence Agency and the NSC suggested that the ROK could soon hold off North Korean ground forces.[85]

South Korea Moves toward Self-Reliance, 1974–1980

The late 1970s resembled the earlier part of the decade in several key respects. Chief among these were continuing economic troubles in the United States and South Korea's rapid economic growth, which were quickly turning it into a middle-income economy. Additionally, while the direct US role in the Vietnam War had ended, its political impact within the United States had not, and in Congress and among the US public there was still little appetite for foreign entanglements. As a result, I would predict US pressure on South Korea to improve its military capabilities to remain intense during the latter part of the 1970s, and to be quite successful, as it had been in earlier years. The evidence largely bears out these predictions. When Gerald Ford assumed the US presidency after Nixon resigned in August 1974, he and his administration continued to push for South Korean military modernization and debated the prospects for further withdrawals internally while declining to actually pull more forces out. Several new developments intervened over the course of his short presidency—most significantly, the collapse of South Vietnam in 1975, as well as the discovery of the ROK's nascent nuclear weapons program—but none of them fundamentally altered the Ford administration's willingness to secure ever-higher levels of South Korean burden-sharing. In turn, Ford's successor, Jimmy Carter, did attempt to withdraw US ground forces from the Korean Peninsula, but ultimately declined to do so, instead trading promises to maintain troop levels in exchange for ROK commitments to increase defense spending.

Table 4.6 Predictions for US burden-sharing pressure toward South Korea, 1974–1980

Latent military potential	External threat	US resource constraints	Prediction	Outcome
Rising to moderate	High	Reduced but still elevated	High US interest in South Korean force improvements, and high South Korean susceptibility to US pressure	US policymakers sought substantial South Korean force improvements and were highly successful.

CONTINUED US CONSTRAINTS

The United States continued to face constraints that caused South Korean officials to doubt its alliance commitment and provided the Ford administration with motivation to seek greater burden-sharing. One of these was the hangover of the Vietnam War, in which the United States had formally ended its combat role in 1973. Sixty thousand Americans had been killed and 150,000 wounded, and the US public and Congress had little appetite for fighting another war.[86] In addition, the US economy was in a period of stagflation, with both inflation and unemployment rates upward of 6 percent, high oil prices in the wake of the 1973 Organization of Petroleum Exporting Countries embargo, and declining GDP from 1973 to 1975.[87]

As a result, Congress continued to exert downward pressure on the defense budget and remained skeptical of the US overseas military footprint, causing unease within the ROK.[88] In particular, Congress's refusal to continue providing material assistance to South Vietnam, coupled with South Vietnam's subsequent takeover by North Vietnam in 1975, caused the South Korean government to formally request assurances that South Korea would not suffer the same fate.[89] A telegram from the US embassy in South Korea described the situation in Seoul in April 1975: "Focal point of concern is Congressional attitudes and fear that in conflict situation Congress (and American public) may—as in case [of] Vietnam—deny funds and use of US forces needed to defend Korea and even force US troop withdrawals before then."[90] In a conversation with his US counterpart in August that year, South Korean defense minister Suh Jyong-chul raised his concern that Kim Il-Sung "may ask, as a result of Vietnam, whether [the US] commitment is reliable."[91]

When it came to congressional opinion on South Korea in particular, there was good reason for Park to worry. Congress continued to scrutinize the amount of US assistance South Korea received, and it more broadly sought to cut military assistance particularly in the form of grant aid.[92] Many in Congress also favored withdrawing forces from the Korean Peninsula. A Department of Defense study in late 1975 noted that "our Korean policy and our defense presence on the Peninsula appear to be losing support of both the US public and the Congress. In part, this is due to the backlash of Vietnam and the fear of another military venture in East Asia. In part, it is due to the increasingly repressive nature of the Park government. As a result, we have witnessed Congressional efforts to remove our troops from Korea." The study likewise speculated that although "Congress should be generally sympathetic to an effort to make the ROK self-sufficient," it was likely to "relate future aid commitments to the US force presence in Korea."[93] Of particular interest to Congress was the presence of a US company in the demilitarized zone, which it feared could result in the United States being drawn into a conflict.[94] Domestic opinion on South Korea further soured as Park escalated his internal repression, especially in the wake of revelations

CHAPTER 4

in 1976 about the "Korea-gate" scandal, in which Park used a lobbyist to bribe numerous US members of Congress to discourage retrenchment from Korea.[95]

US PRESSURE REMAINS INTENSE

Like its predecessor, the Ford administration continued to press the ROK to increase its capacity for self-defense and remained committed to assisting South Korea's military modernization. However, in late 1974 and early 1975, in response to congressional pressure on budgetary appropriations for military assistance, the administration recognized that it would need to shift its assistance away from grant aid and toward FMS credits that the ROK could use to help finance purchases of equipment from the United States.[96] This shift in policy was enshrined in NSDM 282 in January 1975.[97]

US officials did not shy away from emphasizing congressional pressure to motivate South Korean burden-sharing efforts. In the lead-up to Ford's first visit to Seoul in November 1974, the State Department advised him to stress the importance of the military modernization program and the pressure he faced from Congress.[98] During the visit, Ford praised the efforts of the ROK and other countries seeking to "build their countries economically and militarily so that they can become self-sufficient," making clear his intention to continue supporting the ROK's military modernization. However, although he promised to "continue to urge Congress to support allies like South Korea," he lamented that Congress was "not as cooperative as I would have hoped."[99] Ford struck a similar tone when Park visited the White House the following year, emphasizing his continued support for the ROK's modernization despite congressional skepticism.[100] A few months later, Defense Secretary Schlesinger likewise told Park that "to the extent that the ROK increases its own defense effort, it will help with these public and congressional criticisms."[101]

In addition, Ford administration officials gave ambiguous signals about future US troop withdrawals and continued to weigh the prospects for future withdrawals internally. The prevailing view was that further troop withdrawals would be contingent on the security situation on the peninsula—including the pace of South Korea's military modernization, the level of threat posed by North Korea, and whether the United Nations Command in Korea would be disbanded and replaced by a bilateral US-ROK command structure.[102] Nevertheless, policymakers continued to anticipate a process of "gradual disengagement," with US troop levels eventually declining further.[103]

While US officials were generally reassuring about US force levels in the short term, they were ambiguous about force levels in the longer term.[104] When Defense Secretary Schlesinger visited Seoul in August 1975, he told Park that he foresaw "no basic changes over the next five years" in US troop levels, and that the United States would maintain its troop presence to pro-

104

vide cover while the ROK pushed toward self-reliance.[105] In his meeting with the South Korean foreign minister, he reported that there were no plans for changes in US forces "in the period immediately ahead."[106] Habib, for his part, recommended against telling the ROK that troop withdrawals would go hand in hand with South Korean military modernization, lest the United States "create a disincentive for the Koreans" to forge ahead.[107]

Jimmy Carter took an even harder line on South Korean burden-sharing. After years of conflict in Vietnam, Carter, like his predecessors, prioritized reducing the US global military footprint and cutting the US defense budget. Carter targeted South Korea in part because of Park's human rights record and because South Korea's economy and population now far outstripped those of North Korea. While campaigning, Carter pledged to withdraw US ground forces from South Korea and cut the defense budget, and on coming to office he attempted to follow through on these promises almost immediately. His administration viewed the withdrawal plan as a continuation of the trend toward retrenchment and allied self-reliance that had begun with the Nixon Doctrine.[108] Moreover, Carter hoped the removal of US forces from near the demilitarized zone would reduce the chances of South Korea entangling the United States in a conflict.[109]

SOUTH KOREAN BURDEN-SHARING

After the Nixon administration's short-term injection of military aid, South Korea truly began to approach military self-reliance during the latter half of the 1970s. To this end, Park levied a 10 percent income tax to fund a military improvement plan over 1974 to 1981. As a result, the country doubled its military expenditures between 1974 and 1977 and continued to increase spending throughout the late 1970s.[110] Over the course of Ford's and Carter's presidencies, South Korea's military spending continued to soar, accounting for 4 percent of GDP in 1980.[111] In 1976 the Defense Department estimated that Park's push "should bring their forces into rough parity with North Korea."[112]

The evidence strongly suggests that South Korean officials took the possibility of abandonment quite seriously and fully anticipated that there would be more withdrawals of US forces. The briefing materials for Ford's November 1974 trip to Seoul noted that the South Koreans "are concerned about Congressional and public proposals to reduce force levels overseas. They are uncertain about the implications of proposals to designate the Second Infantry Division as a Pacific theater mobile reserve force"—a reference to Defense Secretary Schlesinger's proposal to move the division out of Korea—"and Congressional pressures to relocate the division south of Seoul so as to free it from the possibility of immediate commitment in the event of hostilities."[113] In March the following year, Ambassador Richard Sneider similarly reported that "Park knows that the Administration wants

CHAPTER 4

to keep a US presence in Korea but he does not know if we can deliver the goods."[114]

The threat from North Korea remained a live issue. Despite South Korea's military modernization and rough parity in terms of manpower, North Korea still held a qualitative edge due to its concurrent military buildup.[115] Provocations continued as well. In August 1974 a North Korea sympathizer attempted to assassinate Park; the president narrowly escaped, but his wife was killed. The following year, Park's dread deepened at news that Kim Il Sung had solicited Beijing's support for an attack on South Korea, and in 1976 North Korean soldiers armed with axes killed two US soldiers who were trying to chop down a tree in the demilitarized zone.[116]

Park's fear of abandonment and his assessment of the military balance on the Korean Peninsula served as the rationale for his push toward self-reliance. A May 1974 message from the US embassy noted that the ROK was "moving in the direction of significant defense procurement through its own re-sources," noting that this was a "healthy development" in response to doubts about "Congressional attitudes."[117] During his meeting with Ford later that year, Park told him, "We do not expect the US presence to remain indefinitely, given the mounting US public opinion and pressure in Congress." However, Park worried that US troop withdrawals might come before his defense buildup matched North Korean capabilities.[118] He requested that "Korean self-reliance must be insured before US troop reductions take place. There-fore, I hope for implementation of the Five-Year Modernization Plan with its completion as soon as possible. I also desire help for ROK defense industries, which will build our self-reliance."[119] Events surrounding the fall of South Vietnam in 1975 only further deepened Park's desire for self-reliance.[120]

North Korea's military buildup and continued provocations continually delayed any potential US troop withdrawals, though US officials' assess-ments of the military balance on the peninsula—and their hopes for North-South peace talks—were typically more favorable than those of South Korea, and they still communicated to Park that force levels were contingent on the ROK's own efforts.[121] President Carter, for his part, ultimately shelved his plans to withdraw US ground forces from South Korea in mid-1979, due to a combination of opposition from within his administration, the military, and the Japanese government, along with new intelligence suggesting that North Korean military capabilities exceeded previous estimates such that the ROK would not be able to reach military parity with North Korea until the mid-1980s.[122]

Nevertheless, US officials were still able to use Park's fear of withdrawals as leverage to secure further increases in South Korean defense spending in exchange for promises that US troop levels would remain unchanged for a time.[123] Over the course of a number of meetings between US and South Korean officials—including a summit involving Carter and Park—the Amer-icans urged their ROK counterparts to increase the country's defense efforts. Even though Carter and the rest of his administration had increasingly come to an internal consensus against substantial withdrawals in the near term, US officials did not communicate this consensus to Park, who pleaded with Carter that the new estimates of North Korean strength made the US presence as essential as ever.[124] Instead, they used the prospect of withdrawal to negotiate commitments to increase ROK defense spending and explicitly linked their willingness to adjust the withdrawal timetable—which had effectively become a foregone conclusion anyway—to South Korean defense efforts, with Park further increasing defense spending and initiating plans for a second military improvement plan from 1982 to 1986 before his assassination in 1979.[125] Thus, while he failed to withdraw US forces from the peninsula, Carter was nevertheless able to encourage increased South Korean self-reliance.

SOUTH KOREA AND NUCLEAR WEAPONS: THE PITFALLS OF SELF-RELIANCE?

While Park made a push for self-reliance using conventional military arming in response to perceived US unreliability, South Korea also attempted to obtain nuclear weapons. But its attempt further demonstrated just how limited its leverage was—as well as how potent the US threat of abandonment could be.

Park decided to pursue nuclear weapons in November 1971, and South Korea proceeded to secure nuclear assistance from France and Canada and plan the production of ballistic missiles.[126] India's nuclear test in May 1974 brought proliferation to the top of the US agenda, leading US officials to review which other countries might be considering nuclear weapons. Later that year, the United States detected the South Korean deals for plutonium reprocessing capabilities with France and Canada and proceeded to scrutinize South Korea's nuclear activities.[127] By February 1975, suspicions about South Korea's nuclear intentions had given way to relative certainty that it was attempting to obtain nuclear weapons.[128] The United States saw South Korean proliferation as a potential trigger for either a regional nuclear arms race that could result in North Korea and Japan obtaining nuclear weapons, or a preventive attack by the ROK's neighbors. South Korea's possession of nuclear weapons would also reduce its dependence on the United States—and, in turn, US leverage.[129]

The Ford administration used a multipronged approach to discourage South Korean nuclearization, which included threats to cut off nuclear assistance, pressure on third-party supplier countries—particularly Canada and France—to terminate their nuclear assistance, and efforts to secure ROK ratification of the NPT.[130] Additionally, Ambassador Sneider issued an ultimatum in December 1975 that the "whole range of security and political relationships" between the United States and South Korea would be jeopardized

CHAPTER 4

if it did not cancel the plutonium reprocessing deal with France.[131] The deal was canceled the next month, but over the next several years, similar threats were made by Secretary of Defense Donald Rumsfeld in May 1976 and later by Jimmy Carter, owing to lingering fears about South Korea's nuclear ambitions.[132] The exact end date of South Korea's interest in nuclear weapons is difficult to pin down, but US pressure—both on the supply side and through its threats to cut off economic and security assistance—frustrated South Korea's ambitions. It was forced to simply keep its options open, by investing in missile technologies and its domestic nuclear energy industry, for example, rather than hurtling toward a bomb.[133]

Why did South Korea's pursuit of nuclear weapons not preclude the United States from being able to secure ever-higher levels of burden-sharing? Indeed, in an effort to persuade the ROK to give up its nuclear program, US officials went to some lengths to assuage its fear of abandonment. Both the Department of State and the Department of Defense recognized that the ROK's nuclear weapons program was a reaction to perceived US unreliability.[134] Ambassador Sneider argued in April 1975 that the fall of Saigon was shaking South Korean confidence in the United States, and in June he advocated making very "clear to the Koreans what the prospects are for a continued, long-term US military presence," as uncertainty only encouraged Park "into preparations for what he sees as our eventual withdrawal . . . which include internal repression and plans for the development of nuclear weapons."[135] US officials turned to "pointing up the differences between Vietnam and Korea, with respect to the internal situations in both countries the nature of the US commitments, and their different strategic positions" in order to counteract South Korean fears that the ROK might receive the same treatment as South Vietnam.[136] Additionally, Defense Secretary James Schlesinger publicly declared in July 1975 that the United States had nuclear weapons in South Korea and hinted at their use if South Korea was attacked.[137] June 1976 saw the first of what became the annual Team Spirit joint military exercises between the United States and the ROK, and several months later US forces conducted Operation Paul Bunyan, which deployed US forces to the demilitarized zone to chop down the tree that had been the subject of the "axe murder incident."[138] Even the Carter administration reassured the ROK that the United States would defend the country regardless of any troop withdrawals.[139] Nevertheless, although the United States went to great lengths to deter South Korean nuclearization, this did not prevent it from simultaneously extracting a significant amount of additional burden-sharing from the ROK, as Ford and other US officials continued to invoke the threat to US commitment posed by Congress.[140]

Ultimately, as my theory would predict, the answer lies in the combination of the latent credibility of the Ford administration's threat of abandonment and the ROK's dependence on US protection. The United States had a variety of powerful levers it could push to induce South Korean nuclear restraint—all of which it threatened to use. The ROK was highly dependent on the United States for trade, investment, protection, and its nuclear energy needs.[141] US officials recognized the extent of South Korea's dependence. A telegram from the US embassy in April 1975 reported that "there is no present alternative to continued dependence on us. In the short run, Korea has no other policy options, with any dependence on Japan particularly out of question."[142] Moreover, even as US officials reassured the ROK that it would not be abandoned, these efforts ultimately could not erase the latent credibility of the threat of abandonment. Given domestic pressure within the United States and US attempts to cut costs and limit the risk of foreign entanglements under Nixon and Ford, South Korean officials were not assuaged by US assurances.

South Korea's pursuit of nuclear weapons highlights the dangers of demanding that allies take more responsibility for their own defense, while at the same time illustrating that these dangers vary across cases. The South Korean case suggests that a patron should be careful what it wishes for when it seeks increased self-reliance. Yet, it also reveals that the challenges associated with allied burden-sharing are comparatively more surmountable for allies that are relatively weaker and more dependent. Regardless of its conventional military buildup, South Korea was still an isolated, small-to-middle power, bordered by a hostile neighbor with great power patrons of its own, and it would always have been vulnerable to the threat of abandonment. In principle, nuclear weapons represent a path to self-reliance and independence even for otherwise weak countries. But the path to nuclear weapons acquisition is a perilous one, as it can invite preventive attack, economic sanctions, and abandonment by allies seeking to discourage proliferation.[143] These risks are magnified in the case of weaker states, which may not be able to withstand military or economic coercion.[144] As such, in the case of South Korea, the United States was able to pursue its goals simultaneously: it secured dramatically increased burden-sharing, reduced its military presence, and managed to maintain the ROK's non-nuclear status. Ultimately, of course, the difference is a matter of degree; encouraging allies to become more self-reliant is always a risky business, but some cases are riskier than others.

The case of US burden-sharing pressure on South Korea supports my theory's expectations. US officials routinely used the prospect of reduced protection to pressure the ROK to assume more responsibility for its own defense. US officials never envisioned truly abandoning the ROK by abrogating the MDT, but they hoped that reduced US involvement—fewer US forces on the peninsula and reduced scope of potential US intervention—would lead the ROK to pick up the slack. In this sense, their approach succeeded, as the ROK dramatically increased its defense spending even as US force levels remained effectively constant after the Seventh Infantry Division's withdrawal.

CHAPTER 4

This entailed threading a needle, as US officials hesitated to withdraw forces from the peninsula before the ROK was capable of fending off a North Korean attack itself—a stance further complicated by North Korea's own military buildup—and they worried the ROK might drag its feet in order to convince Washington it needed to stay. As a result, US officials had to persuade the South Koreans that they might withdraw US forces if the ROK did not make sufficient efforts to provide for its own defense.

But the United States' success can be attributed only partly to deft diplomacy. What gave Washington's pressure its bite were the underlying conditions of the case—the looming threat of North Korean attack coupled with the ROK's vulnerability by virtue of its geographic exposure, its small but growing size, and the inherent credibility of abandonment that stemmed from US reluctance to fight another war after Vietnam and pressure from Congress to cut defense spending and reduce the overseas US troop presence. Ultimately, ROK defense burden-sharing was largely a function of US pressure coupled with South Korean officials' fears of reduced US protection.

The case of South Korea illustrates the sorts of outcomes one can expect when the burden-sharing dilemma is less severe. US policymakers had little need to worry about the possibility of South Korea exiting the alliance, and its geographic vulnerability to attack likewise made it quite susceptible to US pressure. As a result, US policymakers were able to use the ROK's fear of abandonment to motivate South Korean burden-sharing. US leverage only increased during the 1970s as a result of US resource and domestic constraints, when US officials were able to coerce the ROK into a dramatic military buildup. Even the ROK's threat of nuclearization did not deter US burden-sharing pressure, because although South Korea could threaten to pursue nuclear weapons, it would still be highly vulnerable to abandonment in the interim, as it would have taken a long time to produce a weapon, let alone a truly robust deterrent.

CHAPTER 5

"Is Iceland Blackmailing Us?"

Icelandic Burden-Sharing, 1949–1960

Iceland is, at first glance, an unlikely member of NATO. The country has no military and a history of seeking neutrality from European conflicts, and it is thousands of miles off the Continent's coast. And with a population of less than 150,000 in 1949, it had little ability to make material contributions to collective defense.

What Iceland has instead is a geostrategically valuable location. Positioned between North America and Northern Europe, Iceland served as a potential staging ground for US reinforcements en route to Europe during a conflict, as well as a forward site for US bombers to reach Soviet targets. Moreover, Iceland sits in the middle of the Greenland-Iceland-United Kingdom (GIUK) Gap, a main thoroughfare for Soviet vessels traveling between the Arctic and the Atlantic Oceans. As a result, Iceland's sole contribution to NATO came in the form of military access.

The United States maintained a base at Keflavik Airport that it used as an Air Force staging ground and a site for surveilling Soviet vessels—particularly submarines—and providing early warning in case of a Soviet air or missile attack. Securing and maintaining this base entailed providing significant compensation to the Icelanders, who repeatedly leveraged the threat of eviction to secure foreign aid packages, grudging US acceptance of expanded Icelandic fishing rights, and material support for operating the airport.

Empirical Predictions

The case of Iceland is seemingly well explained by competing theories. As the smallest NATO member, the economic theory of alliances would predict that Iceland had little to lose from free-riding on the rest of the alliance. Iceland

111

CHAPTER 5

also hosted the largest US troop presence as a percentage of its population, suggesting that Iceland could free-ride more securely. Finally, domestic politics point toward limited Icelandic burden-sharing, owing to the strength of the Socialist Party, particularly in the mid-1950s.

Alliance control theory similarly predicts low levels of Icelandic burden-sharing, but it focuses instead on the role of US pressure—or in Iceland's case, the lack thereof—and Iceland's permissive threat environment (see table 5.1). The country exhibits characteristics of a Benign Neglect case in my theoretical framework. With NATO's smallest economy and population, Iceland's capacity for material contributions to the alliance was limited. I would thus expect to see evidence that US officials primarily sought non-material Icelandic contributions, including political support for the alliance and basing and military access. Because Iceland was more than a thousand miles from the Cold War's front line in Central Europe and was separated from mainland Europe and the Soviet Union by a vast stretch of water, I would also expect that it would prove relatively resistant to US pressure, even for nonmaterial contributions.

The evidence in the case shows that although the economic theory of alliances correctly predicts minimal burden-sharing as a result of Iceland's small size, its comparatively benign threat environment, coupled with minimal US pressure for a conventional Icelandic contribution, played at least as great a role. Moreover, the evidence provides mixed support, at best, for the effects of US troop deployments and Icelandic domestic politics. Far from seeing US forces as an essential source of security, Icelanders accepted the US presence begrudgingly, and only when the Korean War elevated threat perceptions across the US alliance bloc in the early 1950s. Once that immediate danger had passed, Icelandic officials and the Icelandic public grew more skeptical of the US presence and forced the United States to make policy concessions to keep it. Finally, while left-wing parties were in general more skeptical of NATO and the US military presence, the difference in opinion between left- and right-wing parties was fairly small. Additionally, left-wing parties grew in influence during the mid-1950s in part *because of* perceived improvements in the threat environment.

Table 5.1 Iceland's scores on the independent variables

Latent military potential	External threat	US resource constraints	Prediction
Low	Low, but elevated in the early 1950s	Higher in mid-1950s due to the Korean War	Little US interest in Icelandic conventional forces due to the country's small size and benign threat environment

112

Strategic Context

Prior to World War II, Iceland had long preferred to remain neutral in European conflicts. However, Britain's invasion of the island in 1940—intended to keep it out of German hands—upended this tradition of neutrality. The British and subsequently US presence on the island rankled, and as a result, the country looked forward to a return to the prewar status quo. In October 1946, the governments of Iceland and the United States agreed to terminate the 1941 agreement that had granted the Americans use of facilities in Iceland.[1]

Over the next several years, Icelandic officials perceived a growing level of threat from the Soviet Union. However, given Iceland's historical preference for neutrality, coupled with the margin of security it enjoyed from external attack, its government was unsurprisingly skeptical of joining what would become NATO as the United States, Canada, and Western Europe discussed the contours of the alliance throughout 1948 and 1949. While Icelandic policymakers shared many of the concerns about Soviet intentions and were happy to see Western Europe organizing for collective defense, the US ambassador reported in March 1948 that the Icelanders saw NATO as "of no direct concern to Iceland by virtue its geographic position," with Iceland's foreign minister Bjarni Benediktsson claiming that Iceland was "not interested because of Iceland's isolated position and unrelated problems."[2]

Iceland's reluctance did not dissuade US officials from lobbying it to join NATO, which they continued to do throughout 1948 and into 1949.[3] US policymakers viewed Iceland as essential to the defense of Europe for three reasons. First, Iceland, like Greenland (controlled by Denmark) and the Azores (controlled by Portugal), was seen as a "stepping stone" that bridged the gap between North America and Western Europe and could be used as a staging ground for reinforcements en route to Europe from the United States.[4] Indeed, the chairman of the Senate Foreign Relations Committee in early 1949 went so far as to say that "one of the chief values to the United States" of the emerging NATO alliance "was the assurances that it would provide of the use of base facilities in Greenland and Iceland and that if we did not get those we would not be getting very much while we would be giving a great deal."[5] Second, Iceland blocked entry into the GIUK Gap, which served as a chokepoint between the Barents Sea and the North Atlantic that any Soviet vessels would have to pass through in order to reach the Atlantic Ocean from the hub of the Soviet Union's Northern Fleet at the Kola Peninsula, just northeast of Finland.[6] Finally, in the event of conflict, US bombers based in Iceland could strike targets deep in Soviet territory.[7] The US Joint Chiefs of Staff argued that Iceland's was strategically useful for four purposes:

1. Protection of North Atlantic shipping
2. Air transit to and from north west Europe

CHAPTER 5

3. Long-range air operations over Europe and the Soviet Union
4. A fixed submarine detection line from Greenland to the Faroes[8]

Icelandic officials continued to send signals of ambivalence about joining NATO into 1949. Foreign Minister Benediktsson in December 1948 requested advance consultation before the Americans extended a formal invitation to the country, and he told the secretary of state the following year that pro-NATO public officials' primary reservation was the fear of having to host foreign forces.[9] US officials assured their Icelandic counterparts that the United States had no desire for a permanent base in the country.[10] Benediktsson signaled in February 1949 that Icelandic membership might be slipping out of reach, citing increased domestic opposition, but the US ambassador advised that this might be a deliberate attempt "to maneuver Iceland into [a] bargaining position."[11] Following a series of meetings the following month—including a visit from Secretary of State Dean Acheson—Iceland ultimately joined NATO at the end of March 1949, after receiving further assurances that Iceland would not have to accept foreign forces during peacetime and would not be expected to make a direct military contribution to the alliance's collective defense.[12]

Courting Iceland to Secure Military Access, 1949–1951

Iceland's sole contribution to NATO was to offer use of its facilities and territory during a conflict with the Soviet Union. As described above, US defense planners deemed Iceland's position essential to serve as a staging ground for attacking targets in the Soviet Union, reinforcing Europe, and blocking Soviet vessels from reaching the North Atlantic.[13] However, until 1951, the country did not allow permanent, peacetime stationing of US forces.

Otherwise, Iceland made no direct material contributions to NATO. Indeed, prior to signing onto the North Atlantic Treaty, the country insisted that it would have to "occupy a special position" in the alliance wherein it would not have to maintain any armed forces.[14] US officials consciously made no effort to seek an Icelandic military or economic contribution.[15] During the negotiations in the months leading up to the North Atlantic Treaty, for example, US and other allied officials had a working typology of two categories of potential members: "(1) those which would serve as a link between Western Europe and North America, such as Norway, Iceland, Ireland, and Portugal, and (2) those essential to military security from the European standpoint, for example, Italy or Sweden."[16] Allied officials doubted that Iceland would be able to make a meaningful military contribution even if they tried to secure one.[17] A few years later, during the debates over NATO burden-sharing that took place in 1950 and 1951 in response to the Korean War, the other members excused Iceland from the deliberations.[18]

114

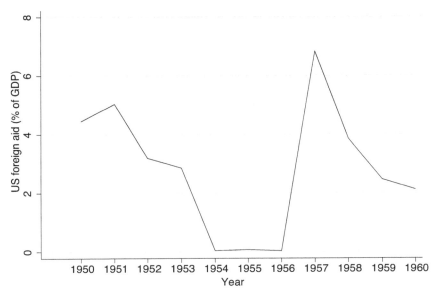

Figure 5.1. US foreign aid to Iceland (% of Iceland's GDP), 1950–1960. Foreign aid data are from the US Agency for International Development's "Greenbook," and GDP data (purchasing power parity) are from Gleditsch 2002.

Iceland not only made no material contributions to the alliance, it was a net recipient of economic assistance.[19] Its geostrategic position was so important to the alliance—and the possibility of its leaving the alliance so damaging—that US officials saw foreign aid as a proactive measure to make NATO membership worthwhile to Iceland.[20] They also saw improving living standards and providing tangible benefits for the Icelandic population as an important way to diminish the appeal of left-wing parties and closer relations with the Soviet Union. During the early 1950s, this was especially important given the country's lingering wartime inflation from the Second World War, which stemmed from the disproportionate size of the US and British presence in the country relative to the size of the country, coupled with the economy's extreme reliance on fishing exports.[21] As a result, US officials provided more than $27 million in foreign aid to Iceland between 1950 and 1953, totaling nearly 4 percent of the country's GDP each year (see figure 5.1).[22]

Toward a Permanent, Peacetime US Military Presence, 1950–1951

In response to North Korea's invasion of South Korea in June 1950, Iceland's opposition to a permanent, peacetime US military presence began to soften. The Korean War marked a watershed in how the United States and its European allies evaluated the threat posed by the Soviet bloc, turning the

CHAPTER 5

NATO alliance from a paper guarantee into a politically and militarily integrated institution.[23] Iceland felt that threat too—Icelandic officials' concern about Soviet ambitions increased in the Korean War's wake.[24]

As a result, the United States and Iceland began discussing what sort of peacetime US presence would be acceptable. The primary point of contention in negotiations was Iceland's insistence on having the right to unilaterally terminate any agreement on US basing rights.[25] The two sides eventually settled on a compromise in May 1951, wherein either party could initiate a review by the North Atlantic Council and terminate the agreement six months later. In the event of war, however, the United States could still use Icelandic facilities.[26] The two sides agreed to having about 3,900 US military forces stationed in the country, with Iceland having the right to deny requests to increase that number. Washington assumed responsibility for Keflavik's operating costs, while Iceland's economy reaped upward of $10 million each year from business generated from US activities at the base.[27]

Paying the Price for Icelandic Support, 1952–1960

While Iceland ultimately accepted permanent, peacetime US access to Keflavik Airport, its government continually chafed at the US presence. Successive Icelandic policymakers considered and even threatened to evict the United States from the base, and they leveraged US fears of losing access to extract a variety of economic concessions, including acceptance of expanded Icelandic fishing rights and foreign aid packages. Meanwhile, the United States continued to show no interest in eliciting an Icelandic military contribution to NATO. This was despite President Eisenhower's ambition, on the heels of what he regarded as an unsustainably high defense buildup due to the Korean War, to rein in US defense budgets and pass more defense responsibility on to NATO. This effort was manifested in Eisenhower's "New Look" approach to defense, which put greater emphasis on the threat of using nuclear weapons owing to their greater "bang for the buck."[28]

ACCOMMODATING ICELAND'S FISHING EXPORTS, 1952–1955

Besides the US presence at Keflavik, perhaps the central issue of contention in the US-Icelandic relationship concerned Iceland's search for ever-expanding export markets for its fisheries. Fish were so central to Iceland's economy that a State Department report characterized the country as having a "one-crop economy," as fish products constituted almost the entirety of the country's exports.[29]

Iceland's ambitions for its fish exports created two intersecting problems for the United States and NATO. First, Iceland's efforts to expand its fishing rights further and further from its coasts created friction with the United

116

Kingdom, which several times imposed boycotts on Icelandic fish and even deployed the Royal Navy to enforce UK fishing rights. Second, Iceland's growing exports to the Soviet Union—in part a response to the shrinking British market for its fish—gave Moscow a potential avenue for exerting influence over Iceland's foreign policy and generated goodwill toward the Soviets and apathy toward NATO among the Icelandic public and political parties.

As a result, ensuring that Iceland had export markets for its fisheries was an area of concern for US policymakers from the first years after World War II. In 1947, for example, fear that the country's inability to sell its fish might cause the governing coalition to collapse and be replaced by one with a greater Communist presence led the United States and the United Kingdom to jointly purchase large quantities of fish.[30] The issue exploded in importance in 1952, as Iceland unilaterally expanded its fishing zone from three to four nautical miles. Britain retaliated by boycotting Icelandic fish imports, which created a void that the Soviet Union was happy to fill. The following year, the two countries signed a trade agreement wherein Iceland received a variety of commodities—notably, cement and petroleum products—in exchange for fish.[31] By mid-1954, the Soviets were importing more than 25 percent of Iceland's exports, up from around 5 percent in 1950.[32] US officials were reluctant to openly oppose the move so soon after the base agreement had been signed, but they were alarmed at the prospect of increased Soviet influence, an Icelandic tilt away from NATO, and restrictions on access to Icelandic territory.[33] The increased Soviet trade provided fuel for Iceland's traditional preference for neutrality and distaste for hosting foreign military forces, and in September 1953 a new, more US-skeptical government came to power.[34] One US official described the problem plainly:

> The Icelanders' basic "anti-foreign army attitude" has received considerable impetus from the Soviet "peace drive" which followed Stalin's death and on which the Communists in Iceland have capitalized. This drive has persuaded many Icelanders—and the belief has mushroomed—that the reasons for putting up with the "evil of a foreign army" have become less cogent. While thus far only a minority would abrogate the Defense Agreement, a majority is apparently in favor of making greater demands on the US and qualifying more sharply the terms under which we are "permitted" to defend Iceland. In brief, the concept of Western defense is finding itself in a "buyers market" in Iceland.[35]

Icelandic skepticism was made possible, as always, by the country's remote position vis-à-vis the central fronts of the Cold War. A report by the NSC noted that Iceland's tendency toward neutralism "has been reinforced by the successful negotiations for [West] German rearmament, which has given rise among prominent Icelanders to a 'continental shield' concept

CHAPTER 5

under which the 'front line' of NATO defense has moved so far east that the stationing of US troops in Iceland may not be required after German rearmament becomes a reality."[36]

While they did not openly condemn Iceland's move, US policymakers took steps to limit the damage.[37] Most significantly, the United States agreed to absorb large quantities of Iceland's fish exports—over the opposition of the US Tariff Commission, which in 1954 recommended increasing tariffs and imposing quotas on Icelandic fish.[38] Additionally, US officials acquiesced to Iceland's desire for a supplementary agreement that increased the use of Icelandic labor in base-related contracts, provided training in construction for Icelandic workers, and gave Iceland's government more control over construction projects around Keflavik.[39]

ICELAND LEVERAGES EVICTION THREATS TO SECURE US AID, 1956–1957

The issue of Keflavik again roiled US-Icelandic relations in 1956, as the centrist Icelandic governing coalition collapsed and the Social Democrats and the Progressive Party united in threatening to evict the US military and transfer control of Keflavik to Iceland. The elections of that summer worsened the crisis, as the Progressives and Social Democrats took power in a left-wing coalition with the Communists.[40] The government used the threat of eviction to extract over $10 million in US aid that year and ultimately relented on plans to push the United States out of Keflavik, even though Icelandic officials continued to suggest that US forces were no longer necessary.[41]

Over the next few years, Iceland continued to bargain for US economic aid. An NSC statement on US policy toward Iceland in May 1957 recommended that the United States "take all feasible actions with respect to Iceland's economy required to achieve US objectives"—namely, Iceland's continued pro-Western orientation, membership in NATO, and US access to Keflavik.[42] Although US imports and a temporary pause in the Iceland-United Kingdom fishing dispute had slowed the growth of Icelandic trade with the Soviet Union, by 1956 the Soviet share of Iceland's exports had increased to 30 percent, and it expanded even more the following year.[43] That same year, Iceland secured another $5 million US aid package (as well as $2 million from West Germany) by threatening to seek economic assistance from the Soviets, prompting US officials to ask, "Is Iceland blackmailing us?"[44]

THE ICELAND-UK FISHING DISPUTE TURNS VIOLENT, 1958–1960

The temporary reprieve in tensions over Icelandic fishing rights ended in spectacular fashion in 1958, when Iceland extended its zone to twelve kilometers beyond its coast. This prompted the United Kingdom to deploy vessels from the Royal Navy to protect and enforce British fishing rights, leading to a series of skirmishes between 1958 and 1961 that became known as the (First) Cod War. As in the previous contest over Iceland's four-kilometer limit, Washington found itself in a bind. It feared openly antagonizing Iceland lest it find itself in another dispute over Keflavik, yet the longer the conflict persisted and the more Iceland alienated not only Britain but other members of NATO, the more tempted it would be to lean on the Soviet Union.[45] The worst-case scenario, as the assistant secretary of state for European affairs put it, was that "this could lead to highly damaging developments such as the building up of pressure on the Government to break its relations with the United Kingdom and withdraw from NATO, and eventually might result in the loss of our base in Iceland."[46]

As a result, the United States undertook a variety of initiatives to mitigate the fallout from the dispute. These included importing more Icelandic fish and encouraging third parties (most successfully Jamaica) to do the same, as well as providing an additional $14 million in economic assistance.[47] Meanwhile, NATO proceeded to mediate the conflict, which was ultimately terminated in the wake of the United Nations Law of the Sea Conference in 1960 and 1961, with Britain accepting Iceland's twelve-mile limit.[48]

As a small country in a comparably benign threat environment, Iceland illustrates the dynamics of a Benign Neglect case with respect to burden-sharing. US ambitions for Iceland's contributions to NATO were modest—it sought only to maintain military access to Icelandic territory, without any sort of material offering to the NATO alliance. It was difficult to secure even this, though, because until their threat perceptions increased following the Korean War, Icelandic officials were reluctant to grant permanent, peacetime access to their territory, and even later they repeatedly threatened to evict Washington from its base at Keflavik. Far from making a material contribution, Iceland instead absorbed millions of dollars in foreign aid from the United States and other NATO members, especially West Germany, as the alliance sought to buy off Iceland's support and dissuade it from restricting access to its territory or tilting toward the Soviet Union. Iceland similarly secured US acceptance of ever-expanding Icelandic fishing rights, even as it encroached on the rights of—and came to blows with—another close US ally, the United Kingdom.

Conclusion

The Enduring Challenges of Burden-Sharing in US Alliances

This book is driven by two central questions. First, why has the United States in some cases gone to great lengths to encourage its allies to bear a larger share of the alliance's defense burdens, while in other cases it has been reluctant to seek burden-sharing or has even actively discouraged it? Second, under what conditions does US burden-sharing pressure succeed?

I argue that the answer to the first question has its roots in the trade-off that great power patrons face between control and cost-sharing in their alliances. When allies shoulder a greater share of the collective defense burden and become more self-reliant, patrons can relieve some of their own burden while maintaining the alliance's military capabilities—but at the price of giving allies more say in the partnership and empowering them to go their own way. A patron thus has good reason to seek burden-sharing contributions from its partners cautiously and selectively, with an eye toward ensuring that allies remain tied to it while simultaneously ensuring that the alliance has sufficient defense capabilities and its own costs are kept in check. Understanding how a patron balances these competing priorities is one of the major objectives of this book. As for the second question, the success of the patron's burden-sharing pressure hinges on whether it can wield a credible, salient threat of abandonment.

I focus on three factors to explain variation in the use and success of US burden-sharing pressure: allies' latent military power, the shared external threat environment, and the level of US resource constraints. In deciding to encourage burden-sharing, the United States faces a Goldilocks problem. Allies that are too small have little capacity to make military contributions, and those that are large enough to significantly contribute to the alliance are also capable of going their own way and redirecting their resources away from collective defense and toward their own priorities. Given the minimal benefits of burden-sharing by smaller allies and the risks of burden-sharing by larger allies, the United States often leans on the contributions of moderate-

CONCLUSION

sized allies. Additionally, the United States is more likely to seek burden-sharing when the level of shared external threat is higher, but whether its pressure succeeds depends on the relative weight of US and allies' perception of that threat. When allies perceive a higher level of threat, the United States has an easier time using their fears of abandonment to press them into making greater contributions. By contrast, when the United States perceives a higher level of threat, its threat of abandonment becomes less credible, because abandoning allies means potentially ceding ground to adversaries who might encroach on them. To disentangle these cross-cutting effects, I focus on allies' geographic proximity to shared adversaries, which varies across allies but is constant for the United States, and I expect that allies more vulnerable to attack—specifically, those that share a land border with an adversary—should be more susceptible to US burden-sharing pressure. Finally, when the United States faces resource and political constraints that bring its reliability into question, it is both more likely to seek greater allied burden-sharing and more likely to succeed in doing so, as its threat of abandonment is inherently more credible.

I tested the theory using qualitative evidence of US burden-sharing pressure on West Germany, South Korea, and Japan during the 1960s and 1970s, as well as Iceland during the 1950s. Several key findings emerge from each case and from a comparison of all cases. First, the German, South Korean, and Japanese cases illustrate the significance of US resource and political constraints during the late 1960s and early 1970s, brought about by the costs of the Vietnam War and an ailing US economy. These constraints encouraged US officials to seek greater burden-sharing from US partners and raised allies' concerns about US reliability, which bolstered the effectiveness of US pressure. Second, a cross-case comparison reveals several patterns. For example, Washington had greater success in encouraging burden-sharing by South Korea and West Germany, as opposed to Japan and Iceland, because their land contiguity to adversary states resulted in a greater perception of threat. Additionally, the Japanese case and to a lesser extent the West German case showed that US officials were quite reluctant to seek dramatically increased burden-sharing—even during the period of the Nixon Doctrine in the 1970s—for fear that doing so would enable the allies to become more independent. US policymakers likewise put little pressure on Iceland to make a military contribution to NATO, but for the opposite reason: because Iceland effectively lacked the capacity to do so. This contrasted with the approach taken with South Korea, which faced an enormous amount of US pressure to become self-reliant because it was a Goldilocks case—powerful enough to provide a substantial contribution, but not so powerful that it could confidently exit the alliance. But even the case of South Korea illustrates the risks that come with encouraging allies to become more self-reliant, because for the South Korean government, self-reliance meant obtaining nuclear weapons. Nevertheless, because South Korea was so dependent on

121

CONCLUSION

US protection, US officials were able to simultaneously discourage South Korean nuclear efforts while successfully encouraging South Korea to vastly increase its conventional military arming.

Comparison with Alternative Explanations

Overall, the findings provide stronger support for alliance control theory than for the three alternative explanations described in chapter 1: public goods theory, which predicts that smaller allies tend to free-ride on the contributions of larger allies; the effect of US signals of support, which expects allied burden-sharing to vary inversely with US troop levels; and allied domestic politics, which would expect variation in the success of US burden-sharing pressure to be driven by the relative political influence of alliance-skeptical political parties and leaders, domestic economic conditions, or antimilitarist norms (see table 6.1). To be sure, despite these explanations being more mono-causal than this book's own theory, when combined, they can account for important details in each case, as I discuss below. Nevertheless, alliance control theory provides a more complete account, since it is able to explain many of the same events that competing explanations can explain as well as additional details they cannot.

PUBLIC GOODS AND THE LOGIC OF ALLIANCE ASYMMETRY

First, the findings offer mixed support for the conventional wisdom, rooted in the logic of public goods and alliance asymmetry presented by scholars such as Mancur Olson, Richard Zeckhauser, and James Morrow, that larger allies devote more resources to defense because their contributions matter more.[1] South Korea contributed a very high portion of its resources to defense during the 1970s despite being small to moderate in size, driven largely by the fear that it might have to face an escalating threat from North Korea alone due to a potentially unreliable US patron. This fear was stoked by the United States, which wielded the threat of abandonment to encourage the ROK to assume more responsibility for its own defense. The threat environment and US pressure, then, substantially motivated ROK burden-sharing. Indeed, the country was responsive to US pressure even in the early stages of its meteoric economic growth, and it used its contributions to the Vietnam War to attempt to ward off US troop withdrawals from the Korean Peninsula. By contrast, Japan's enormous latent military potential meant that it was the US ally most capable of playing a decisive role in the regional balance of power. However, US officials consciously avoided asking Japan to assume a substantially larger military role, and the Japanese showed little interest in playing such a role, except as a hedge against US abandonment. As a result, in spite of the Nixon Doctrine, US decision mak-

122

Table 6.1 Summary of case study findings

	US burden-sharing pressure	West Germany		Japan		South Korea		Iceland	
		Willingness	*Success*	*Willingness*	*Success*	*Willingness*	*Success*	*Willingness*	*Success*
Support for explanation	Alliance control theory	Strong	Strong	Strong	Strong	Strong	Strong	Strong	Strong
	Asymmetry	N/A	Moderate	N/A	Weak	N/A	Weak	N/A	Strong
	US signals of support	N/A	Weak	N/A	Moderate	N/A	Moderate	N/A	Weak
	Domestic politics	Moderate; evidence suggests that US officials feared driving hard bargains or threatening troop withdrawals from governments with greater left-wing influence. This influence often was either the result of resentment at US pressure and concern about US reliability (e.g., West Germany, Japan) or downstream of a more benign external threat environment (e.g., Iceland). Left-wing governments were generally no less responsive to US burden-sharing pressure, on average.							

Note: Each cell indicates whether the evidence from each case provided strong, moderate, or weak support for alliance control theory and alternative explanations.

CONCLUSION

ers declined to seek more than modest, qualitative improvements in Japanese defense capabilities.

The cases that fit the public goods logic of alliance asymmetry better are Iceland, which was the weakest NATO member and thus had no military, and to a lesser extent West Germany, NATO's largest member and one of its larger contributors. Nevertheless, even in these cases, the decision-making calculus behind their defense efforts reflected other considerations. West Germany's contributions were frequently coerced rather than voluntary, with US pressure succeeding due to the FRG's vulnerability to Soviet attack. Relatively high levels of defense effort by the FRG were thus less the result of its size and more the result of its threat environment and US pressure. Indeed, the FRG's size partly pushed in the opposite direction. Although the United States sought—and secured—quite a bit of West German burden-sharing, there is also evidence that Washington balked at seeking a truly self-reliant FRG out of fear that it would reduce its attachment to NATO. As a result, the overall size of the West German military was smaller relative to the country's population than that of any NATO member save Iceland and Luxembourg, and what forces it did have were tightly bound to NATO and armed with military equipment purchased from the United States (under duress). In the case of Iceland, it was able to avoid fielding a military in large part not because of its small size, but rather because of its geographic insularity. My theory also correctly predicts that Iceland's size would lead US officials to set their ambitions for Icelandic burden-sharing quite low. Iceland's lack of military contributions, in other words, was not entirely the result of its making a rational decision to free-ride in light of its small size.

US SIGNALS OF SUPPORT

Second, the cases show little evidence that deployments of US forces suppressed burden-sharing by these allies. Rather, what was more decisive was the degree to which allies feared that these forces might be reduced, or that the US commitment might have been unreliable due to other factors. West Germany hosted the largest numbers of peacetime US military forces of any country, received numerous verbal assurances of US support, and participated in military exercises with the United States. Nevertheless, the United States was able to pressure the FRG into significant burden-sharing contributions by wielding the threat of withdrawal. Japan and South Korea hosted the second- and third-largest US forces among US allies. Yet, even though they hosted comparable numbers of total US forces—with South Korea hosting more than twice as many as Japan on a per capita basis—the ROK devoted significantly more of its GDP to defense during the 1970s, in large part because of its more acute perception of threat due to sharing a land border with the Communist bloc. And while all three countries experienced partial troop withdrawals between 1967 and 1971, this cannot fully explain the

124

CONCLUSION

timing and magnitude of changes in their defense spending. In all three cases, rising defense investment lasted long after withdrawals of US forces and was motivated more by the fear of potential future withdrawals than by the current level of US forces.

The size of the US troop presence can only indirectly explain Icelandic burden-sharing. While it is possible that Iceland would have established an independent military capability in the absence of the US presence—or, for that matter, the NATO security guarantee—Iceland's behavior and perception of threat suggests that this is unlikely. Iceland had no military before the US permanent presence was established, and in the 1950s it was not nervously seeking assurances that US forces would stay, but rather threatening to evict them in order to extract other concessions. Icelandic politicians who favored evicting the United States typically favored rapprochement with the Soviet Union rather than unilateral arming.

ALLIED DOMESTIC POLITICS

Third, allies' domestic politics did contribute to US officials' fears that demanding burden-sharing would fail, or that it would encourage allies to seek outside options like nuclear weapons, rapprochement with adversaries, or even alliance exit. But domestic alliance skepticism tended to be downstream of other factors, including those my theory considers to be causally prior. In particular, alliance-skeptical leaders and parties, particularly those on the left, tended to gain influence when the external threat environment was more benign, when US reliability seemed in doubt, or when US burden-sharing pressure seemed especially heavy handed.

In the case of West Germany, the left-wing Social Democratic Party was a leading proponent of rapprochement with the Communist bloc, and rising Social Democratic strength in the late 1960s and early 1970s correlated with efforts to seek détente with the Soviet Union, and with US unease about the course of German foreign policy.[2] Nevertheless, Chancellor Willy Brandt's Social Democratic government (1969–1974) proved quite responsive to the Nixon administration's pressure for offset and conventional force improvements, and the Social Democrats had gained power in part *because of* perceived US bullying and unreliability. Ludwig Erhard's government fell in October 1966 in no small part because of his willingness to cave in to US pressure over offset payments. In the "Grand Coalition" that followed under Chancellor Kiesinger, both the Gaullists within the Christian Democratic Party and the Social Democrats had more prominent roles, with Willy Brandt becoming foreign minister.[3] The first signs of détente started under Kiesinger and accelerated when Brandt became chancellor in 1969.[4] Thus, the partisan balance of power was partly downstream of US burden-sharing pressure and unreliability. Indeed, US officials were wary of pushing the FRG too hard on offset for fear of political repercussions in Germany, and in the aftermath of

125

CONCLUSION

Erhard's failed trip in late 1966, the percentage of Germans who believed that the FRG's interests aligned with those of Washington dropped to 16 percent, down from over 70 percent in June 1965.[5]

Similarly, variation in Japan's susceptibility to US burden-sharing pressure generally cannot be explained by shifts in the partisan balance of power. The major left-wing Japanese parties, the JSP and the JCP, were skeptical of US protection, and they favored pursuing a more nonaligned foreign policy more than the dominant, conservative LDP did.[6] The LDP was generally more open to US concerns about burden-sharing than the JCP and JSP, but it was a conservative LDP politician who articulated the Yoshida Doctrine that formulated the basis for relying on the United States for defense.[7]

The left-wing political gains during the early 1970s that raised concerns about Japanese neutralism were partly a by-product of Japanese fears about US reliability that arose from Washington's resource and domestic political constraints.[8] Both US and Japanese officials had long warned that troop withdrawals would damage the LDP and undermine Japanese support for the alliance.[9] Moreover, the shift in Japanese foreign policy thinking was not purely the result of left-wing gains. The LDP itself began to de-emphasize the importance of the US alliance in the late 1960s and early 1970s and increasingly favored an independent foreign policy, as conservatives felt that despite their loyalty, they had been let down by the United States.[10] During the 1969 election, for example, many LDP candidates openly complained about the United States in their campaigns.[11] US officials recognized that increased Japanese skepticism toward the US alliance was largely a response to US behavior and doubts about US reliability.[12] Finally, despite the growth in JSP and JCP influence, the 1970s still saw substantial growth in Japanese military spending, though this shift was highly incremental and did not result in quantitative growth in the size of the Japanese SDF.

Additionally, Japan and West Germany's emerging antimilitarist cultures can only partly explain their defense investments. While the size of West Germany's military was modest relative to its population and economy, and smaller than those of comparably sized Britain and France, unlike these two countries, the FRG did not have military obligations outside of Europe, and along with the United States it supplied the majority of NATO forces on the front lines with the Soviet Union. Indeed, whereas most NATO allies were relatively unmoved by US pressure throughout much of the 1960s, the FRG consistently proved more receptive to US burden-sharing requests, whether it was completing its rearmament plans, bolstering the capabilities and readiness of its forces in Central Europe, or offsetting the costs of US deployments in Germany. FRG defense spending rose in response to US pressure during the early 1970s despite growing public support for détente and continued majority support for maintaining or reducing defense spending, as well as the shift in elite opinion in favor of *Ostpolitik* and détente.[13] More broadly, West German officials were quite interested in possessing military

126

CONCLUSION

capabilities that could allow them to both hedge against US abandonment and gain greater say in NATO—including, but not limited to, access to nuclear weapons, whether in unilateral or multilateral form.

Antimilitarist norms fare better in the Japanese case, as they may be able to account for the degree of opposition to Yasuhiro Nakasone's more ambitious arming plans, which raised concerns that they could push Japan on the road to militarism and antagonize Japan's neighbors.[14] Nevertheless, the Japanese responded to US pressure and doubts about US reliability by increasing their defense spending to pursue qualitative improvements in their capabilities, and they did so explicitly through domestic arms production, seeking self-reliance in military production.[15] Moreover, one major reason Japan did not dramatically expand the SDF was its lower threat perception. The possibility of invasion was deemed remote, especially compared to the risk faced by allies in more vulnerable positions, such as West Germany and South Korea.

In terms of South Korean domestic politics, political ideology played a permissive but not decisive role. President Park was staunchly anticommunist and used the prospect of US withdrawal to solidify his hold on power, pursue a campaign of military modernization, declare a state of emergency in 1971, and justify his use of repression under the revised Yushin Constitution beginning in 1972.[16] US officials did regard Park's rule as preferable to many alternatives.[17] Nevertheless, it is clear from the available evidence that the core reason US officials were not very worried about South Korean alliance exit was the ROK's comparative weakness, and that the South Korean government was responsive to US pressure because they feared abandonment as a result of both their external threat environment and resource and domestic political constraints in the United States. Indeed, the causality to some extent ran in reverse, with domestic politics being shaped by security concerns. Park's declaration of a national emergency and institution of the Yushin Constitution was in large part motivated by his feelings of insecurity in the aftermath of the withdrawal of the US Seventh Infantry Division, doubts around the credibility of US protection, and a series of North Korean provocations, some of which targeted Park and his family.[18]

Domestic politics in Iceland mattered at the margins. Most notably, the Communist Party—which favored withdrawing from NATO and ejecting foreign forces from the country—held substantial sway, though its influence varied over time.[19] The Communist Party's influence derived not only from its strength in the legislature but also from its connections to the country's major labor unions.[20] Other parties approached the alliance with similar skepticism.[21] The pro-NATO Conservatives were the largest party during the 1940s and 1950s, but the second-largest Progressive Party had strong neutralist leanings.[22] As a result, the United States generally approached Iceland with a soft touch and calibrated its approach in response to the strength of left-wing parties over time. During the late 1940s and early 1950s, the Communist Party

CONCLUSION

claimed about 20 percent of the national vote and seats in the legislature, and during this period the United States provided around 4 percent of Iceland's GDP in foreign aid each year.[23] In 1951, for example, Washington approved an injection of aid in response to an economic crisis that US officials feared could rally the population around Communist-led strikes.[24] After a left-wing government took power in 1956, the United States similarly provided large amounts of aid after the left-wing coalition government threatened to evict it from Keflavik Airport and lean closer to Moscow.[25]

But while Icelandic domestic politics magnified US fears over losing its access to Keflavik and intensified its efforts to compensate Iceland, the basic reasons why US policymakers sought a military base—but not Icelandic conventional military contributions—were structural and derived from the combination of Iceland's small size, its geostrategic position, and its distance from Soviet military power. The variation in Iceland's willingness to host a permanent, peacetime US presence can ultimately be traced to its threat perceptions. Increased perception of threat in the wake of the Korean War led the Icelandic government to accept a permanent US presence, but by the mid-1950s, as the period of highest threat waned, the Icelandic parties began to see less need for it and were more confident in their ability to wield the threat of eviction to extract compensation.[26]

Economic conditions can explain aspects of these cases but fall short overall, as defense spending did not always rise and fall proportionally to economic growth. The West German recession during 1966 and 1967 contributed to Erhard's difficulty in meeting US offset requests, but US pressure prevented the dramatic cuts in FRG defense spending that many West German politicians had called for to redress budgetary shortfalls.[27] South Korea's economic conditions can partially explain rising South Korean military capabilities, as the country's fast growth during the 1960s and 1970s meant that the country could more easily afford to invest more in defense. However, South Korean military spending did not rise in a purely mechanical way, but rather because of deliberate decisions made by both US and South Korean officials. After a final burst of military assistance in the early 1970s, South Korea was effectively left to pay its own way, and it drove toward self-reliance in response to US pressure coupled with fears of US disengagement. Japan experienced meteoric growth during the 1960s and 1970s, yet for much of the period its military spending did not fully keep pace, leading to a slight decline in Japanese defense expenditures as a percentage of GDP from 1966 to 1970. It was not until the early 1970s, when Japanese policymakers made the explicit decision to seek a more self-reliant defense capability, that Japan's defense efforts accelerated considerably.

Finally, the only allied leaders of these countries with previous executive-level business experience were Erhard in West Germany and Tanaka in Japan. Neither of them proved noticeably less susceptible to US pressure. Erhard ultimately lost power in no small part because he could not resist

128

CONCLUSION

US offset demands in the face of threats of drastic troop withdrawals. Indeed, when Johnson met with Kiesinger in 1967, the chancellor referred to Erhard as "naïve," to which Johnson replied that Erhard was not a "softie," but instead someone "who was wise to see the danger of an isolationist trend which was growing in the US."[28] Similarly, Tanaka's tenure (1972–1974) saw the beginning of the substantial rise in Japanese defense spending throughout the 1970s.[29]

Generalizing the Findings: Burden-Sharing in Comparative Perspective

A natural question arises as to whether the book's findings can be generalized beyond its four case studies. While a systematic analysis of all cases of asymmetric alliance burden-sharing is ultimately beyond the scope of a single book, I can nevertheless briefly attempt to show that my theory's underlying logic can explain dynamics in other cases. Elsewhere, I have reported quantitative results confirming that US allies bordering shared adversaries by land do indeed spend more on defense than other allies—about 1 percent of GDP more, on average.[30] Here, I further demonstrate the findings' generalizability by discussing two sets of cases that extend beyond US Cold War alliances. The first looks at a different set of cases across a similar time period: burden-sharing in Soviet alliances during the Cold War. The second examines a contemporary case: NATO burden-sharing after Russia's February 2022 invasion of Ukraine.

SOVIET ALLIANCES IN THE COLD WAR

The Soviet Union's approach to burden-sharing differed from that of the United States in important respects. In particular, the Soviets were far less constrained in exercising direct control over the foreign and domestic policies of its allies than the United States. Soviet and Soviet-trained officers were directly integrated into Warsaw Pact members' chains of command, a Soviet supreme commander stood atop the pact's military hierarchy, and Moscow militarily intervened on a number of occasions—most notably in Hungary (1956) and Czechoslovakia (1968)—when Communist rule was threatened. Nevertheless, the Soviets still encountered the burden-sharing dilemma. Soviet domination required that the USSR have the capacity to impose discipline in its bloc. As a result, the Soviet Union's share of contributions to the Warsaw Pact's capabilities was even more disproportionate than the United States' to NATO, and it offered the Warsaw Pact members little autonomy in the event of conflict with NATO.[31]

Like the United States, the Soviets generally found that their most cooperative partners were those situated close to NATO countries, which depended on Moscow for survival—namely, East Germany, Poland, Bulgaria,

129

CONCLUSION

and Czechoslovakia. East Germany in particular bound itself closely to the Soviet Union due to its insecurity over its legitimacy and recognition in the face of West Germany, while Poland and Czechoslovakia harbored long-running suspicions of Germany, with whom they had unsettled border disputes. These countries formed the core of the Warsaw Pact's "Northern Tier," and along with Bulgaria, which bordered NATO members Greece and Turkey, they tended to be more receptive to higher defense spending and to planning for coalition warfare with Moscow.[32] By contrast, the Soviets had far more difficulty wrangling contributions from Romania, which bordered other Communist countries only and sought to maximize its flexibility by playing the Soviet Union, NATO, and China against each other, pursuing an autonomous defense posture, and opposing Soviet efforts to impose control over the Warsaw Pact.[33]

Soviet efforts to solicit greater Warsaw Pact military contributions frequently proved to be a double-edged sword. The challenges were evident after Joseph Stalin's death in 1953. Soviet officials wanted Eastern Europe to assume more of the burden for their own security, and they allowed the Soviet satellites to gain more control over their military officer corps, which made it more difficult for the Soviets to exercise direct influence over their foreign and security policies. Romania ultimately negotiated a withdrawal of Soviet forces from its territory, Poland extracted pledges of nonintervention in Polish affairs in exchange for hosting Soviet troops, and the presence of Soviet officers in pact members' chains of command diminished.[34] Under Nikita Khrushchev and Leonid Brezhnev during the 1960s, in part as a reaction to the pressures of the Sino-Soviet split and NATO's Flexible Response doctrine, the Soviets sought to consolidate Warsaw Pact military power through institutional reforms to streamline political and military decision-making in the pact, establish greater military integration, and create a unified general staff under the Soviet supreme commander. But objections from other members, particularly Romania, forced the Soviets to compromise on reforms that instead created a multinational Committee of Ministers of Defense and a Military Council in addition to the Soviet supreme commander, ensuring that decision-making about pact military operations was subject to input and voting from all Warsaw Pact members, which were not strictly bound by their decisions. Moreover, each member's forces would remain under national control in wartime. The reforms thus shifted the Warsaw Pact in the direction of being a truly multilateral organization in which non-Soviet members had a voice; while they hardly offered much safeguard against unilateral Soviet action, they nevertheless did not allow Moscow to use the other pact members' military forces as extensions of Soviet power without their consent.[35] It was not until the late 1970s, after a decade of an intense Soviet military buildup that led it to assume a substantially larger share of Warsaw Pact military responsibilities, along with intensifying concern about internal challenges to communist rule, that the pact members—

130

CONCLUSION

with the exception of Romania—accepted Soviet plans to grant the Soviet supreme commander broad wartime authority over coalition forces.[36]

Like the United States during the 1970s, the Soviet Union sought to reduce its own military burdens during the 1980s in response to economic stagnation in the Soviet economy and the costs of the arms race and the war in Afghanistan. By the early 1980s, the Soviet economy was in deep relative decline, and Soviet defense spending, military commitments, and massive subsidies to Eastern Europe were draining the Soviet treasury. As a result, Moscow pursued arms control with Washington, ultimately withdrew from Afghanistan, and shrank the Soviet military footprint in Eastern Europe. The Soviets also encouraged other pact members to assume more of the burden for their own defense, both internal and external, and were increasingly reluctant to intervene militarily in other pact countries. But the Soviets had limited success in encouraging increased defense spending (except in East Germany), in no small part because, like Moscow, other Warsaw Pact capitals saw ensuring economic welfare at home as more crucial to regime survival than deterring a NATO offensive.[37] They were ultimately unable to stave off the revolutions and independence movements that swept across the Soviet bloc in 1989, which the Soviets did not put down with force like they had in previous decades.

The Soviet Union thus faced problems in managing burden-sharing within the Warsaw Pact that were not dissimilar from those the United States faced in its alliances. Although none of the Soviet satellites in Eastern Europe had the latent power of a Japan or West Germany, and consequently most had limited ability to resist Soviet demands, the Soviets still faced a trade-off between military cost-sharing and political control. Moreover, geography played a crucial role in shaping Warsaw Pact members' relative dependence on Soviet protection. East Germany, Poland, and Bulgaria looked to Moscow for support and were generally more pliant partners, whereas Romania played a role much like that of Gaullist France—which, not coincidentally, was also insulated from direct attack—in resisting its patron's attempts to impose order in the alliance.

The challenges of burden-sharing were, if anything, even more acute when it came to the Soviet alliance with China. From the beginning of their alliance in 1950, the Soviets looked to China as a counterweight to the United States and its partners. As a result, Moscow provided Beijing with substantial amounts of economic and especially military assistance to help jump-start China's industrialization and defense production so that it could more effectively burden-share.[38] Stalin also encouraged China and North Korea to prolong the stalemate in the Korean War from 1951 to 1953 in order to drain and distract the United States.[39]

Beginning in the late 1950s and early 1960s, however, the Sino-Soviet relationship rapidly deteriorated. The proximate cause of their rupture stemmed from their divergent approaches to confrontation with the US-led bloc—especially over Taiwan—and to revolutionary movements worldwide,

CONCLUSION

coupled with ideological disagreements related to Stalin's legacy.[40] But the Sino-Soviet split had a structural component as well. Although China was initially the junior partner, its size and rapid growth during the 1950s made it virtually inevitable that it would demand a greater degree of autonomy and equality in the alliance. The Soviet Union could not simultaneously hope for China to be both a pliant partner and its "chief lieutenant in Asia."[41] Having expended a massive amount of blood and treasure in the Korean War and having made progress toward industrialization and military self-sufficiency, by the late 1950s Chinese Communist Party chairman Mao Zedong aspired to a position equal to that of the Soviet Union in the international Communist movement. Mao's push for self-reliance was further propelled by increasing Soviet suspicion and hostility toward China's growing strength and assertiveness, which manifested in reduced military and technical assistance, especially when it came to missile and nuclear technology, as well as attempts to constrain the Chinese navy by proposing a joint submarine fleet.[42] By the 1960s, China was an outright competitor for influence—not only in Asia and Africa, but also among some members of the Warsaw Pact like Romania and Albania.[43] The end of that decade saw China and the Soviet Union on the brink of war, ultimately culminating in Sino-American normalization in the 1970s and a de facto alliance between the United States and China in the 1980s.

NATO BURDEN-SHARING AFTER RUSSIA'S INVASION OF UKRAINE

Russia's invasion of Ukraine in February 2022 provided both new urgency for debates over burden-sharing in the NATO alliance and an opportunity for President Joseph Biden's administration to redress long-standing US grievances about insufficient European defense spending.[44] Prior to the invasion, the NATO members who perceived the greatest level of threat from Russia all bordered on Russia: Estonia, Latvia, Lithuania, and Poland.[45] Not coincidentally, these four countries were among the nine non-US NATO members that spent at least 2 percent of their GDP on defense in 2021.[46] Furthermore, all four countries have pledged to increase defense spending to at least 2.5 percent of GDP (5% in Poland's case) in light of Russia's invasion of Ukraine, which would make Poland NATO's top spender as a percentage of GDP and the Baltic states behind only the United States, Greece, and Croatia in relative defense burdens among NATO members.[47] As of summer 2022, Poland, Estonia, and Latvia were in the top ten non-US providers of military aid to Ukraine in NATO, surpassing France, Italy, and Spain.[48] Poland and the three Baltic states are also, as of December 2022, the largest providers of aid to Ukraine as a percentage of their GDP.[49] Other NATO members, including Belgium, Czechia, Italy, Norway, Romania, and perhaps most significantly Germany, also pledged to increase defense spending, and

CONCLUSION

Denmark backpedaled from opting out of the European Union's Common Security and Defense Policy.[50]

Nevertheless, events since February 2022 also point to the challenges of encouraging burden-sharing—especially, as this book expects, among allies more insulated from Russian attack. A poll across ten European countries by the European Council on Foreign Relations found that it was only in Poland—the only NATO member surveyed that borders Russia—that more respondents favored pursuing a decisive defeat of Russia over offering up Ukrainian territory in exchange for peace, and a clear majority supported increasing defense spending.[51] Domestic politics forced Italy, for example, to delay defense investments.[52] Germany similarly faced political pushback against the defense investments promised by Chancellor Olaf Scholz, who dragged his feet on supplying weapons to Ukraine.[53] As of February 2023, the governing coalition has approved the creation of a hundred-billion euro supplemental defense fund with the goal of reaching NATO's 2 percent of GDP defense spending target. However, it remains unclear how much Germany will ultimately spend, for how long, and on what, as the supplemental fund is to be spent over multiple years and may be used to cover preexisting commitments.[54] Germany has long overinvested in personnel at the expense of equipment, resulting in severe shortages in combat readiness that will take years of sustained investment to reverse.[55] Indeed, Germany has pledged to invest more in defense in the past, particularly after Russia's initial invasion of Ukraine and annexation of Crimea in 2014, only for it to ultimately fall short. Even with the new fund, Germany has pledged to spend only 2 percent of GDP—the minimum NATO target and substantially less than Poland and the Baltic states, let alone the United States—over a "multi-year average" rather than every year, and estimates as of early 2023 suggest that it is not clear when Germany will reach 2 percent of GDP, even with the supplemental fund.[56]

As for the other two largest European economies, both France and Britain have pledged increases to defense spending since Russia's invasion of Ukraine. In Britain's case, however, the bulk of its spending increases will stem from inflation and economic growth, and it is unclear as of December 2022 whether the country will spend substantially more as a percentage of GDP by 2030, though it has provided substantial military assistance to Ukraine.[57] Both countries have long had ambitions to play a security role outside of Europe—particularly in Africa, in France's case—and it remains to be seen whether these commitments will divert attention and resources away from Russia.[58] French president Emmanuel Macron has spent a great deal of time and energy attempting to broker a political settlement with Moscow and cautioning against the risks of escalation and humiliating Russia.[59] France and Britain's responses are largely in keeping with the historical norm, with France long being a spoiler in NATO. During the early Cold War, it attempted to co-opt the alliance to play a role in securing its overseas empire, and throughout the

133

CONCLUSION

1960s it challenged US leadership in the alliance, ultimately withdrawing from NATO command in 1966.[60] Both during and immediately after the Cold War, France viewed the Soviet Union and Russia as counterweights to German power.[61] The United Kingdom, meanwhile, has historically made substantial contributions to US-led military coalitions, which some scholars attribute to the two countries' "special relationship" and cultural affinity.[62] Nevertheless, US policymakers have often struggled to wield the threat of abandonment to coerce British burden-sharing when it was not voluntarily forthcoming—for example, they failed to ward off UK defense cuts during the 1960s and 1970s, even after they temporarily cut off intelligence sharing.[63]

While the United States cannot control geography or the ways in which allies perceive Russian capabilities and intentions, it can influence NATO burden-sharing in the coming months and years by communicating its own intentions toward Europe. As discussed in chapter 1, one of the challenges to encouraging burden-sharing is that even an elevated level of external threat is not necessarily a guarantee of success, because the shared threat is likely to increase not just allies' desire for protection but also the United States' commitment to them. Events since Russia's invasion of Ukraine illustrate this tendency. NATO moved to increase the size of its multinational battlegroups present in Poland and the three Baltic states from battalions to brigades, and it created four new multinational battlegroups in Bulgaria, Hungary, Romania, and Slovakia. But the United States has punched above its weight in reinforcing NATO's Eastern Flank.[64] Washington increased its presence on the Continent from around 80,000 to 100,000, especially in Eastern Europe, and established its first permanent presence in Poland.[65] The United States likewise accounts for half of global aid committed to Ukraine.[66] The NATO secretary general announced at the June 2022 Madrid Summit that the NATO Response Force would be substantially increased, but as of February 2023, the details of these new forces are unclear, and the evidence suggests that some NATO capitals were caught off guard by the announcement.[67]

However, what could both constrain an increased US presence and give European capitals incentive to burden-share despite the already-existing US footprint is the long-standing US ambition to devote more resources to the Asia-Pacific to counter a rising China. Of course, most NATO members did not reach the alliance's target of 2 percent of GDP after the 2014 Russian invasion, despite the Obama administration's erstwhile "pivot to Asia." But whether European decision makers expect events in Asia to fundamentally alter the resources that Washington is willing to devote to Europe will likely play a key role in determining whether "this time is different" for NATO burden-sharing. This is not to suggest US behavior will be the sole or even most important determinant of burden-sharing in NATO in the coming decade. Achieving European strategic autonomy would take time, and some scholars doubt whether NATO members are sufficiently aligned in their threat perceptions to ever act cohesively.[68] Nevertheless, as the Continent's

134

decades-long security guarantor, the United States is in a unique position to influence European governments' military arming.

Aside from the question of whether Europe could fend for itself, this book points to what is perhaps just as unclear: whether Washington will want it to. It would require relinquishing some influence over European countries and accepting that they may implement policies and forge partnerships against Washington's wishes.[69] Despite their stated ambitions for trans-Atlantic burden-sharing, US policymakers have routinely met previous European efforts to forge a more independent defense identity with concerns that these might allow Europe to decouple from NATO; these concerns date back to French efforts to seek an autonomous European bloc during the Cold War and continued through to the establishment of the joint European Defense Fund in 2018.[70] Secretary of State Madeleine Albright, for example, warned against the "three Ds" in European defense initiatives: (1) delinking from NATO; (2) duplicating NATO capabilities and structures; and (3) discriminating against countries outside Europe.[71] There are signs that the Biden administration, driven by its desire to reorient US foreign policy toward the Asia-Pacific and cognizant of the United States' diminishing share of global economic output, may be more willing than its predecessors to embrace European strategic autonomy.[72] However, it remains to be seen whether this reflects a permanent change of heart or whether, in keeping with the historical norm, the administration will instead ultimately backpedal when faced with the reality of an independent European defense policy.

Avenues for Future Research

In addition to providing and empirically testing a theory of asymmetric alliance burden-sharing, this book suggests numerous avenues for future research.[73] First, although the book focuses primarily on the effectiveness of negative inducements—and in particular, threats of abandonment—further research could investigate their effectiveness relative to other forms of persuasion. These could include, but are not limited to, economic coercion, promises of rewards and positive inducements, and efforts to "name and shame" states that undercontribute to their alliances. Scholars have emphasized such factors mostly in the context of multilateral military interventions and coalition-building, but less so in the literature on general defense burden-sharing.[74] A related line of research could focus on allies' willingness to contribute to collective goods for reasons unrelated to bargaining or the contributions of other allies.[75]

Second, this book suggests that the United States is much more likely to seek more contributions from its partners—and much more likely to be successful in doing so—when it faces domestic political constraints on its ability to maintain its foreign commitments. Additional research could be done on

CONCLUSION

the conditions under which burden-sharing is a salient political issue to domestic actors, as well as how much burden-sharing is "enough" to deter an anti-alliance backlash. Political psychology scholarship could shed light on micro-foundations to help understand characteristics that make individuals predisposed to seeing free-riding by allies as unacceptable.[76]

Third, further research could explore other mechanisms by which allies can encourage partner burden-sharing without sacrificing political influence. In principle, for example, allies might reduce the chances of defection by having each member of the alliance specialize in some military capabilities but not others, increasing their efficiency in fighting together but making it more difficult to fight alone.[77] Future scholars could identify the conditions under which allies ask their partners to specialize in a particular capability portfolio, as opposed to obtaining a more balanced force.[78]

Theoretical Implications

This book suggests new ways of thinking about the effect of alliance guarantees on partners' behavior, particularly the risk of "moral hazard." Scholars have long discussed the potentially pernicious side effects of security assurances and have argued that assurances can both embolden partners to provoke their adversaries and encourage them to free-ride.[79] This study complicates this perspective in two key ways. First, alliances can mitigate partners' adventurism by allowing them to meet their security needs without relying on their own efforts. States in alliances can thus afford to refrain from proactive military arming or preventive war, thereby diminishing the influence of the security dilemma on their own and their neighbors' foreign policies.[80] My findings show that while alliances might in some cases increase the risk of aggressive behavior due to greed (i.e., moral hazard), they also reduce the hazard of aggressive behavior due to insecurity. Second (and relatedly), free-riding is not necessarily an inevitable consequence of alliances that patron countries are forced to tolerate, or at least not one that is constant across cases and over time. Patrons have agency in shaping their partners' contributions, and burden-sharing in asymmetric alliances is possible to the extent that a patron is willing and able to pressure its allies to do more. However, it may not always elect to do so. Thus, some of what we consider free-riding can stem from a patron's conscious choices.[81]

More broadly, this book informs scholarly understanding of global order and great power politics by studying how great powers maintain their alliances and manage their costs and benefits. Classic works in the international relations literature argue that free-riding is inherent in great powers' alliances with weaker partners, and that the costs of maintaining these asymmetric partnerships can even contribute to overextension and long-term economic decline.[82] This insight has contributed to debates about the course

136

of US grand strategy. Some scholars prescribe retrenchment as a way to mitigate free-riding and rein in escalating costs of US commitments.[83] Others argue that the consequences of free-riding are overstated, and that the benefits of alliances far outweigh their costs.[84] This book contributes to this debate by studying the conditions under which great powers are able to maintain cohesion and loyalty in their alliances while simultaneously promoting burden-sharing. In this regard, the book offers room for both optimism and pessimism. On the one hand, patrons can in many cases encourage burden-sharing without shedding its alliances. In particular, patrons are best positioned to obtain allied burden-sharing when they need it most—namely, when their own resources are constrained, and when the alliance's external threat environment is most dangerous. On the other hand, encouraging allied self-reliance can act as a centrifugal force in the alliance, leading allies to seek greater say in the partnership or even to go their own way. Most regrettably, from the patron's perspective, the allies most capable of carrying their own weight may be the ones for which this risk is the greatest and thus the allies the patron is least willing to ask to become self-reliant.

Policy Implications

This book also has implications for understanding the role of alliances in US foreign policy. Below, I discuss five concrete policy implications. The first four draw attention to the conditions under which US burden-sharing pressure is more or less likely to succeed, and shed light on the factors that might shape the United States' ability to encourage burden-sharing in the coming years. The fifth suggests policymakers should be aware of the unavoidable trade-offs inherent to burden-sharing and highlights the conditions under which policymakers are likely to find these dilemmas most severe.

REASSURING ALLIES DOESN'T NECESSARILY UNDERMINE BURDEN-SHARING

The United States is not helpless in encouraging allied burden-sharing, even when it goes to some length to reassure them by, for example, stationing troops on their territory. Assurances of protection do not preclude burden-sharing; rather, when used in tandem with threats of abandonment, they play a central role in inducing allies to contribute more because it is the combination of threats and assurances that makes coercion most effective.[85] If an ally needs reassurance because it fears abandonment, then the patron is in a good position to leverage this fear to encourage burden-sharing, even as it assures the ally that it will be protected if it complies. In such circumstances—for example, during periods in which patrons face

CONCLUSION

domestic pressure to retrench and reduce their commitments—the patron's challenge is to simultaneously convince allies that it will reduce its commitment if allies do not comply and that it will not reduce its level of commitment if they do comply. Otherwise, allies may hedge and avoid increasing their share of the defense burden rather than become more self-reliant and thus give the patron an excuse to retrench. Alternatively, the ally might seek other means of achieving security, such as forming alliances with third parties, jumping on the bandwagon with adversaries, or seeking nuclear weapons.[86] Ultimately, as Thomas Schelling famously argued, threats must be combined with assurances, since if targets of coercion expect to be punished no matter what they do, they have little reason to behave as requested.[87]

BURDEN-SHARING IS STRUCTURALLY LIMITED, ESPECIALLY BY GEOGRAPHY

The second policy implication of this book is an important caveat to the first—namely, that the United States' room for maneuver is bounded, often structurally constrained by factors largely out of its control. Periods of sustained pressure for retrenchment, for example, are unlikely to be deliberately manufactured. When they stem from the costs of the United States' foreign wars, resource constraints that make burden-sharing pressure more successful may even be less potent in the twenty-first century, as the heavier reliance on defense contractors and unmanned weapons systems reduces war's visible costs and makes security commitments easier for domestic audiences to ignore.[88] Additionally, while the findings of this book suggest that the United States tends to be more successful in encouraging burden-sharing by allies that have a high perception of threat, not all allies will fit this description—including the ones that the United States most needs to contribute. One consistent finding in this book relates to the importance of geography, with allies contiguous to adversaries by land (West Germany, South Korea) being more susceptible to US burden-sharing than allies separated from adversaries by water (Iceland, Japan).[89] In terms of policy implications, this suggests that expanding an alliance's geographic frontiers might diminish the incentive to burden-share for allies situated further away from shared adversaries. This may be a particularly salient problem if it is larger allies—which have the greatest potential to contribute—that are insulated. Germany, for example, transitioned from being a frontline state that contributed a great deal during the Cold War to one whose margin of security allowed it to chronically underinvest in defense in the decades that followed.[90] Germany's incentive to supply military resources to NATO may increase in the coming years—for example, if it perceives greater hostility from Russian intentions, or if the United States appears unable or unwilling to act as Europe's security guarantor. But the analysis presented in this book suggests that its incentive will always be less than those of allies bor-

138

CONCLUSION

dering Russia directly, many of which (e.g., Estonia, Latvia, and Lithuania) are among NATO's smallest members.

FEAR OF CHINA AND RUSSIA DOESN'T GUARANTEE UNIVERSALLY GREATER BURDEN-SHARING

One might expect rising Chinese power in East Asia and Russian expansionism in Europe to trigger substantially greater investments in self-defense among US allies in these regions. However, this book suggests that the amount of allied burden-sharing may disappoint. The presence of a shared adversary—even one that is powerful and has aggressive intentions—is no guarantee of success. Although allies with an elevated perception of threat are likely to be inclined toward greater burden-sharing, an elevated US perception of threat may reduce allies' incentives for greater burden-sharing, because it is more difficult for US officials to credibly threaten to reduce US protection—by withdrawing forces, for example—when allies face an external threat that threatens the regional status quo. US success is likely to be undercut to the extent that its own perception of threat matches or outweighs those of allies, as this is likely to reduce allies' fears of abandonment and thus their incentive to burden-share. As described in chapter 2, changes in Soviet capabilities and behavior had only a weak relationship to NATO burden-sharing. With the exception of West Germany, NATO allies' proclivity to burden-share did not increase substantially in the wake of the Berlin Crisis in 1961 and 1962 or the Soviet invasion of Czechoslovakia in 1968. Counterintuitively, it was during the period of rapprochement with the Communist bloc during the 1970s that many European NATO members increased their defense spending in response to US pressure and concerns about US troop withdrawals—which were themselves in part the result of improvements in the threat environment, as many in the US Congress viewed détente as an excuse to draw down US forces. US officials should not be surprised, then, when allies are less receptive to US pressure than either party's perception of threat might otherwise imply.

WASHINGTON CAN'T ALWAYS GET WHAT IT WANTS, BUT IT SOMETIMES GETS WHAT IT NEEDS

The presence of powerful, revisionist competitors does not guarantee that allies will be responsive to US burden-sharing pressure. What might provide more incentive for burden-sharing are constraints on US resources and allies' doubts about US reliability. Many observers expect that US economic and military power will decline in relative terms over the course of the twenty-first century.[91] If this is the case, and the United States has fewer resources to devote to its foreign commitments, its partners may be willing pick up some of the slack. The evidence in this book suggests that the

139

CONCLUSION

perception of a relative decline in US power during the late 1960s and 1970s led many US allies to take more seriously Washington's overtures to burden-share. The upside is that the potentially negative consequences of US decline for the ability of its alliances to deter and win wars may be offset by increased allied contributions. The downside, of course, is that US leaders would in many cases surely prefer that allies contribute more before the United States faces acute decline.

BURDEN-SHARING PRESENTS UNAVOIDABLE TRADE-OFFS

Finally, this book suggests that allied burden-sharing is ultimately a mixed blessing. The conventional wisdom, informed by the economic theory of alliances, suggests that unequal alliance burden-sharing is in important ways automatic; smaller allies free-ride because their larger patron is both able and willing to disproportionately contribute to the alliance's collective defense, while at the same time incapable of discouraging allies to increase their own contributions.[92] The argument I present here, however, suggests that the problem is often not whether the United States *can* convince its allies to contribute more—a combination of threats of abandonment coupled with assurances of protection can be a powerful coercive tool under the right circumstances—but rather whether it is *willing* to do so, as allies that are more capable of contributing to the alliance are also more capable of leaving it. The problem of equitable alliance burden-sharing cannot be definitively solved through threats of abandonment. Indeed, the argument I present here suggests that it is a problem that can rarely if ever be totally resolved. The patron's desire for cost-sharing frequently runs up against its competing priority of maintaining alliance control, and the balance it strikes between the two is an ever-evolving one. Thus, the oft-derided free-riding in US alliances is not an accident, nor is it entirely beyond the control of the United States. Policymakers have long complained about lacking contributions from US allies and will almost certainly continue to do so. But historically, they have always settled on accepting the trade-off of sacrificing some cost-sharing for the sake of influence and control.

APPENDIX

Selected US Economic Statistics, 1950–1980

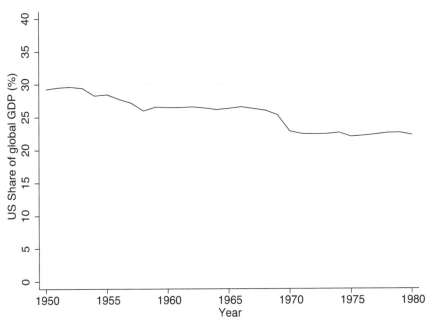

Figure A.1. US share of global gross domestic product, 1950–1980. Source: Gleditsch 2002.

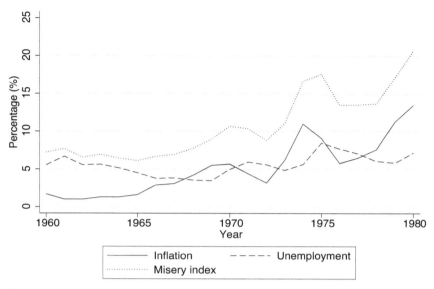

Figure A.2. US unemployment, inflation, and the "misery index"—the combination of inflation and unemployment—between 1960 and 1980. Source: US Bureau of Labor Statistics, "CPI-All Urban Consumers (Current Series)" (2019), and US Bureau of Labor Statistics, "Labor Force Statistics from the Current Population Survey" (2019).

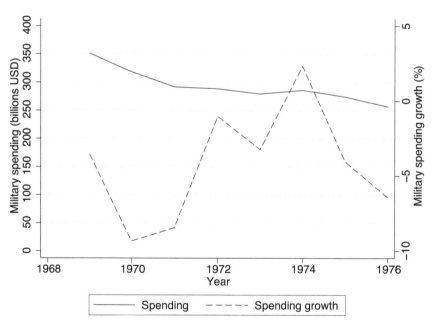

Figure A.3. US military spending (in billions of constant 2005 US dollars) and spending growth (% change), 1969–1976. Military spending data are from Version 5.0 of the Correlates of War's National Material Capabilities Dataset (Singer 1987).

Notes

Introduction

1. Jeffrey Goldberg, "The Obama Doctrine: The U.S. President Talks Through His Hardest Decisions about America's Role in the World," *The Atlantic*, March 10, 2016. Portions of this chapter are adapted from Blankenship 2021 (691–95) with permission from *Security Studies*.

2. Ben Jacobs, "Donald Trump Reiterates He Will Only Help NATO Countries That Pay 'Fair Share,'" *Guardian*, July 27, 2016.

3. Michael Birnbaum, "Gates Rebukes European Allies in Farewell Speech," *Washington Post*, June 10, 2011.

4. Driver 2016, 6.

5. Summary Record of NSC Executive Committee Meeting No. 38 (Part II), January 25, 1963, *FRUS*, 1961–1963, vol. 13, 486, 489.

6. Lee and Heo 2002, 111–52.

7. Dumbrell 1996; O'Hara 2003.

8. Komine 2014.

9. Schake 1998; Posen 2006; Shifrinson 2020.

10. Olson and Zeckhauser 1966; Sandler 1993.

11. Dorussen, Kirchner, and Sperling 2009; Zyla 2015.

12. Christensen 2011.

13. Gilpin 1981; Kennedy 1987.

14. Oatley 2015; Cappella Zielinski 2016.

15. Olson and Zeckhauser 1966; Gilpin 1981; Posen 2014. By assuring them of security, promises of support can also lead allies to take other risks such as provoking an adversary or prioritizing internal threats over preparedness for external threats in the knowledge that their partner will bail them out. Fearon 1997; Posen 2014; Boutton 2019.

16. Morrow 1991; Lake 2009.

17. Olson 1965; Olson and Zeckhauser 1966; Oneal and Elrod 1989; Palmer 1990a, 1990b; Plümper and Neumayer 2015.

18. Lake 2009; Martínez Machain and Morgan 2013; Posen 2014.

19. Lanoszka 2015.

20. Sandler and Forbes 1980; Murdoch and Sandler 1984; Palmer 1990a, 1990b; Sandler 1993; Sandler and Shimizu 2014.

143

NOTES TO PAGES 4–8

21. See, for instance, Lee and Heo 2002; Thies 2003. For exceptions, see Fang and Ramsay 2010; Kim 2016. The other exceptions come from the literature on alternative forms of burden-sharing outside of defense spending, such as participation in multilateral military interventions postconflict reconstruction peacekeeping and foreign aid, but this is largely beyond the scope of this book which focuses on general defense burden-sharing. On multilateral military coalition-building, see Bennett, Lepgold, and Unger 1994; Tago 2007, 2008, 2014; Kreps 2010; Henke 2019. On other forms of burden-sharing, see Khanna and Sandler 1997; Khanna, Sandler, and Shimizu 1998; Dorussen, Kirchner, and Sperling 2009; Zyla 2015, 2016, 2018; Sandler 2017.

22. Studies that find that the presence of US troops has a negative effect on burden-sharing include Lake 2007; Martínez Machain and Morgan 2013; Jakobsen and Jakobsen 2018; and DiGiuseppe and Shea 2021. Studies that do not find such an effect include Bennett, Lepgold, and Unger 1994; Allen, VanDusky-Allen, and Flynn 2016; and Blankenship 2021.

23. Large 1996.

24. Art 1996; Howorth and Keeler 2003; Posen 2006; Steven Erlanger, "U.S. Revives Concerns about European Defense Plans Rattling NATO Allies," *New York Times*, February 18, 2018; Erik Brattberg and Jamie Fly, "Two Cheers for European Defense Cooperation," *Foreign Policy*, March 9, 2018; Ronja Kempin and Barbara Kunz, "Washington Should Help Europe Achieve 'Strategic Autonomy,' Not Fight It," *War on the Rocks*, April 12, 2018.

25. The term *alliance control theory* originally appeared in Blankenship 2020. I have adopted it again here with permission from *International Studies Quarterly* and Oxford University Press.

26. See also Christensen 2011; Douglas 2014. Stein 1984 describes a similar "hegemon's dilemma" in the realm of international political economy between what Mastanduno 2009 calls "system making" and "privilege taking," wherein leading states are forced to accept some degree of exploitation by other more protectionist states in exchange for freer trade overall.

27. Sandler and Forbes 1980; Murdoch and Sandler 1984; Oneal and Elrod 1989; Oneal 1990; Palmer 1990a, 1990b; Plümper and Neumayer 2015.

28. Rapp-Hooper 2020, 77–85.

29. Zyla 2015.

30. Notably, the definition of alliance I use here differs from that of Stephen Walt, who uses the terms *alliance* and *alignment* interchangeably and defines an alliance as "a formal or informal arrangement for security cooperation between two or more sovereign states" (1987, 12). My definition more closely resembles that of Leeds, Long, and Mitchell: "a written agreement signed by official representatives of at least two independent states that includes promises to aid a partner in the event of military conflict remain neutral in the event of conflict refrain from military conflict with one another or consult/cooperate in the event of international crises that create a potential for military conflict" (2000, 690).

31. Waltz 1979; Kim 2016.

32. Harrison 2005.

33. Doyle 1986; Russett 1994; Owen 1997.

34. Fearon 1994; Kydd 1997; Schultz 1998; Bueno de Mesquita et al. 1999; Reiter and Stam 2002.

35. Gaubatz 1996; Gartzke and Gleditsch 2004; Leeds Mattes and Vogel 2009; Digiuseppe and Poast 2018.

36. Levy and Thompson 2010.

37. Boulding 1962; Mearsheimer 2001.

38. Bak 2018; Schuessler and Shifrinson 2019; van Hooft 2020.

39. Olson and Zeckhauser 1966; Lanoszka 2015.

40. Snyder 1965.

41. Lieber and Press 2020.

42. Schelling 1966; Jervis 1989.

43. Lanoszka 2022, ch. 4.

44. Data are from version 5 of the ATOP dataset. Leeds et al. 2002.

45. On the influence of the nuclear revolution, see Lanoszka 2022, ch. 6. On the influence of bipolarity and unipolarity, see Snyder 1997; Walt 2009; Selden 2013; Kim 2016. On the greater number of democracies, see Leeds and Savun 2007. On the greater institutionalization of alliances, see Haftendorn, Keohane, and Wallander 1999; Kuo 2021.

144

NOTES TO PAGES 9–17

46. Fearon 1998.
47. Blankenship 2020, 2021.
48. Davis 2000; Kydd and McManus 2015; Sechser 2018; Cebul, Dafoe, and Monteiro 2021.
49. Olson and Zeckhauser 1966.
50. Snyder 1997; Kim 2016; Poast 2019.
51. Morrow 1994, 2000; Signorino and Ritter 1999. On alliance formation, see Waltz 1979; Walt 1987; Snyder 1997; Barnett 1996; Haas 2005; Schroeder 1976; Morrow 1991. On the effects of alliance treaties, see Leeds 2003b; Benson 2012; Jo and Gartzke 2007; Reiter 2014. On alliance design, see Leeds et al. 2002; Leeds and Anac 2005; Long and Leeds 2006; T. Kim 2011; Mattes 2012; Benson 2012; Cha 2016.
52. Schroeder 1976; Weitsman 2004; Bearce, Flanagan, and Floros 2006; Gelpi 1999; Crawford 2003; Pressman 2008; T. Kim 2011; Benson 2012; Owsiak and Frazier 2014; Fang, Johnson, and Leeds 2014; Cha 2016.
53. Jervis 1976; Monteiro 2014.

1. The Strategic Logic of Coercive Burden-Sharing

1. Portions of the next several paragraphs are drawn from Blankenship 2020 (1019) with permission from *International Studies Quarterly* and Oxford University Press.
2. Morrow 1991; Lake 2009.
3. Gilpin 1981; Kennedy 1987; MacDonald and Parent 2018.
4. Mearsheimer 2001; Montgomery 2016.
5. Snyder 1997; Jervis 1997; Crawford 2003.
6. Gilpin 1971; Mastanduno 1992; Norrlof 2010; Bove, Elia, and Sekeris 2014; Selden 2013
7. Rosato 2015.
8. Morrow 1994, 2000.
9. T. Kim 2011; Benson 2012.
10. Beckley 2015.
11. Rapp-Hooper 2015, 27–31.
12. Leeds et al. 2002. These were the Helsinki Accord in 1975, which became the Paris Charter in 1990; NATO between 1949 and 1951; and the Southeast Asia Treaty Organization (SEATO), which lost the bulk of its members in 1977 and thereafter is coded as a bilateral United States-Thailand alliance.
13. Leeds 2003a; Leeds and Savun 2007.
14. Siverson and King 1980; Bennett 1997; Leeds 2003a; Gartzke and Gleditsch 2004; Leeds, Mattes, and Vogel 2009.
15. Snyder 1997.
16. Schelling 1966; Snyder 1997; Morgan 1983; Benson, Meirowitz, and Ramsay 2014; McManus 2014, 2018; Izumikawa 2018; Blankenship 2020; Miller 2014; Gerzhoy 2015; Gavin 2015; Lanoszka 2018; Crawford 2021.
17. Posen 2014.
18. Olson and Zeckhauser 1966; Morrow 1991.
19. Cesa 2010; Christensen 2011; Douglas 2014.
20. David M. Herszenhorn, "Macron Wants Europe to Buy Its Own Military Hardware," *Politico*, November 11, 2018, https://www.politico.eu/article/macron-wants-europe-to-build-its-own-military-hardware/.
21. Gilli and Gilli 2019; Lanoszka 2022, ch. 4; Biddle 2004; Horowitz 2010.
22. Morrow 1994.
23. Large 1996, 8, 133–34, 219–20; Trachtenberg 1999, 118.
24. Cohen and Scheinmann 2014, 45–48.
25. Davis 2000; Carnegie 2015; Sechser 2018; Cebul, Dafoe, and Monteiro 2021.
26. Schelling 1966, 74.
27. Snyder 1997; Kim 2016; Izumikawa 2018; Blankenship 2020.

NOTES TO PAGES 18–27

28. Latent military potential is distinct from the status of "major" or "great" power, which often takes into account states' actual capabilities and behavior. Fordham 2011.

29. Note that I am excluding nonmaterial forms of military power such as leadership, training, and doctrine. These forms of power may be accessible regardless of material strength, though evidence suggests that regime type may be an important determinant of governments' willingness to implement what Stephen Biddle refers to as the "modern system of force employment." Biddle 2004; Talmadge 2015.

30. Mearsheimer 2001, 60–67; Deni 2021, 12–15.

31. Singer 1987.

32. Beckley 2018.

33. Anders, Fariss, and Markowitz 2020.

34. Beckley 2018. Data are from Gleditsch's Expanded GDP and Trade dataset (2002).

35. Olson and Zeckhauser 1966.

36. Haynes 2015.

37. Lee 2020.

38. Barnett and Levy 1991; Morrow 1991.

39. Jervis 1997. 200–203; Harrison 2005.

40. Lundestad 2003, 45–48, 55–57.

41. Sayle 2019, 20–27.

42. Mearsheimer 1983; Handel 1990, 91–97.

43. Hirschman 1945; Rector 2009, 20–21.

44. Bueno de Mesquita and Smith 2007.

45. Fuhrmann and Kreps 2010; Monteiro and Debs 2017; Ludvik 2018.

46. Yost 1985a, 1–13; Yost 1985b, 2–5, 32–33.

47. Portions of this section are drawn from Blankenship 2021 (699–703) with permission from *Security Studies* and Taylor and Francis.

48. Walt 1987.

49. Snyder 1997.

50. Fox 1959; Handel 1990, 71–74.

51. Catalinac 2010.

52. McLean 2001; Curran 2015.

53. Snyder 1997.

54. Waltz 1979; Mearsheimer 2001.

55. Christensen 2011.

56. Handel 1990, 149.

57. Lundestad 2003, 211–12.

58. Fang and Ramsay 2010.

59. Yarhi-Milo, Lanoszka, and Cooper 2016.

60. Helene Cooper, "Pentagon Chief Ashton Carter Adds 'Secretary of Reassurance' to His Portfolio," *New York Times*, August 3, 2015.

61. Haas 2005; Yarhi-Milo 2014.

62. Mearsheimer 2001; Biddle 2004; Levy and Thompson 2010.

63. Fazal 2007.

64. Senese 2005; Starr 2005; Fazal 2007; Reed and Chiba 2010.

65. Uslu 2003, ch. 4.

66. Vasconcelos 1988; Intelligence Memorandum Prepared in the Central Intelligence Agency, "Current Problems in NATO," January 21, 1969, *FRUS*, 1969–1976, vol. 41, 9.

67. Mearsheimer 1983.

68. Blankenship and Lin-Greenberg 2022.

69. Curran 2015.

70. Curran 2014.

71. Catalinac 2010.

72. Portions of this section are drawn from Blankenship 2020 (1021) with permission from *International Studies Quarterly*.

73. Gilpin 1981; Kennedy 1987; Friedberg 1988; MacDonald and Parent 2018; Shifrinson 2018.

146

NOTES TO PAGES 27–39

74. Clark Nordstrom and Reed 2008; Chapman, McDonald, and Moser 2015.

75. Haynes 2015; MacDonald and Parent 2018.

76. Krebs and Spindel 2018.

77. Waltz 1979; Gilpin 1981; Kennedy 1987; Friedberg 1988; Mearsheimer 2001; Shifrinson 2018.

78. MacDonald and Parent 2018.

79. Rockoff 2012; Oatley 2015; Cappella Zielinski 2016; Kreps 2018.

80. Mueller 1973; Gelpi, Feaver, and Reifler 2009.

81. Chanley 1999; Chapman, McDonald, and Moser 2015.

82. Pfundstein Chamberlain 2016; Flores-Macias and Kreps 2017.

83. Treisman 2004; MacDonald and Parent 2018.

84. Putnam 1988.

85. Fang and Ramsay 2010; Yarhi-Milo, Lanoszka, and Cooper 2016.

86. Simmons 1978, 6–13; Cha 1999, 63–65; Yong Lee 2011, 420–21.

87. Williams 1985.

88. Olson and Zeckhauser 1966; Sandler 1993.

89. Morrow 1991.

90. See, for example, Posen 2014.

91. Schelling 1966; Lake 2009; Martínez Machain and Morgan 2013; Allen, VanDusky-Allen, and Flynn 2016; Hunzeker and Lanoszka 2016.

92. Blankenship 2021.

93. Fuhrmann 2020.

94. Budge and Hofferbert 1990; Russett 1990; Klingemann, Hofferbert, and Budge 1994; Eichenberg 1996; Palmer, London, and Regan 2004; Foster 2008; Clark, Fordham, and Nordstrom 2011.

95. Liska 1962, 90, 187, 191; Haas 2005, 2014.

96. Schmitz 1999.

97. Berger 1993, 1998.

98. King, Keohane, and Verba 1994, 137–38; George and Bennett 2005, 180–83.

99. Stravers 2021; Blankenship 2021. These include the Danish Straits (Germany), the Greenland-Iceland-United Kingdom Gap (Iceland), the Korea Strait (South Korea and Japan), and the Soya and Tsugaru Straits (Japan).

100. Waltz 1979.

101. Cha 2016, 10–11.

102. George and Bennett 2005, 75; Lieberman 2005; Seawright 2016.

2. "A Legitimate Role in the Defense of the Alliance, but on a Leash"

1. Portions of this chapter are adapted from Blankenship 2021 (718–21) with permission from *Security Studies*.

2. Gleditsch 2002.

3. Telegram from U.S. Embassy (Bonn) to William Rogers, "The European Balance in the Early 1970s," January 1969, Folder "Germany, Vol. I [2 of 2]," NSC Files, Country Files, Box 681, RMNL; Statement of Policy by the National Security Council, *FRUS*, 1952–1954, vol. 7, 511.

4. NIE 20-1-69, December 4, 1969, *FRUS*, 1969–1976, vol. 41, 87.

5. Large 1996; Creswell and Kollmer 2013.

6. Letter from Finletter to Kennedy, May 29, 1961, *FRUS*, 1961–1963, vol. 13, doc. 106.

7. Trachtenberg, 1999, ch. 5; Lundestad 2003, 67–71; Sayle 2019, 24; Lanoszka, 2018, 58–60.

8. Sayle 2019, 83–84.

9. Lundestad 2003, 67–71.

10. Trachtenberg 1999, ch. 4.

11. Duffield 1995, chs. 4–5; Trachtenberg 1999, ch. 8.

12. Kelleher 1975, 37–44, 76–78, 84–85; Duffield 1995, 124–25.

13. Kelleher 1975, 89–94, 126–27; Trachtenberg 1999, chs. 5–6; Lanoszka 2018, 49–50.

NOTES TO PAGES 39–46

14. Trachtenberg 1999, 105, 113–14, 128–30, quote at 105.

15. Sayle 2019, 18.

16. Large 1996, 96–107; Trachtenberg 1999, 106–13, 125–28; Lundestad 2003, 80–83.

17. Duffield 1995, 130, 145, 161.

18. Kelleher 1975, 33–37.

19. Kelleher 1975, 48–49, 79–81, 87.

20. Duffield 1995, 134–37.

21. Duffield 1995, 137–42.

22. As Francis Gavin (2012, ch. 2) has noted, the United States never truly backed up its stated commitment to flexible response with a substantial increase in its own conventional forces on the order of what would have been required to mount a conventional defense of Europe. Nevertheless, it used flexible response as a cudgel to encourage allies to fill the gap. See Strategy Paper Prepared in the Department of State, May 17, 1963, *FRUS*, 1961–1963, vol. 13, doc. 196.

23. Duffield 1995, 158–62; Trachtenberg 1999, ch. 7; Sayle 2019, 76–77, 83–85, 89–99; Telegram from Rusk to the Department of State, December 15, 1962, *FRUS*, 1961–1963, vol. 13, doc. 159.

24. Schwartz 2003, 63–65; Gavin 2004, esp. 23–25, 36–37.

25. Gavin 2004, 36–41, 60–64.

26. Duffield 1995, 113–17, 153–56; Trachtenberg 1999, 286–89, 292–95, 315–19; Scope Paper Prepared for the NATO Ministerial Meeting, December 6, 1962, *FRUS*, 1961–1963, vol. 13, doc. 158.

27. Kelleher 1975, 109, 158–61, 166–76, 208–10, 213; Duffield 1995, 160–65.

28. Lanoszka 2018, 53; Memorandum of Conversation, February 6, 1962, *FRUS*, 1961–1963, vol. 13, 361.

29. Sayle 2019, 111.

30. Gavin 2004, 114, 154–55; Memorandum of Conversation, April 30, 1962, *FRUS*, 1961–1963, vol. 15, doc. 44.

31. Memorandum of Conversation, February 6, 1962, *FRUS*, 1961–1963, vol. 13, doc. 126; Letter from Taylor to Kennedy, April 3, 1962, *FRUS*, 1961–1963, vol. 13, doc. 131; Memorandum from Secretary of State Rusk to President Kennedy, April 13, 1962, *FRUS*, 1961–1963, vol. 13, doc. 132.

32. Memorandum for the President, undated, *FRUS*, 1961–1963, vol. 13, 430–34; Memorandum of Conversation, October 16, 1963, *FRUS*, 1961–1963, vol. 13, 619–24; Telegram from the Department of State to the Mission to the North Atlantic Treaty Organization and European Regional Organizations, April 16, 1962, *FRUS*, 1961–1963, vol. 13, doc. 134; Telegram from the Department of State to the Mission to the North Atlantic Treaty Organization and European Regional Organizations, June 14, 1962, *FRUS*, 1961–1963, vol. 13, doc. 141; Memorandum of Conversation, June 22, 1962, *FRUS*, 1961–1963, vol. 13, doc. 145.

33. Trachtenberg 1999, 213–15, 284–85, 304–5, 309–14, 321–29; Lanoszka 2018, 40–41; Memorandum of Conversation, October 31, 1964, *FRUS*, 1964–1968, vol. 13, 95–100; Telegram from the Department of State to the Embassy in Germany, February 18, 1966, *FRUS*, 1964–1968, vol. 13, 314–15.

34. Sayle 2019, ch. 5.

35. Zimmermann 2002, 135–36, 147–51, 164–65, 222; Gavin 2004, 112–13; Creswell and Kollmer 2013, 83–84.

36. Peters 2010, 98.

37. Gavin 2004, 63–67.

38. Zimmermann 2002, 149.

39. Gavin 2004, 94–95, 103, 107–11.

40. Summary Record of NSC Executive Committee Meeting, No. 38 (Part II), January 25, 1963, *FRUS*, 1961–1963, vol. 13, 486, 489. See also Trachtenberg 1999, 374.

41. Zimmermann 2002, 151–54, 159, 162–63, 215–16.

42. Gavin 2004, 111–12.

43. Kelleher 1975, 163–64, 168, 171, 209–10, 214–15; Duffield 1995, 124–25, 167–68; Gavin 2004, 112–13; Sayle 2019, 83–84.

44. Kelleher 1975, 176.

45. Kelleher 1975, 37, 44, 55, 75–78, 91–93.

46. Trachtenberg 1999, 371–79; Lundestad 2003, 123–25, quote at 124.

NOTES TO PAGES 46–51

47. Kelleher 1975, 161–69, 176; Duffield, 1995, 153, 158–62; Trachtenberg 1999, 274–86, 329–31, 339–51; Lanoszka 2018, 66–67; Sayle 2019, 76–77.

48. Gerzhoy 2015, 117; Gavin 2004, 113–14; Schwartz 2003, 16; Memorandum of Conversation, June 1, 1961, *FRUS*, 1961–1963, vol. 13, 313; Memorandum of Conversation, NATO and East-West Relations, April 12, 1961, *FRUS*, 1961–1963, vol. 13, 273.

49. Kelleher 1975, 99–102, 220–22.

50. Haftendorn 1996, 121.

51. Duffield 1995, 171–72.

52. Trachtenberg 1999, ch. 9.

53. Kaplan 1999, 122; Lundestad 2003, 170.

54. Sayle 2019, ch. 7.

55. Gavin 2004, 136–37.

56. Williams 1985, 200–201.

57. Kaplan 1999, 138.

58. Williams 1985, 130–34, 142, 162–64, 170, 216–18; Kissinger 1979, 939–40; Zelizer 2010, 533–34.

59. Gavin 2004, 144, 147, 153.

60. Zimmermann 2002, 223–24; Telegram from the Embassy in Germany to the Department of State, November 2, 1966, *FRUS*, 1964–1968, vol. 15, 447.

61. Powaski 1994, 71–72; Haftendorn 1996, 154–55; Gavin 2004, 112–13.

62. Lepgold 1990, 144, 147.

63. Gavin 2004, 154–55, 176–77.

64. McGhee to State, September 20, 1966, *FRUS*, 1964–1968, vol. 15, 418.

65. Gavin 2004, 143, 154–55.

66. Zimmermann 2002, 210; Memorandum of Conversation, September 26, 1966, *FRUS*, 1964–1968, vol. 13, 473.

67. Memorandum of Conversation, September 25, 1966, *FRUS*, 1964–1968, vol. 15, 427.

68. Zimmermann 2002, 173–76.

69. Kaplan 1999, 139; Gavin 2004, 141, 156–57.

70. Zimmermann 2002, 223–24.

71. Telegram from the Embassy in Germany to the Department of State, November 2, 1966, *FRUS*, 1964–1968, vol. 15, 447.

72. Gavin 2004, 149; Schwartz 2003, 44–45, 111–12.

73. Gavin 2004, 142–44, 149, 162–64; Gerzhoy 2015, 121–23.

74. Zimmermann 2002, 233; Schwartz 2003, 156.

75. Blechman and Kaplan 1978, 499–500.

76. Blackwill and Legro 1989.

77. Duffield 1995, 181–82.

78. Lepgold 1990, 127; Gavin 2004, 135–41, quote at 139.

79. Zimmermann 2002, 165, 172.

80. Zimmermann 2002, 151, 166.

81. Zimmermann 1996, 337, 339–40.

82. Lepgold 1990, 150–51; Gavin 2004, 151, 160–61; Zimmermann 2009, 17–18, 23.

83. Zimmermann 2002, 176–77, 190–203.

84. Gavin 2004, 140, 150–51.

85. Memorandum from the President's Special Assistant (Rostow) to President Johnson, September 19, 1966, *FRUS*, 1964–1968, vol. 15, 413–16.

86. Text of Telegram from the Embassy in Germany to the Department of State, September 20, 1966, *FRUS*, 1964–1968, vol. 15, 416–20.

87. Sayle 2019, 142.

88. Telephone Conversation between President Johnson and Secretary of Defense McNamara, September 26, 1966, *FRUS*, 1964–1968, vol. 15, 435.

89. Zimmermann 2002, 202–5, quote at 205.

90. Zimmermann 2002, 216–20; Gavin 2004, 140–41; McGhee to State, September 20, 1966, *FRUS*, 1964–1968, vol. 15, 418.

149

NOTES TO PAGES 52–56

91. Lepgold 1990, 146; Zimmermann 2002, 216.
92. Schwartz 2003, 155.
93. Schwartz 2003, 163.
94. Zimmermann 2002, 222–33.
95. Duffield 1995, 186–87.
96. Kelleher 1975, 220–27; Schwartz 2003, 98.
97. Duffield 1995, 173–74, 181–82.
98. Duffield 1995, 187–88; Schwartz 2003, 183–84.
99. Kelleher 1975, 213–14; Duffield 1995, 177–81.
100. Memorandum from Bowie to Rusk, July 20, 1967, *FRUS*, 1964–1968, vol. 13, 598.
101. Theodore S. Eliot to Henry Kissinger, "Political Consequences of SPD-FDP Coalition in the Federal Republic," October 6, 1969, Folder "Germany, Vol. III [3 of 3]," NSC Files, Country Files, Box 682, RMNL.
102. Schwartz 2003, 87–90.
103. Lundestad 2003, 160.
104. Pelt 2006, esp. 26–30, 80–81, 127, 167–69, 357–60.
105. Williams 1985, 158–59; Brady 2004, 139; Memorandum of Conversation, February 13, 1969, *FRUS*, 1969–1976, vol. 40, 19–22; Draft Memorandum of Conversation, February 26, 1969, *FRUS*, 1969–1976, vol. 40, 42–48; Memorandum of Conversation, "Meeting of Secretary Laird with the Secretary General of NATO, 14 February 1969," February 14, 1969, *FRUS*, 1969–1976, vol. 41, 31–36; Memorandum of Conversation, November 14, 1968, *FRUS*, 1964–1968, vol. 13, 787–90.
106. Duffield 1995, 183, 188–89; Herring 1998, 51; Intelligence Memorandum No. 2049/68, November 4, 1968, *FRUS*, 1964–1968, vol. 13, 778–80; Laird to Nixon, February 20, 1969, *FRUS*, 1969–1976, vol. 41, 41; Intelligence Memorandum Prepared in the Central Intelligence Agency, January 21, 1969, *FRUS*, 1969–1976, vol. 41, 1–12.
107. Memorandum of Conversation, February 14, 1969, *FRUS*, 1969–1976, vol. 41, 32.
108. Memorandum of Conversation, November 14, 1968, *FRUS*, 1964–1968, vol. 13, 788.
109. Nelson 2019, 17–26.
110. Nichter 2015, ch. 2; Nelson 2019, 34–41, 98–99.
111. Rostow to Kissinger, December 23, 1968, Folder "4. World Situation," NSC Files, Kissinger Office Files, HAK Administrative and Staff Files, Box 4, RMNL.
112. Report by President Nixon to the Congress, U.S. Foreign Policy for the 1970s, February 18, 1970, *FRUS*, 1969–1972, vol. 1, doc. 60.
113. Caldwell 2009, 634–35; Nichter 2015, 11–12; Nelson 2019, 53–56, 78–79.
114. Litwak 1986, 52–55, 75–76.
115. Haftendorn 1996, 155–56; Memorandum of Conversation, "Mr. Kissinger's Discussion of U.S.-Japan Political and Economic Relations with Mr. Fukuda," June 11, 1972, Folder "3. Japan Trip Memcons—the President," NSC Files, Kissinger Office Files, HAK Trip Files, Box 22, RMNL.
116. Nelson 2019, 76–83.
117. Williams 1985, 150–51; Litwak 1986, 119–20.
118. Kissinger 1979, 213–15; Lepgold 1990, 147–48.
119. Powaski 1994, 80.
120. Memorandum for the Record, "Luncheon Conversation between Henry Kissinger and Egon Bahr, April 8, 1970," April 8, 1970, Folder "Germany, Vol. IV [1 of 2]," NSC Files, Country Files, Box 683, RMNL. See also Kissinger 1979, 945.
121. Telegram from U.S. Embassy (Bonn) to William Rogers, "Secretary Laird's Talk with FRG Defense Minister Helmut Schmidt," June 1970, Folder "Germany, Vol. V [2 of 2]," NSC Files, Country Files, Box 683, RMNL.
122. Powaski 1994, 90–91.
123. NIE 20-72, December 14, 1972, *FRUS*, 1969–1976, vol. 41, 349–50.
124. Powaski 1994, 98–99, 102–3; Kaplan 1999, 116–17; Kissinger to Ford, "Meeting with Permanent Representatives of the North Atlantic Council," June 19, 1975, Folder "North Atlantic Treaty Organization (NATO), 1975 (3) WH," National Security Adviser's Files, NSC Europe, Canada, and Ocean Affairs Staff Files, Box 53, GRFL.

NOTES TO PAGES 56–60

125. Clift to Kissinger, "Reported Reactions in FRG Cabinet to US-USSR Agreement on the Prevention of Nuclear War," June 30, 1973, Folder "Germany, Vol. XIII [2 of 3]," NSC Files, Country Files, Box 687, RMNL.

126. Haftendorn 1996, 154, 159. Kissinger (1979, 94) put the matter well in his memoirs: "In times of relaxing tension, [the Europeans] dreaded a U.S.–Soviet condominium."

127. Williams 1985, 215–16.

128. Memorandum for the Record, May 13, 1971, *FRUS*, 1969–1976, vol. 41, 275.

129. Information Memorandum from the Assistant Secretary of State for European Affairs (Hillenbrand) to Rogers, November 15, 1971, *FRUS*, 1969–1976, vol. 41, 326.

130. Lepgold 1990, 138; Zimmermann 2009, 20; Minutes of a Legislative Interdepartmental Group Meeting, May 12, 1971, *FRUS*, 1969–1976, vol. 41, 270.

131. Trachtenberg 1999, 128–30; Gavin 2012, 50–51.

132. Cha 1999, 69.

133. Kissinger 1979, 88–89, 921–22; Williams 1985, 165.

134. Lepgold 1990, 149; Gavin 2004, 190.

135. Telegram from U.S. Embassy to William Rogers, "Allied Consultation on SALT," June 1969, NSC Files, Country Files, Box 681, RMNL; "Memorandum of Conversation between President Nixon and Chancellor Kiesinger at the White House," August 7, 1969, NSC Files, Country Files, Box 682, RMNL.

136. Minutes of a National Security Council Meeting, November 19, 1970, *FRUS*, 1969–1976, vol. 41, 230.

137. Memorandum for the Record, May 13, 1971, *FRUS*, 1969–1976, vol. 41, 275.

138. Bitzinger 1989, 24–32; Trachtenberg 2012, 169–70.

139. Duffield 1995, 204–8.

140. Memorandum of Conversation, April 11, 1969, *FRUS*, 1969–1976, col. 41, doc. 12; Telegram from the Mission to the North Atlantic Treaty Organization to the Department of State, December 3, 1970, *FRUS*, 1969–1976, vol. 41, doc. 55.

141. Report on a NATO Commanders Meeting, September 30, 1970, *FRUS*, 1969–1976, vol. 41, 190–94; Paper Prepared by the National Security Council Staff, undated [1969], *FRUS*, 1969–1976, vol. 41, doc. 52; Memorandum for the Record, May 13, 1971, *FRUS*, 1969–1976, vol. 41, doc. 63; Draft Memorandum of Conversation, February 26, 1969, *FRUS*, 1969–1976, vol. 40, doc. 15.

142. Sayle 2019, 147.

143. Klitzing 2009, 82.

144. Lundestad 2003, 171–72; Juneau 2011, 279–80; Lanoszka 2018, 74–75; Editorial Note, *FRUS*, 1969–1976, vol. 40, doc. 57; Memo from Sonnenfeldt to Kissinger, December 19, 1970, *FRUS*, 1969–1976, vol. 40, doc. 150.

145. Nixon 1971, 5.

146. Nixon 1971, 7–8.

147. Duffield 1995, 229–31; Laird to Nixon, February 20, 1969, *FRUS*, 1969–1976, vol. 41, doc. 8; Memorandum for the Record by the Director of the Office of International Security Policy and Planning, July 18, 1973, FRUS, 1969–1976, vol. E–15 (pt. 2), doc. 266.

148. Duffield 1995, 206–10; Minutes of a Combined Senior Review Group and Verification Panel Meeting, October 28, 1970, *FRUS*, 1969–1976, vol. 41, doc. 51; Minutes of a National Security Council Meeting, November 19, 1970, *FRUS*, 1969–1976, vol. 41, doc. 53; Memorandum for the Record, May 13, 1971, *FRUS*, 1969–1976, vol. 41, doc. 63; Minutes of a Defense Program Review Committee Meeting, August 4, 1971, *FRUS*, 1969–1976, vol. 41, doc. 70.

149. National Intelligence Estimate, December 14, 1972, *FRUS*, 1969–1976, vol. 41, doc. 86; Memorandum for the President's File by Kissinger, May 1, 1973, *FRUS*, 1969–1976, vol. E–15 (pt. 2), doc. 265.

150. Laird to Nixon, February 20, 1969, *FRUS*, 1969–1976, vol. 41, 39–40; Paper Prepared by the National Security Council Staff, May 14, 1971, *FRUS*, 1969–1976, vol. 41, 287 (emphasis added).

151. Paper Prepared by the National Security Council Staff, May 14, 1971, *FRUS*, 1969–1976, vol. 41, 287 (emphasis added).

152. Telegram from the Department of State to All North Atlantic Treaty Organization Capitals, December 11, 1971, *FRUS*, 1969–1976, vol. 41, 335 (emphasis added).

151

NOTES TO PAGES 60–62

153. NSDM 133, September 22, 1971, *FRUS*, 1969–1976, vol. 41, 306. See also NSDM 142, December 2, 1971, *FRUS*, 1969–1976, vol. 41, 329–30.

154. Laird to Nixon, February 20, 1969, *FRUS*, 1969–1976, vol. 41, doc. 8; Minutes of a Combined Senior Review Group and Verification Panel Meeting, October 28, 1970, *FRUS*, 1969–1976, vol. 41, doc. 51; Paper Prepared by the National Security Council Staff, undated [1969], *FRUS*, 1969–1976, vol. 41, doc. 52; Minutes of a National Security Council Meeting, November 19, 1970, *FRUS*, 1969–1976, vol. 41, doc. 53; NSDM 95, November 25, 1970, *FRUS*, 1969–1976, vol. 41, doc. 54; Telegram from U.S. Embassy (Bonn) to William Rogers, "Burden Sharing," October 1970, Folder "Germany, Vol. VII [3 of 3]," NSC Files, Country Files, Box 684, RMNL.

155. Report on a NATO Commanders Meeting, September 30, 1970, *FRUS*, 1969–1976, vol. 41, 192–93.

156. Memorandum of Conversation, September 30, 1970, *FRUS*, 1969–1976, vol. 39, doc. 34; Memo from Sonnenfeldt to Kissinger, October 5, 1970, *FRUS*, 1969–1976, vol. 40, doc. 128.

157. Memorandum of Conversation, April 11, 1969, *FRUS*, 1969–1976, vol. 41, 51.

158. Report on a NATO Commanders Meeting, September 30, 1970, *FRUS*, 1969–1976, vol. 41, 192–93.

159. Minutes of a Defense Program Review Committee Meeting, August 4, 1971, *FRUS*, 1969–1976, vol. 41, 301.

160. Rogers to U.S. Embassy in Bonn, "Offset," May 1971, Folder "4. Germany, Chancellor Brandt (1971)," NSC Files, Presidential Correspondence, 1969–1974, Box 753, RMNL; Nixon to Brandt, January 18, 1974, Folder "1. Germany, Willy Brandt 1972," NSC Files, Presidential Correspondence, 1969–1974, Box 754, RMNL.

161. Williams 1985, 252–53.

162. Williams 1985, 239.

163. Report on a NATO Commanders Meeting, September 30, 1970, *FRUS*, 1969–1976, vol. 41, 190–94; NSDM 133, September 22, 1971, *FRUS*, 1969–1976, vol. 41, 306–8; NSDM 142, December 2, 1971, *FRUS*, 1969–1976, vol. 41, 329–30.

164. See *FRUS*, 1969–1976, vol. 41, 31–36, 240–41, 282–87, 315–22, 346–47.

165. Telegram from the Embassy in Germany to the Department of State, October 29, 1969, *FRUS*, 1969–1976, vol. 40, 110.

166. Memorandum of Conversation, September 29, 1973, Box 2, National Security Adviser Memoranda of Conversations, 1973–1977, GRFL; Memorandum for the Record, Meeting between Dr. Kissinger and Italian Ambassador Ortona, November 19, 1971, *FRUS*, 1969–1972, vol. 41, doc. 216.

167. Henry Kissinger to Richard Nixon, "Offset Negotiations with Germany," undated [May 1969], Folder "Germany, Vol. I [2 of 2]," NSC Files, Country Files, Box 681, RMNL.

168. Helmut Sonnenfeldt, "Your Meeting with Ambassador Pauls, Wednesday at 12," June 1, 1971, Folder "Germany, Vol. IX [2 of 3]," NSC Files, Country Files, Box 685, RMNL.

169. Sonnenfeldt to Kissinger, "Your Meeting with German Finance Minister Helmut Schmidt, July 31, 1973, 4 p.m.," July 30, 1973, Folder "Germany, Vol. XIII [2 of 3]," NSC Files, Country Files, Box 687, RMNL; Henry A. Kissinger, "Meeting with Walter Scheel," Folder "Germany, Vol. XIII [2 of 3]," July 12, 1973, NSC Files, Country Files, Box 687, RMNL; Henry A. Kissinger, "Meeting with Rainer Barzel," April 18, 1973, Folder "Germany, Vol. XIII [2 of 3]," NSC Files, Country Files, Box 687, RMNL.

170. Kissinger 1979, 400; Lepgold 1990, 153–54; Powaski 1994, 93; Kaplan 1999, 155–57; Bergsten to Kissinger, July 9, 1969, *FRUS*, 1969–1976, vol. 41, 68–69; Telegram from the Mission to the North Atlantic Treaty Organization to the Department of State, December 3, 1970, *FRUS*, 1969–1976, vol. 41, 236–40; Editorial Note, *FRUS*, 1969–1976, vol. 41, doc. 77; Telegram from Rogers to the Department of State, December 10, 1971, *FRUS*, 1969–1976, vol. 41, doc. 78; Memo from Eagleburger to Richardson, *FRUS*, 1969–1976, vol. E–15 (pt. 2), doc. 262; Telegram from the Department of State to the Embassy in the Federal Republic of Germany, March 22, 1974, *FRUS*, 1969–1976, vol. E–15 (pt. 2), doc. 278; Telegram from U.S. Consul (Munich) to Rogers, "FRG Defense Budget for 1972," December 27, 1971, Folder "Germany, Vol. X [1 of 2]," NSC Files, Country Files, Box 686, RMNL.

NOTES TO PAGES 62–70

171. Williams 1985, 154–59, 165–67; Duffield 1995, 194, 197–201, 210–11; Telegram from the Department of State to All North Atlantic Treaty Organization Capitals, December 11, 1971, *FRUS*, 1969–1976, vol. 41, doc. 79; Telegram from U.S. consul (Munich) to Rogers, "FRG Defense Budget for 1972," December 27, 1971, Folder "Germany, Vol. X [1 of 2]," NSC Files, Country Files, Box 686, RMNL; Telegram from the Mission to the North Atlantic Treaty Organization to the Department of State, February 2, 1969, *FRUS*, 1969–1976, vol. 40, doc. 6; Telegram from U.S. Embassy to Secretary of State, July 1970, Folder "Germany, Vol. V [2 of 2]," NSC Files, Country Files, Box 683, RMNL.

172. Lundestad 2003, 171–73.

173. Laird to Nixon, November 9, 1971, *FRUS*, 1969–1976, vol. 41, doc. 74.

174. Hunt 2015, 313; Gavin 2012, 48.

175. Telegram from U.S. Embassy (Bonn) to William Rogers, "Defense Burden Sharing," June 1970, Folder "Germany, Vol. V [2 of 2]," NSC Files, Country Files, Box 683, RMNL.

176. Telegram from U.S. Embassy (Bonn) to William Rogers, "Schmidt on NATO and Burden Sharing," October 1970, Folder "Germany, Vol. VII [3 of 3]," NSC Files, Country Files, Box 684, RMNL; Telegram from U.S. Embassy (Bonn) to William Rogers, "Burden Sharing," October 1970, Folder "Germany, Vol. VII [3 of 3]," NSC Files, Country Files, Box 684, RMNL; Telegram from U.S. Consul (Munich) to Rogers, "Offset—Discussion with Foreign Minister Scheel," May 1971, Folder "Germany, Vol. IX [3 of 3]," NSC Files, Country Files, Box 685, RMNL; Telegram from U.S. Consul (Munich) to Rogers, "Offset: Conversation with Herbst," October 1971, Folder "Germany, Vol. IX [3 of 3]," NSC Files, Country Files, Box 685, RMNL.

177. Williams 1985, 239–41; State Department Briefing Paper, "President Nixon's Visit to Brussels," June 1974, Folder "NAC Summit—Brussels the President," NSC Files, HAK Office Files, Country Files, Box 54, RMNL; Memo from Odeen and Sonnenfeldt to Kissinger, September 20, 1973, *FRUS*, 1969–1976, vol. E–15 (pt. 2), doc. 269; Memo from Scowcroft to Nixon, January 16, 1974, *FRUS*, 1969–1976, vol. E–15 (pt. 2), doc. 276; Telegram from the Department of State to the Embassy in the Federal Republic of Germany, March 22, 1974, *FRUS*, 1969–1976, vol. E–15 (pt. 2), doc. 278.

3. "Between Scylla and Charybdis"

1. Portions of this chapter are adapted from Blankenship 2021 (721–22) with permission from *Security Studies*.

2. Rusk to Gilpatric, February 23, 1963, *FRUS*, 1961–1963, vol. 22, 772.

3. Greene 1975, 30–33.

4. Smith 2019, 49.

5. Cha 1999, 71, 75–77; Memorandum of Conversation, November 14, 1967, *FRUS*, 1964–1968, vol. 29 (pt. 2), 227–32; Memorandum of Conversation, September 1, 1971, *FRUS*, 1969–1976, vol. 19 (pt. 1), 272–77.

6. Greene 1975, 5–6, 8, 23, 39–41.

7. Swenson-Wright 2005, 187.

8. Welfield 1988, 49–52; Samuels 2007, 31–35, 39–40, 46–47.

9. Welfield 1988, 70, 98–108.

10. Green 2017, 247, 252–53, 265, 272–73; *FRUS*, 1964–1968, vol. 29 (pt. 2), docs. 35, 65, 86; *FRUS*, 1969–1972, vol. 19 (pt. 2), docs. 4, 8, 49, 121; Kissinger to Rockefeller, "Courtesy Call on Japanese Prime Minister Takeo Miki," August 6, 1975, Folder "Prime Minister Miki of Japan, August 6–7, 1975 (4)," National Security Adviser's Files, NSC East Asia and Pacific Affairs Staff Files, Box 22, GRFL.

11. Department of State Guidelines Paper, undated, *FRUS*, 1961–1963, vol. 22, 732.

12. Izumikawa 2018.

13. Memorandum from the Ambassador to Japan (Reischauer) to Secretary of State Rusk, July 14, 1965, *FRUS*, 1964–1968, vol. 29 (pt. 2), 104–5.

14. Welfield 1988, 51, 98.

15. *FRUS*, 1964–1968, vol. 29 (pt. 2), docs. 5–7.

153

NOTES TO PAGES 70–75

16. *FRUS*, 1964–1968, vol. 29 (pt. 2), docs 16, 52.

17. *FRUS*, 1964–1968, vol. 29 (pt. 2), doc. 58.

18. Telegram from the Embassy in Japan to the Department of State, August 20, 1964, *FRUS*, 1964–1968, vol. 29 (pt. 2), 30.

19. Airgram from the Embassy in Japan to the Department of State, December 4, 1964, *FRUS*, 1964–1968, vol. 29 (pt. 2), 47–51. An NIE in 1965 similarly concluded that a more powerful Japan would likely take a more independent stance on issues ranging from the United States' use of bases on Okinawa to US conduct in Vietnam. SNIE 41-65, November 26, 1965, *FRUS*, 1964–1968, vol. 29 (pt. 2), doc. 64.

20. Action Memorandum from the Assistant Secretary of State for Far Eastern Affairs (Bundy) to Secretary of State Rusk, January 6, 1965, *FRUS*, 1964–1968, vol. 29 (pt. 2), 60.

21. Memorandum from Bundy to Thompson, August 20, 1965, *FRUS*, 1964–1968, vol. 29 (pt. 2), 117.

22. Memorandum from Bundy to Thompson, August 20, 1965, *FRUS*, 1964–1968, vol. 29 (pt. 2), 117–18.

23. Memorandum from Bundy to Thompson, August 20, 1965, *FRUS*, 1964–1968, vol. 29 (pt. 2), 120.

24. Memorandum of Conversation, June 30, 1964, *FRUS*, 1964–1968, vol. 29 (pt. 2), 19–22; Action Memorandum from Bundy to Ball, November 9, 1964, *FRUS*, 1964–1968, vol. 29 (pt. 2), 42. See also Action Memorandum from Bundy to Rusk, January 6, 1965, *FRUS*, 1964–1968, vol. 29 (pt. 2), 58–62; Memorandum From the Joint Chiefs of Staff to Secretary of Defense Secretary McNamara, July 8, 1965, *FRUS*, 1964–1968, vol. 29 (pt. 2), 100–101.

25. Memorandum from Rusk to Johnson, September 4, 1967, *FRUS*, 1964–1968, vol. 29 (pt. 2), 206.

26. Telegram from the Embassy in Japan to the Department of State, June 5, 1968, *FRUS*, 1964–1968, vol. 29 (pt. 2), 282–83.

27. *FRUS*, 1964–1968, vol. 29 (pt. 2), docs. 35, 58, 95, 96, 98, 104, 106; Memorandum of Conversation, July 9, 1974, Box 4, National Security Adviser Memoranda of Conversations, 1973–1977, GRFL; *FRUS*, 1969–1972, vol. 19 (pt. 2), doc. 42.

28. Action Memorandum from Bundy to Rusk, January 6, 1965, *FRUS*, 1964–1968, vol. 29 (pt. 2), 60.

29. Lanoszka 2018, 83–85.

30. Memorandum of Conversation, July 7, 1966, *FRUS*, 1964–1968, vol. 29 (pt. 2), 150. See also Memorandum Prepared by Counselor and Chairman of the Policy Planning Council (Owen), July 12, 1966, *FRUS*, 1964–1968, vol. 29 (pt. 2), 153–54.

31. Volpe 2018, 326–27.

32. Airgram from the Embassy in Japan to the Department of State, December 4, 1964, *FRUS*, 1964–1968, vol. 29 (pt. 2), 48.

33. Memorandum of Conversation, January 12, 1965, *FRUS*, 1964–1968, vol. 29 (pt. 2), 66–74.

34. Greene 1975, 33; Memorandum of Conversation, November 14, 1967, *FRUS*, 1964–1968, vol. 29 (pt. 2), 227–32; Memorandum of Conversation, November 15, 1967, *FRUS*, 1964–1968, vol. 29 (pt. 2), 232–34; Memorandum of Conversation, November 15, 1967, *FRUS*, 1964–1968, vol. 29 (pt. 2), 235–44.

35. Welfield 1988, 191–96.

36. Welfield 1988, 364; "US Defense Issues in East Asia," December 3, 1976, p. 7, Digital National Security Archives.

37. Welfield 1988, 143; Lanoszka 2018, 87–88; National Security Council Report, April 9, 1955, *FRUS*, 1955–1957, vol. 23, 52–62; Memorandum from the Assistant Secretary of State for Far Eastern Affairs to the Secretary of State, July 28, 1955, *FRUS*, 1955–1975, vol. 23, 79–80; Memorandum of Conversation, June 20, 1961, *FRUS*, 1961–1963, vol. 22, 380–82.

38. *FRUS*, 1964–1968, vol. 29 (pt. 2), doc. 58.

39. *FRUS*, 1964–1968, vol. 29 (pt. 2), doc. 58.

40. Samuels 2007, 43; *FRUS*, 1964–1968, vol. 29 (pt. 2), docs. 35, 58, 95, 96, 98, 104, 106; Memorandum of Conversation, July 9, 1974, Box 4, National Security Adviser Memoranda of Conversations, 1973–1977, GRFL.

NOTES TO PAGES 75–78

41. Greene 1975, 80–81; Welfield 1988, 365; Gilpatric to Kennedy, February 8, 1963, *FRUS*, 1961–1963, vol. 9, 766–71; Dillon to Rusk, March 8, 1963, *FRUS*, 1961–1963, col. 22, 165–66; Telegram from the Embassy in Japan to the Department of State, November 1, 1963, *FRUS*, 1961–1963, vol. 22, 795–98; Letter from Secretary of Defense McNamara to Secretary of State Rusk, November 16, 1963, *FRUS*, 1961–1963, vol. 22, 801–3; *FRUS*, 1964–1968, vol. 29 (pt. 2), docs. 94–96, 98, 103, 104, 106, 109.

42. Memorandum from Gilpatric to President Kennedy, February 8, 1963, *FRUS*, 1961–1963, vol. 22, 769.

43. Memorandum from Fowler to Johnson, August 31, 1967, *FRUS*, 1964–1968, vol. 29 (pt. 2), docs. 95, 106.

44. Swenson-Wright 2005, 197–204.

45. Smith 2019, 173–80.

46. Yoda 2006.

47. Zelizer 2010, 530–35; Nelson 2019, 34–35, 39–41, 98–99.

48. Editorial Note, *FRUS*, 1964–1968, vol. 29 (pt. 2), 270.

49. Memorandum from the Department of State's Country Director for Japan (Sneider) to the Assistant Secretary of State for East Asian and Pacific Affairs (Bundy), April 26, 1968, *FRUS*, 1964–1968, vol. 29 (pt. 2), 273.

50. Telegram from the Embassy in Japan to the Department of State, June 5, 1968, *FRUS*, 1964–1968, vol. 29 (pt. 2), 278, 282.

51. Memorandum of Conversation, "Mr. Kissinger's Discussion of US–Japan Political and Economic Relations with Mr. Fukuda," June 11, 1972, Folder "3. Japan Trip Memcons—the President," NSC Files, Kissinger Office Files, HAK Trip Files, Box 22, RMNL.

52. Memorandum from Shakespeare to Kissinger, February 16, 1971, *FRUS*, 1969–1976, vol. 19 (pt. 2), 184–85.

53. "Japan Adjusts to an Era of Multipolarity in Asia," April 21, 1972, Folder "Japan, March 6–June 6 1972 (4 of 5)," NSC Files, Kissinger Office Files, Country Files, Far East, Box 102, RMNL; Tokyo Embassy to Rogers, June 1972, Folder "Japan, March 6–June 6 1972 (2 of 5)," NSC Files, Kissinger Office Files, Country Files, Far East, Box 102, RMNL; Holdridge and Lord to Kissinger, "HAK Statement to Japan–US Economic Council," June 8, 1972, Folder "2. HAK's Japan Visit June 1972 Talking Points JUSEC Luncheon (1 of 7)," NSC Files, Kissinger Office Files, HAK Trip Files, Box 21, RMNL.

54. Greene 1975, 14–15; Welfield 1988, 275–80, 325–29; Cha 1999, 69–72; Komine 2014, 93–94.

55. Cha 1999, 61.

56. Cha 1999, 71.

57. Cha 1999, 147–48; Memo from Kissinger to the President, August 2, 1975, *FRUS*, 1969–1976, vol. E–12, doc. 205.

58. Nelson 2019, 75–82, 96–99.

59. See *FRUS*, 1969–1976, vol. 19 (pt. 2), docs. 74, 81, 82; Attachment to Memorandum from Rostow to Johnson, March 1, 1967, *FRUS*, 1964–1968, vol. 29 (pt. 2), 168.

60. Attachment to Memorandum from Rostow to Johnson, March 1, 1967, *FRUS*, 1964–1968, vol. 29 (pt. 2), 166.

61. Memo from Kissinger to Nixon, "Meeting with Japanese Prime Minister Kakuei Tanaka," July 31, 1973, Folder "Prime Minister Kakuei Tanaka of Japan, July 31–August 1, 1975 (3)," National Security Adviser's Files, NSC East Asia and Pacific Affairs Staff Files, Box 21, GRFL.

62. Memorandum from Lord to Kissinger, "Highlights of the 19th US–Japan Planning Talks and My Trip to Korea," July 31, 1974, Folder "Japan (4)," National Security Adviser's Files, NSC East Asia and Pacific Affairs Staff Files, Box 4, GRFL.

63. Greene 1975, 11; Welfield 1988, 295, 309–10; quote at 295; Cha 1999, 104, 107.

64. Greene 1975, 8, 10–11, 19, 21; "Japan Adjusts to an Era of Multipolarity in Asia," April 21, 1972, Folder "Japan, March 6—June 6, 1972 [4 of 5]," NSC Files, HAK Office Files, Box 102, RMNL; Holdridge to Kissinger, "Your Meetings with Tanaka and Ohira," August 10, 1972, Folder "Japan, June 13, 1972—," NSC Files, HAK Office Files, Country Files, Box 102, RMNL.

65. Welfield 1988, 296–336.

66. Summary Paper Prepared by the Interdepartmental Group for East Asia, August 2, 1971, *FRUS*, 1969–1976, vol. 19 (pt. 2), 232.

NOTES TO PAGES 78–82

67. Komine 2014, 116; Sonnenfeldt and Hyland to Kissinger, "Soviet-Japanese Relations," April 7, 1972, Folder "HAK's Japan Visit June 1972 Talking Points JUSEC Luncheon [6 of 7]," NSC Files, HAK Office Files, HAK Trip Files, Box 21, RMNL.

68. Greene 1975, 8, 10; Cha 1999, 103–9, 147, 152–54.

69. Lanoszka 2018, 100–106.

70. Komine 2014, 106; Memorandum from Richard Finn to Winston Lord, "Study on Forces at Work in Japan," April 23, 1974, Folder "Japan—NSSM 172 (5)," National Security Adviser's Files, NSC East Asia and Pacific Affairs Staff Files, Box 4, GRFL, 7–18, quote at 7–8.

71. Minutes of Senior Review Group Meeting, August 6, 1971, FRUS, 1969–1976, vol. 19 (pt. 2), 259.

72. Memo from Kissinger to Nixon, August 29, 1972, FRUS, 1969–1976, vol. 19 (pt. 2), 461–65.

73. Memorandum for the Record, July 20, 1971, FRUS, 1969–1976, vol. 19 (pt. 2), 223.

74. Memo from Sonnenfeldt and Hyland to Kissinger, April 7, 1972, FRUS, 1969–1976, vol. 19 (pt. 2), 416.

75. Welfield 1988, 252–53, 289, 332; Zubok 2013; Komine 2014, 105–9, 113, 118.

76. Greene 1975, 95–98; Komine 2014, 95, 115.

77. NIE 41-69, February 17, 1969, FRUS, 1969–1976, vol. 19 (pt. 2), 11.

78. Cha 1999, 69–72; Komine 2014, 88, 93, 117.

79. Greene 1975, 78–81; Rusk to Johnson, September 4, 1967, FRUS, 1964–1968, vol. 29 (pt. 2), 206–7; Memorandum of Conversation, November 14, 1967, FRUS, 1964–1968, vol. 29 (pt. 2), 227–32; Jenkins to Rostow, June 14, 1968, FRUS, 1964–1968, vol. 29 (pt. 2), 284–85.

80. Telegram from the Embassy in Japan to the Department of State, August 21, 1968, FRUS, 1964–1968, vol. 29 (pt. 2), 297.

81. Laird to Nixon, July 19, 1971, FRUS, 1969–1976, vol. 19 (pt. 2), 213–21.

82. Greene 1975, 80–81, 87–91; Welfield 1988, 447; Komine 2014, 95–97, 102, 114, 116.

83. Memorandum of Conversation, June 23, 1970, FRUS, 1969–1976, vol. 19 (pt. 2), 133.

84. Komine 2014, 114.

85. Editorial Note, FRUS, 1969–1976, vol. 19 (pt. 2), 26–27; Laird to Nixon, July 19, 1971, FRUS, 1969–1976, vol. 19 (pt. 2), 216.

86. Greene 1975, 80–81, 87–91; Welfield 1988, 447; Komine 2014, 95–97, 102, 114, 116.

87. Zubok 2013, 56.

88. Memorandum from Rogers to Nixon, September 22, 1970, FRUS, 1969–1976, vol. 19 (pt. 1), 185.

89. Summary Paper Prepared by the Interdepartmental Group for East Asia, August 2, 1971, FRUS, 1969–1976, vol. 19 (pt. 1), 237–39.

90. Minutes of Senior Review Group Meeting, August 6, 1971, FRUS, 1969–1976, vol. 19 (pt. 1), 259, 266.

91. Minutes of Senior Review Group Meeting, August 6, 1971, FRUS, 1969–1976, vol. 19 (pt. 1), 261.

92. Minutes of a Senior Review Group Meeting, August 27, 1971, FRUS, 1969–1976, vol. 19 (pt. 1), 285, 293.

93. Minutes of a Senior Review Group Meeting, August 27, 1971, FRUS, 1969–1976, vol. 19 (pt. 1), 287.

94. Minutes of a Senior Review Group Meeting, August 27, 1971, FRUS, 1969–1976, vol. 19 (pt. 1), 289.

95. Minutes of a Senior Review Group Meeting, August 27, 1971, FRUS, 1969–1976, vol. 19 (pt. 1), 290.

96. Letter from Meyer to Nixon, March 14, 1972, FRUS, 1969–1976, vol. 19 (pt. 2), 289.

97. Komine 2014, 96, 112; Laird to Nixon, July 19, 1971, FRUS, 1969–1976, vol. 19 (pt. 2), 213–21; NSDM 13, "Policy toward Japan," Box H–208, National Security Council Institutional Files, RMNL; Memorandum from W. R. Smyser to Robert Ingersoll, "Policy Statement for the Japan PARA," February 15, 1974, Folder "Japan—NSSM 172 (2)," National Security Adviser's Files, NSC East Asia and Pacific Affairs Staff Files, Box 4, GRFL; Memorandum from W. R. Smyser to Richard L. Sneider, "List of Objectives for Japan NSSM," April 4, 1974, Folder "Japan—NSSM

NOTES TO PAGES 82–84

172 (1)," National Security Adviser's Files, NSC East Asia and Pacific Affairs Staff Files, Box 4, GRFL; Memorandum from Richard Finn to Winston Lord, "Study on Forces at Work in Japan," April 23, 1974, Folder "Japan—NSSM 172 (5)," National Security Adviser's Files, NSC East Asia and Pacific Affairs Staff Files, Box 4, GRFL; Memo from Kissinger to Nixon, "Meeting with Japanese Prime Minister Kakuei Tanaka," July 31, 1973, Folder "Prime Minister Kakuei Tanaka of Japan, July 31–August 1, 1975 (3)," National Security Adviser's Files, NSC East Asia and Pacific Affairs Staff Files, Box 21, GRFL.

98. "HAK Statement before Japan–US Economic Council," June 8, 1972, Folder "HAK's Japan Visit June 1972 Talking Points JUSEC Luncheon [1 of 7]," NSC Files, HAK Office Files, HAK Trip Files, Box 21, RMNL. See also Kissinger to Nixon, "My Trip to Japan," June 19, 1972, Folder "HAK's Japan Visit June 1972 Talking Points JUSEC Luncheon [2 of 7]," NSC Files, HAK Office Files, HAK Trip Files, Box 21, RMNL.

99. Memorandum of Conversation, "Mr. Kissinger's Discussion of US-Japan Political and Economic Relations with Mr. Fukuda," June 11, 1972, Folder "Japan Trip Memcons—the President," NSC Files, HAK Office Files, HAK Trip Files, Box 22, RMNL.

100. Komine 2014, 112–16; Study Prepared by the NSC Interdepartmental Group for East Asia and Pacific Affairs, undated, *FRUS*, 1969–1976, vol. E–12, doc. 190.

101. Memorandum for Major General Brent Scowcroft, "Briefing for President on Japan," August 26, 1974, Folder "Japan (1)," Presidential Country Files for East Asia and the Pacific, Box 6, GRFL; Memorandum of Conversation, "US-Japan Relations," July 1, 1976, Box 20, National Security Adviser Memoranda of Conversations, 1973–1977, GRFL; Philip Habib to Brent Scowcroft, "Submission of Response to NSSM 210," October 21, 1974, Folder "Japan—NSSM 210," National Security Adviser's Files, NSC East Asia and Pacific Affairs Staff Files, Box 5, GRFL, 66–70.

102. Komine 2014, 117; Memo from Kissinger to the President, August 2, 1975, *FRUS*, 1969–1976, vol. E–12, doc. 205. See also doc. 197.

103. Fred Greene, "US Relations with Japan," October 1974, Folder "Japan—NSSM 172 (9)," National Security Adviser's Files, NSC East Asia and Pacific Affairs Staff Files, Box 4, GRFL.

104. Memorandum from John Froebe and Robert Hormats of the NSC Staff to Secretary of State Kissinger, November 9, 1974, *FRUS*, 1969–1976, vol. E–12, doc. 196.

105. Greene 1975, 14; Welfield 1988, 330–32; Cha 1999, 69.

106. Cha 1999, 108; "Your Schedule and Talking Points for Your Meetings with the Japanese Leaders," Folder "Henry A. Kissinger's Trip to Japan—Talking Points," NSC Files, Kissinger Office Files, HAK Trip Files, Box 22, RMNL.

107. Memorandum of Conversation, July 23, 1971, *FRUS*, 1969–1976, vol. 19 (pt. 2), 226; Letter from Nixon to Sato, August 3, 1971, *FRUS*, 1969–1976, vol. 19 (pt. 2), 252; Memorandum of Conversation, October 22, 1971, *FRUS*, 1969–1976, vol. 19 (pt. 2), 345–53.

108. Memorandum from Acting Secretary of State Johnson to President Nixon, December 29, 1971, *FRUS*, 1969–1976, vol. 19 (pt. 2), 372.

109. "Your Japan Visit—Scope Paper," June 1972, Folder "1. Henry Kissinger's Trip to Japan," NSC Files, Kissinger Office Files, HAK Trip Files, Box 22, RMNL; Memo from Kissinger to Nixon, June 19, 1972, *FRUS*, 1969–1976, vol. 19 (pt. 2), 437.

110. Memo from Kissinger to Nixon, August 29, 1972, *FRUS*, 1969–1976, vol. 19 (pt. 2), 461.

111. Campbell and Sunohara 2004, 222; Memorandum of Conversation, "Overall View of US-Japan Relations and Global Situation," April 10, 1975, Folder "Japan (5)," National Security Adviser's Files, NSC East Asia and Pacific Affairs Staff Files, Box 4, GRFL.

112. Memo from Kissinger to Nixon, undated, *FRUS*, 1969–1976, vol. 19 (pt. 2), 211.

113. Johnson to Kissinger, June 7, 1972, Folder "Japan, March 6–June 6, 1972 [2 of 5]," NSC Files, HAK Office Files, Box 102, RMNL.

114. Lanoszka 2018, 99–102; Memorandum of Conversation, May 21, 1974, National Security Adviser Memoranda of Conversations, 1973–1977, Box 4, GRFL; Briefing Memorandum from Robert Ingersoll to Kissinger, "Your Meeting with Foreign Minister Ohira Monday, May 20, 1974," May 1974, Folder "Japan (2)," National Security Adviser's Files, NSC East Asia and Pacific Affairs Staff Files, Box 3, GRFL.

NOTES TO PAGES 84–90

115. Smith 2019, 36–41.

116. Greene 1975, 78–79.

117. Cha 1999, 71–72; Laird to Nixon, July 19, 1971, *FRUS*, 1969–1976, vol. 19 (pt. 2), doc. 80; Memorandum for the President's File, January 7, 1972, *FRUS*, 1969–1976, vol. 19 (pt. 2), doc. 112; Memo from Laird to Kissinger, June 7, 1972, *FRUS*, 1969–1976, vol. 19 (pt. 2), doc. 119.

118. Komine 2014, 98–101, 110–12, 116, 119–22.

119. Green 1995, 57–71; Smith 2019, 39–41.

120. Greene 1975, 78–87.

121. Komine 2014, 126–27.

122. Memorandum from W. R. Smyser to Robert Ingersoll, "List of Objectives for Japan NSSM," April 4, 1974, Folder "Japan—NSSM 172 (1)," National Security Adviser's Files, NSC East Asia and Pacific Affairs Staff Files, Box 4, GRFL.

123. Minutes of Senior Review Group Meeting, "Japan NSSM 122," August 6, 1971, *FRUS*, 1969–1976, vol. 19 (pt. 2), 266.

124. Memorandum from Richard Finn to Winston Lord, "Study on Forces at Work in Japan," April 23, 1974, Folder "Japan—NSSM 172 (5)," National Security Adviser's Files, NSC East Asia and Pacific Affairs Staff Files, Box 4, GRFL, 4–6; Philip Habib to Brent Scowcroft, "Submission of Response to NSSM 210," October 21, 1974, Folder "Japan—NSSM 210," National Security Adviser's Files, NSC East Asia and Pacific Affairs Staff Files, Box 5, GRFL, 66–70; Memorandum for Major General Brent Scowcroft, "Briefing for President on Japan," August 26, 1974, Folder "Japan (1)," Presidential Country Files for East Asia and the Pacific, Box 6, GRFL.

125. Minutes of Senior Review Group Meeting, August 6, 1971, *FRUS*, 1969–1976, vol. 19 (pt. 2), 264; Minutes of Senior Review Group Meeting, August 27, 1971, *FRUS*, 1969–1976, vol. 19 (pt. 2), 289; US Information Agency, "US-Japan Security Relations: Their Place in US Strategic Thinking," November 1974, Folder "President Ford's Trip to Tokyo, November 1974 (3)," National Security Adviser's Files, NSC East Asia and Pacific Affairs Staff Files, Box 18, GRFL.

126. Ha and Guinasso 1980, 250, 256, 260; Cha 1999, 147, 152–54; Lind 2004, 107–11; Lanoszka 2018, 107–8; Memorandum of Conversation, "President Ford—Prime Minister Tanaka—Second Meeting," November 20, 1974, Folder "President Ford Memcons (1)," National Security Adviser's Files, NSC East Asia and Pacific Affairs Staff Files, Box 16, GRFL; "Japanese Perceptions of the Asian Military Balance," June 23, 1976, Folder "Japan (11)," National Security Adviser's Files, Presidential Country Files for East Asia and the Pacific," Box 6, GRFL; Memorandum of Conversation, "Ford-Miki Luncheon Conversation," June 30, 1976, National Security Adviser's Memoranda of Conversation, 1973–1977, Box 20, GRFL; Memorandum of Conversation, July 1, 1976, *FRUS*, 1969–1976, vol. E–12, doc. 226.

127. Greene 1975, 8–10; Welfield 1988, 353–56; Cha 1999, 108–9; Komine 2014, 120–22; Smith 2019, 40–42.

4. "They Live at Our Sufferance"

1. Current-year dollars; equivalent of about $2,200 in 2022 dollars.

2. Yong Lee 2011, 405; Gul Hong 2011, 503–4; Lee and Heo 2002, 77–81, 101; Lanoszka 2018, 111, 115, 119.

3. Jervis 1980; Draft Study Prepared by the Ad Hoc Inter–Departmental Working Group for Korea, May 2–June 11, 1969, *FRUS*, vol. 19, doc. 26.

4. *FRUS*, 1964–1968, vol. 29 (pt. 1), docs. 92 and 99; *FRUS*, 1969–1972, vol. 19 (pt. 1), doc. 164; *FRUS*, 1969–1972, vol. 19 (pt. 2), doc. 3.

5. Lee and Heo 2002, 74–76, 82, 93–94.

6. Memorandum from Barnett to Black, October 5, 1964, *FRUS*, 1964–1968, vol. 29 (pt. 1), doc. 25; National Security Action Memorandum No. 298, May 5, 1964, *FRUS*, 1964–1968, vol. 29 (pt. 1), doc. 9.

7. *FRUS*, 1964–1968, vol. 29 (pt. 1), docs. 25, 42, 50, 52, 183, 201, 209.

8. Airgram From the Embassy in Korea to the Department of State, February 5, 1964, *FRUS*, 1964–1968, vol. 29 (pt. 1), doc. 3.

NOTES TO PAGES 91–94

9. Yong Lee 2011, 410–14.

10. *FRUS*, 1964–1968, vol. 29 (pt. 1), docs. 37, 43, 47–48, 66, 68.

11. Yong Lee 2011, 409–13; Notes on Conversation between President Johnson and President Pak, December 21, 1967, *FRUS*, 1964–1968, vol. 29 (pt. 1), doc. 140; Memorandum from Rostow to Johnson, December 29, 1967, *FRUS*, 1964–1968, vol. 29 (pt. 1), doc. 141.

12. Memorandum of Conversation, May 12, 1965, *FRUS*, 1964–1968, vol. 29 (pt. 1), 88.

13. Yong Lee 2011, 416–19; Telegram from the Embassy in Korea to the Department of State, February 10, 1968, *FRUS*, 1964–1968, vol. 29 (pt. 1), doc. 174; Telegram from the Department of State to the Embassy in Korea, February 11, 1968, *FRUS*, 1964–1968, vol. 29 (pt. 1), doc. 175; Memorandum from Cyrus R. Vance to President Johnson, February 20, 1968, *FRUS*, 1964–1968, vol. 29 (pt. 1), doc. 181; Telegram from Rostow to Johnson, February 20, 1968, *FRUS*, 1964–1968, vol. 29 (pt. 1), doc. 190.

14. Memorandum of Conversation, May 12, 1965, *FRUS*, 1964–1968, vol. 29 (pt. 1), 88.

15. Thomson to Johnson, May 17, 1965, *FRUS*, 1964–1968, vol. 29 (pt. 1), 96. See also Memorandum of Conversation, May 17, 1965, *FRUS*, 1964–1968, vol. 29 (pt. 1), 97–99. Similar exchanges, in which the South Koreans sought an assurance of troop levels while the United States promised only that it had no current plans to withdraw forces and that it would consult the ROK prior to withdrawal, pervaded the 1960s. See, for example, Telegram from the Embassy in Korea to the Department of State, October 19, 1966, *FRUS*, 1964–1968, vol. 29 (pt. 1), 199–200; and Memorandum of Conversation between President Johnson and President Pak, November 1, 1966, *FRUS*, 1964–1968, vol. 29 (pt. 1), 205–7.

16. Yong Lee 2011, 410.

17. Notes of the President's Meeting with Cyrus R. Vance, February 15, 1968, *FRUS*, 1964–1968, vol. 29 (pt. 1), 378.

18. Telegram from Rostow to Johnson, April 13, 1968, *FRUS*, 1964–1968, vol. 29 (pt. 1), 412.

19. Intelligence Memorandum, November 8, 1966, *FRUS*, 1964–1968, vol. 29 (pt. 1), doc. 98; Telegram from the Embassy in Korea to the Department of State, August 23, 1967, *FRUS*, 1964–1968, vol. 29 (pt. 1), doc. 125.

20. Nam 1986, 86; Lee and Heo 2002, 80–81; Telegram from the Department of State to the Embassy in Korea, February 7, 1968, *FRUS*, 1964–1968, vol. 29 (pt. 1), doc. 159.

21. Yong Lee 2011, 420–21; Memorandum to Holders of Special National Intelligence Estimate Number 14.2-671, February 29, 1968. *FRUS*, 1964–1968, vol. 29 (pt. 1), doc. 184; Telegram from the Embassy in Korea to the Department of State, March 15, 1968, *FRUS*, 1964–1968, vol. 29 (pt. 1), doc. 188; Summary of Conversations between President Johnson and President Pak, April 17, 1968, *FRUS*, 1964–1968, vol. 29 (pt. 1), doc. 194.

22. Information on the annual financial cost of military operations in Vietnam is difficult to come by, but estimates suggest that the cumulative cost of the war was $111 billion in current-year dollars ($738 billion in 2011 dollars). See Stephen Daggett, *Costs of Major Wars*, Congressional Research Service RS22926, June 29, 2010, https://fas.org/sgp/crs/natsec/RS22926.pdf

23. Nelson 2019, 34–35, 39–41, 98–99.

24. Gavin 2004.

25. Williams 1985, 142, 162, 170, 200–201; Litwak 1986, 119–20; Lee and Heo 2002, 82–89, 102–5; Zelizer 2010; Nelson 2019, 17–24.

26. Study Prepared by the Office of International Security Affairs in the Department of Defense, undated, *FRUS*, 1969–1976, vol. E–12, doc. 274; Telegram from the Department of State to the Embassy in Korea, April 23, 1970, *FRUS*, 1969–1976, vol. 19 (pt. 1), 151.

27. Litwak 1986, 52–55, 75–76; Caldwell 2009, 634–35; Nelson 2019, 34–43, 53–56, 78–79, 98–99.

28. Nam 1986, 83; Hunt 2015, 349.

29. Memorandum from Nixon to Kissinger, November 24, 1969, *FRUS*, 1969–1972, vol. 19, 117; Telegram from the Department of State to the Embassy in Korea, January 29, 1970, *FRUS*, 1969–1972, vol. 19, 121–22; Minutes of a National Security Council Review Group Meeting, *FRUS*, 1969–1972, vol. 19, 125–31; Draft Minutes of a National Security Council Meeting, *FRUS*, 1969–1972, vol. 19, 142–47.

30. Kim 2001, 55; Memorandum of Conversation, March 3, 1970, *FRUS*, 1969–1972, vol. 19, 139–42.

159

NOTES TO PAGES 94–96

31. Draft Memorandum from Rusk to Johnson, June 8, 1964, *FRUS*, 1964–1968, vol. 29 (pt. 1), doc. 17; Memorandum from Katzenbach to Johnson, December 23, 1968, *FRUS*, 1964–1968, vol. 29 (pt. 1), doc. 211.

32. NSSM 211, "Security Assistance to the ROK," Folder "Korea (8)," NSC East Asia and Pacific, Box 5, GRFL, 3–4; State Department, Memo for Scowcroft, "Issues Paper on Korea," October 19, 1974, Folder "Korea (1)," National Security Adviser's Files, Presidential Country Files for East Asia and the Pacific, Box 9, GRFL.

33. Nam 1986, 68–81, 109–14, 126, quote at 81; Nelson 2019, 75–82, 96–99.

34. Paper Prepared by the Policy Planning Council of the Department of State, June 15, 1968, *FRUS*, 1964–1968, vol. 29 (pt. 1), doc. 201; Memorandum from Katzenbach to Johnson, December 23, 1968, *FRUS*, 1964–1968, vol. 29 (pt. 1), doc. 211.

35. Rogers to Nixon, "Your Meeting with President Park Chung Hee of Korea, August 21, 1969, 11:30 a.m.," Folder "Background Papers Korean Visit, August 19, 1969," NSC Files, HAK Office Files, Country Files, Box 102, RMNL.

36. Memorandum of Conversation, August 21, 1969, *FRUS*, 1969–1976, vol. 19 (pt. 1), 96–102; Letter from President Nixon to Korean President Park, May 26, 1970, *FRUS*, 1969–1976, vol. 19 (pt. 1), 152–54; Laird to Nixon, July 19, 1971, *FRUS*, 1969–1976, 19 (pt. 1), 254–63.

37. NSDM 48, March 20, 1970, *FRUS*, 1969–1976, vol. 19 (pt. 1), 148–50.

38. Nam 1986, 67, 76–78, 97, 101–2; Telegram from the Department of State to the Embassy in Korea, January 29, 1970, *FRUS*, 1969–1976, vol. 19 (pt. 1), 121–22; Kissinger to Nixon, "Five-Year Korea Plan," undated, Folder "Korea—NSDM 48" National Security Adviser's Files, NSC East Asia and Pacific Affairs Staff Files, Box 5, GRFL; "Special Message to the Congress Proposing Supplemental Foreign Assistance Appropriations," November 18, 1970, American Presidency Project, https://www.presidency.ucsb.edu/documents/special-message-the-congress -proposing-supplemental-foreign-assistance-appropriations; Memo from Nixon to Kissinger, August 22, 1970, *FRUS*, 1969–1972, vol. 19 (pt. 1), doc. 70.

39. Rogers to Nixon, "Your Meeting with President Park Chung Hee of Korea, August 21, 1969, 11:30 a.m.," Folder "Background Papers Korean Visit, August 19, 1969," NSC Files, HAK Office Files, Country Files, Box 102, RMNL; Letter from President Nixon to Korean President Park, May 26, 1970, *FRUS*, 1969–1976, vol. 19 (pt. 1), 152–54; Letter from President Nixon to Korean President Park, July 7, 1970, *FRUS*, 1969–1976, vol. 19 (pt. 1), 164–65.

40. Telegram from the Embassy in Korea to the Department of State, May 29, 1970, *FRUS*, 1969–1976, vol. 19 (pt. 1), 154–57.

41. Nam 1986, 86; Jang 2016, 512; Memorandum from Holdridge to Kissinger, November 16, 1970, *FRUS*, 1969–1976, vol. 19 (pt. 1), 198–99.

42. Memorandum of Conversation, September 28, 1971, *FRUS*, 1969–1976, vol. 19 (pt. 1), 281–85; Letter from President Nixon to Korean President Park, November 29, 1971, *FRUS*, 1969–1976, vol. 19 (pt. 1), 293–95; Telegram from the Embassy in Korea to the Department of State, December 13, 1971, *FRUS*, 1969–1976, vol. 19 (pt. 1), 302–5.

43. Cha 1999, 67.

44. Hunt 2015, 349. Emphasis in original.

45. Nam 1986, 77–79, 97–99.

46. NSDM 48, "US Programs in Korea," March 20, 1970, Box H-208, National Security Council Institutional Files, RMNL; Smith and Holdridge to Kissinger, September 1, 1971, *FRUS*, 1969–1976, vol. 19 (pt. 1), 270–71.

47. Nam 1986, 83; Hayes 1991, 55–56; Oberdorfer 1997, 86; Memorandum from Rogers to Nixon, September 22, 1970, *FRUS*, 1969–1976, vol. 19 (pt. 1), 184–85.

48. Memorandum of Conversation, December 2, 1970, *FRUS*, 1969–1976, vol. 19 (pt. 1), 213.

49. Nam 1986, 78; Laird to Nixon, July 19, 1971, *FRUS*, 1969–1976, Vol. 19 (pt. 1), 254–63.

50. Telegram from the Department of State to the Embassy in Korea, October 26, 1970, *FRUS*, 1969–1976, vol. 19 (pt. 1), 188.

51. Memorandum of Conversation, September 28, 1971, *FRUS*, 1969–1976, vol. 19 (pt. 1), 281–85; Letter from President Nixon to Korean President Park, November 29, 1971, *FRUS*, 1969–1976, vol. 19 (pt. 1), 293–95; Irwin to Nixon, March 21, 1972, *FRUS*, 1969–1976, vol. 19 (pt. 1), 321–22;

NOTES TO PAGES 96–99

Kissinger to Nixon, March 31, 1972, *FRUS*, 1969–1976, vol. 19 (pt. 1), 326–28; Letter from President Nixon to Korean President Park, May 19, 1972, *FRUS*, 1969–1976, vol. 19 (pt. 1), 351–53.

52. Telegram from the Embassy in Korea to the Department of State, June 13, 1972, *FRUS*, 1969–1976, vol. 19 (pt. 1), 362–65; Miller to Kissinger, July 3, 1972, *FRUS*, 1969–1976, vol. 19 (pt. 1), 366–68; Holdridge to Kissinger, "State's Analysis of North Korean Premier Kim Il–Song's Proposals of June 21," July 4, 1972, 369–70; Telegram from the Embassy in Korea to the Department of State, July 7, 1972, *FRUS*, 1969–1976, vol. 19 (pt. 1), 371–76; Kennedy to Kissinger, January 16, 1973, *FRUS*, 1969–1976, vol. E–12, doc. 231; Kissinger to Rogers and Schlesinger, July 18, 1973, *FRUS*, 1969–1976, vol. E–12, doc. 241.

53. Memorandum of Conversation, February 24, 1973, *FRUS*, 1969–1976, vol. E–12, doc. 232, 3.

54. Memo from Smyser to Kissinger, "Your Meeting with South Korean Foreign Minister Kim on March 20, 1974 at 6:00 p.m.," March 19, 1974, Folder "Korea (3)," National Security Adviser's Files, NSC East Asia and Pacific Affairs Staff Files, Box 5, GRFL.

55. Memorandum of Conversation, May 28, 1974, *FRUS*, 1969–1976, vol. E–12, doc. 254.

56. NSDM 48, March 20, 1970, *FRUS*, 1969–1976, vol. 19 (pt. 1), 148–50.

57. Letter from President Nixon to Korean President Park, May 26, 1970, *FRUS*, 1969–1976, vol. 19 (pt. 1), 152–54.

58. Letter from President Nixon to Korean President Park, May 26, 1970, *FRUS*, 1969–1976, vol. 19 (pt. 1), 152–54.

59. Telegram from the Department of State to the Embassy in Korea, January 29, 1970, *FRUS*, 1969–1976, vol. 19 (pt. 1), 121–22.

60. Draft Minutes of a National Security Council Meeting, March 4, 1970, *FRUS*, 1969–1976, vol. 19 (pt. 1), 142–47.

61. Laird to Nixon, July 19, 1971, *FRUS*, 1969–1976, vol. 19 (pt. 1), 254–63.

62. Paper Prepared by the Policy Planning Council of the Department of State, June 15, 1968, *FRUS*, 1964–1968, vol. 19 (pt. 1), 433–36.

63. National Intelligence Estimate, December 2, 1970, *FRUS*, 1969–1976, vol. 19 (pt. 1), 210. See also Telegram from the Department of State to the Embassy in Korea, December 2, 1971, *FRUS*, 1969–1976, vol. 19 (pt. 1), 295–96; Telegram from the Embassy in Korea to the Department of State, June 13, 1972, *FRUS*, 1969–1976, vol. 19 (pt. 1), 362–65; Airgram from the Embassy in Korea to the Department of State, December 10, 1972, *FRUS*, 1969–1976, vol. 19 (pt. 1), 436–45.

64. Conversation among President Nixon, Secretary of the Treasury Connally, the Under Secretary of State for Political Affairs (Johnson), and Others, April 17, 1971, *FRUS*, 1969–1976, vol. 19 (pt. 1), 237.

65. Memorandum of Conversation, March 3, 1970, *FRUS*, 1969–1976, vol. 19 (pt. 1), 142.

66. Telegram from the Embassy in Korea to the Department of State, December 23, 1971, *FRUS*, 1969–1976, vol. 19 (pt. 1), 312.

67. Cha 1999, 111–12; Telegram from the Department of State to the Embassy in Korea, April 23, 1970, *FRUS*, 1969–1976, vol. 19 (pt. 1), 151.

68. McLaurin 1988, 170–71; Telegram from the Embassy in Korea to the Department of State, December 22, 1971, *FRUS*, 1969–1976, vol. 19 (pt. 1), 307–10.

69. Simmons 1978, 6–13, 25–27; Nam 1986, 83–85; Nelson 2019, 53–56, 78–79; Draft Study Prepared by the Ad Hoc Inter-Departmental Working Group for Korea, May 2–June 11, 1969, *FRUS*, vol. 19 (pt. 1), doc. 26.

70. Simmons 1978, 21–33; Cha 1999, 63–65; Yong Lee 2011, 405, 420–21; Lanoszka 2018, 111–12, 119–20; Minutes of a National Security Council Meeting, April 16, 1969, *FRUS*, 1969–1976, vol. 19 (pt. 1), doc. 13; Telegram from the Department of State to the Embassy in Korea, February 7, 1968, *FRUS*, 1964–1968, vol. 29 (pt. 1), doc. 159.

71. Vance to Johnson, February 20, 1968, *FRUS*, 1964–1968, vol. 29 (pt. 1), 385.

72. Lee and Heo 2002, 76–77, 93–94.

73. Cha 1999, 110.

74. Nam 1986, 126; Telegram from the Embassy in Korea to the Department of State, December 13, 1971, *FRUS*, 1969–1976, vol. 19 (pt. 1), 302–5.

NOTES TO PAGES 99–104

75. Kim 2001, 55.

76. Telegram from the Embassy in Korea to the Department of State, December 22, 1971, *FRUS, 1969–1976*, vol. 19 (pt. 1), 308–10.

77. Minutes of the Secretary of State's Staff Meeting, Washington, January 25, 1974, *FRUS, 1969–1976*, vol. E–12, doc. 249.

78. Laird to Nixon, July 19, 1971, *FRUS, 1969–1976*, vol. 19 (pt. 1), 254–63.

79. Airgram from the Embassy in Korea to the Department of State, December 10, 1972, *FRUS, 1969–1976*, vol. 19 (pt. 1), 439.

80. Nam 1986, 101; Yong Lee 2011, 421–25.

81. Gul Hong 2011, 487–88.

82. Lee and Heo 2002, 38–40, 74, 100–101; Study Prepared by the Office of International Security Affairs in the Department of Defense, undated, *FRUS, 1969–1976*, vol. E–12, doc. 274.

83. Memorandum Porter to Nixon, June 15, 1973, *FRUS, 1969–1976*, vol. E–12, doc. 237.

84. Memorandum from Kissinger to Nixon, July 25, 1973, *FRUS, 1969–1976*, vol. E–12, doc. 242; NSDM 227, July 27, 1973, *FRUS, 1969–1976*, vol. E–12, doc. 243; Smyser and Kennedy to Scowcroft, "Proposed Sale of F-4 Squadron to Republic of Korea," July 5, 1974, Folder "Korea (6)," NSC East Asia and Pacific Files, Box 5, GRFL.

85. National Intelligence Analytical Memorandum 14.2-1-74, Washington, July 15, 1974, *FRUS, 1969–1976*, vol. E–12, doc. 255; NSSM 211, "Security Assistance to the ROK," Folder "Korea (8)," NSC East Asia and Pacific, Box 5, GRFL, 4.

86. Vietnam War US Military Fatal Casualty Statistics, National Archives and Records Administration, https://www.archives.gov/research/military/vietnam-war/casualty-statistics (accessed August 31, 2020).

87. Darby 1982.

88. McLaurin 1988, 170, 176; Lee and Heo 2002, 102–3.

89. Cha 1999, 148–49. According to Lieutenant General James F. Hollingsworth, who was in command of the ROK / US I Corps in Seoul during 1973, Park had asked him, "Are you going to do the same thing here you did in Vietnam?" (Oberdorfer 1997, 61).

90. Telegram 2685 from the Embassy in the Republic of Korea to the Department of State, April 18, 1975, *FRUS, 1969–1976*, vol. E–12, doc 267.

91. Memorandum of Conversation, August 26, 1975, Folder "Korea (11)," National Security Adviser's Files, Presidential Country Files for East Asia and the Pacific, Box 9, GRFL.

92. Memorandum of Conversation, May 28, 1974, *FRUS, 1969–1976*, vol. E–12, doc. 254; Memorandum from Kissinger to Ford, January 3, 1975, *FRUS, 1969–1976*, vol. E–12, doc. 260.

93. Study Prepared by the Office of International Security Affairs in the Department of Defense, Washington, undated, *FRUS, 1969–1976*, vol. E–12, doc. 274.

94. Memo for the Deputy Assistant to the President for National Security Affairs, "US Company on the Demilitarized Zone," February 19, 1975, Folder "Korea (3)," Presidential East Asia and Pacific Files, Box 9, GRFL.

95. Nam 1986, 156–57; Moon 1988, 111–12; Y. Kim 2011, 462–64, 473–76; Kissinger to Ford, January 3, 1975, *FRUS*, vol. E–12, doc. 260; Memorandum of Conversation, June 12, 1975, *FRUS*, vol. E–12, doc. 269; Telegram 9567 from Embassy in the Republic of Korea to the Department of State, December 3, 1976, *FRUS*, vol. E–12, doc. 290; Memo from Froebe to Scowcroft, "Request by Eight Congressmen to Call on the President Prior to His Visit to South Korea," November 5, 1974, Folder "Korea (7)," National Security Adviser's Files, NSC East Asia and Pacific Affairs Staff Files, Box 5, GRFL.

96. McLaurin 1988, 177–78; Kennedy and Smyser to Kissinger, "Future US Military Assistance to South Korea," December 20, 1974, Folder "Korea (8)," National Security Adviser's Files, NSC East Asia and Pacific Affairs Staff Files, Box 5, GRFL; Kissinger to Ford, "Future US Military Assistance to South Korea," undated [January 1975], Folder "Korea (8)," National Security Adviser's Files, NSC East Asia and Pacific Affairs Staff Files, Box 5, GRFL; NSSM 211, "Security Assistance to the Republic of Korea," Folder "Korea (8)," National Security Adviser's Files, NSC East Asia and Pacific Affairs Staff Files, Box 5, GRFL; Kissinger to Ford, "Future US Military Assistance to South Korea," undated [December 1974], Folder "Korea (8)," National Security Adviser's Files, NSC East Asia and Pacific Affairs Staff Files, Box 5, GRFL.

NOTES TO PAGES 104–106

97. NSDM 282, Washington, January 9, 1975, *FRUS*, 1969–1976, vol. E–12, doc. 262.

98. Department of State, "President Ford's Visit to Korea, November 22–23, 1974: Issues and Talking Points," Folder "President Ford's Trip to Seoul, November 1974 (2)," National Security Adviser's Files, NSC East Asian and Pacific Affairs Staff Files, Box 18, GRFL; Memo from Kissinger to Ford, "Your Visit to Korea," October 1974, Folder "Korea (7)," National Security Adviser's Files, NSC East Asia and Pacific Affairs Staff Files, Box 5, GRFL.

99. Memorandum of Conversation, "South Korean Dependence on US Support," November 22, 1974, Folder "President Ford Memcons (1)," National Security Adviser's Files, NSC East Asia and Pacific Affairs Staff Files, Box 16, GRFL.

100. Memorandum of Conversation, May 8, 1975, National Security Adviser's Memoranda of Conversation Collection, Box 11, GRFL.

101. Memorandum for the Record, "Meeting with President Pak Chung Hee in Seoul, Korea 27 August 1975," September 2, 1975, Folder "Korea (10)," National Security Adviser's Files, Presidential Country Files for East Asia and the Pacific, Box 9, GRFL.

102. Froebe to Scowcroft, "Your Meeting with Ambassador Sneider on September 12, 1974," September 11, 1974, Folder "Korea (6)," NSC East Asia and Pacific Files, Box 5, GRFL; Memorandum from Kissinger to Schlesinger, October 8, 1974, *FRUS*, 1969–1976, vol. E–12, doc. 257; Department of State, "President Ford's Visit to Korea, November 22–23, 1974: Issues and Talking Points," Folder "President Ford's Trip to Seoul, November 1974 (2)," National Security Adviser's Files, NSC East Asian and Pacific Affairs Staff Files, Box 18, GRFL.

103. Hayes 1991, 55–56; Oberdorfer 1997, 86; Springsteen to Scowcroft, "Issues Paper on Korea," October 19, 1974, Folder "Korea (1)," Presidential East Asia and Pacific Files, Box 9, GRFL; Memorandum from Kissinger to Nixon, March 25, 1974, *FRUS*, 1969–1976, vol. E–12, doc. 252; NSDM 251, Washington, March 29, 1974, *FRUS*, 1969–1976, vol. E–12, doc. 253; Minutes of the Secretary of State's Staff Meeting, January 6, 1975, *FRUS*, 1969–1976, vol. E–12, doc. 261, 10.

104. Memorandum from the President's Assistant for National Security Affairs (Kissinger) to President Ford, Washington, January 3, 1975, *FRUS*, 1969–1976, vol. E–12, doc. 260, 1; Memorandum of Conversation, November 22, 1974, 3:00 p.m., National Security Adviser's Memoranda of Conversation Collection, Box 7, GRFL; Memorandum of Conversation, "Meeting with the Speaker of the South Korean National Assembly Chung Il-Kwon," May 8, 1975, Box 11, National Security Adviser Memoranda of Conversations, 1973–1977, GRFL.

105. Memorandum of Conversation, August 27, 1975, *FRUS*, 1969–1976, vol. E–12, doc. 271.

106. Memorandum of Conversation, August 26, 1975, Folder "Korea (11)," National Security Adviser's Files, Presidential Country Files for East Asia and the Pacific, Box 9, GRFL.

107. Memorandum from Richard Smyser of the National Security Council Staff to Secretary of State Kissinger, Washington, undated [July–October 1974], *FRUS*, 1969–1976, vol. E–12, doc. 256.

108. Suhrke and Morrison 1977, 367–69.

109. Niksch 1981, 326–28; Nam 1986, 148, 155; Choi 2018, 934–36, 940–41.

110. McLaurin 1988, 179; Cha 1999, 148–49; Gul Hong 2011, 487–88.

111. Lee and Heo 2002, 99–101.

112. Study Prepared by the Office of International Security Affairs in the Department of Defense, undated, *FRUS*, 1969–1976, vol. E–12, doc. 274.

113. Department of State, "President Ford's Visit to Korea, November 22–23, 1974: Issues and Talking Points," Folder "President Ford's Trip to Seoul, November 1974 (2)," National Security Adviser's Files, NSC East Asian and Pacific Affairs Staff Files, Box 18, GRFL.

114. Memorandum of Conversation, March 27, 1975, *FRUS*, 1969–1976, vol. E–12, doc. 265.

115. Gul Hong 2011, 488; National Intelligence Analytical Memorandum 14.2-1-74, Washington, July 15, 1974, *FRUS*, 1969–1976, vol. E–12, doc. 255; Study Prepared by the Office of International Security Affairs in the Department of Defense, Washington, undated, *FRUS*, 1969–1976, vol. E–12, doc. 274; Minutes of Washington Special Actions Group Meeting, August 18, 1976, *FRUS*, 1969–1976, vol. E–12, doc. 282.

116. Cha 1999, 110, 148–49; Y. Kim 2011, 463–65; Lanoszka 2018, 129–30; Ria Chae, "East German Documents on Kim Il Sung's April 1975 Trip to Beijing," May 2012, North Korea International Documentation Project, Wilson Center, https://www.wilsoncenter.org/publication/east-german-documents-kim-il-sungs-april-1975-trip-to-beijing.

163

NOTES TO PAGES 106–108

117. Telegram from US Embassy (Seoul) to Secretary of State, May 1974, "ROK Defense Procurement: Implications for US Policy," Folder "Korea (6)," National Security Adviser's Files, NSC East Asia and Pacific Affairs Staff Files, Country File, 1969–1976, Box 5, GRFL.

118. Y. Kim 2011, 469–70.

119. Memorandum of Conversation, November 22, 1974, *FRUS*, 1969–1976, vol. E–12, doc. 258.

120. Telegram 2685 From the Embassy in the Republic of Korea to the Department of State, April 18, 1975, *FRUS*, 1969–1976, vol. E–12, doc. 267.

121. *FRUS*, 1969–1976, vol. E–12, docs. 241, 252–56, 258–59, 271, 274, 278, 282.

122. Niksch 1981, 328–34; Nam 1986, 159–61; Choi 2018, 942–54; Sungjoo 1980, 1079–80; Memorandum for the Secretary of Defense from Russell Murray, Assistant Secretary of Defense, Program Analysis & Evaluation, Subject PRM-45 (TS), June 6, 1979, National Security Archive, https://nsarchive.gwu.edu/document/23916-memorandum-secretary-defense-russell-murray-assistant-secretary-defense-program; Franz-Stefan Gady, "How the 'Deep State' Stopped a US President from Withdrawing US Troops from Korea," *The Diplomat*, June 15, 2018, https://thediplomat.com/2018/06/how-the-deep-state-stopped-a-us-president-from-withdrawing-us-troops-from-korea/.

123. Y. Kim 2011, 478–80.

124. Suhrke and Morrison 1977, 371–72.

125. Memorandum for the Secretary of Defense from Russell Murray, June 6, 1979, National Security Archive, https://nsarchive.gwu.edu/document/23916-memorandum-secretary-defense-russell-murray-assistant-secretary-defense-program; Memorandum for the Secretary of Defense from Assistant Secretary of Defense for International Security Affairs, David E. McGiffert, Subject: Korean Troop Withdrawals—Action Memorandum, June 20, 1979, Secret, National Security Archive, https://nsarchive.gwu.edu/document/22881-document-07-memorandum-secretary; Cable, Mike Armacost to Deputy Secretary of Defense Claytor, Subject: Report to President of Secret Discussions in Korea, October 20, 1979, Secret, National Security Archive, https://nsarchive.gwu.edu/document/22884-document-10-cable-mike-armacost-deputy; Memoranda of Conversation, President Jimmy Carter, South Korean President Park Chung Hee, et al., June 30, 1979, Secret, National Security Archive, https://nsarchive.gwu.edu/document/22882-document-08-memoranda-conversation-president.

126. Gul Hong 2011, 488, 491–95.

127. Gul Hong 2011, 496–97.

128. Memorandum from Smyser and Elliott to Kissinger, *FRUS*, 1969–1976, vol. E–12, doc. 264.

129. Nam 1986, 106; Gul Hong 2011, 497–98.

130. Oberdorfer 1997, 71; Lanoszka 2018, 121–25; Study Prepared by the Office of International Security Affairs in the Department of Defense, undated, *FRUS*, 1969–1976, vol. E–12, doc. 274; Memo from Lodal and Elliott to Kissinger, "Approach to South Korea on Reprocessing," July 24, 1975, Folder "Korea (9)," National Security Adviser's Files, Presidential Country Files for East Asia and the Pacific, Box 9, GRFL.

131. Gul Hong 2011, 501.

132. Oberdorfer 1997, 72; Gul Hong 2011, 498–503.

133. Kim 2001, 67–68; Lanoszka 2018, 125–29.

134. Nam 1986, 106; Study Prepared by the Office of International Security Affairs in the Department of Defense, undated, *FRUS*, 1969–1976, vol. E–12, doc. 274; Draft Department of State Cable, "ROK Plans to Develop Nuclear Weapons and Missiles," February 24, 1975, Folder "Korea (4)," National Security Adviser, Presidential Country Files for East Asia and the Pacific, Box 9, GRFL.

135. Oberdorfer 1997, 65; Telegram from Kissinger to US Embassy (Seoul), "ROK Plans to Develop Nuclear Weapons and Missiles," March 1975, Folder "Korea—State Department Telegrams from SECSTATE—NODIS (3)," National Security Adviser's Files, Presidential Country Files for East Asia and the Pacific, Box 11, GRFL.

136. Telegram 2685 from the Embassy in the Republic of Korea to the Department of State, April 18, 1975, *FRUS*, 1969–1976, vol. E–12, doc. 267. See also Memorandum from Kissinger to Ford, "Meeting with the Speaker of the South Korean National Assembly Chung Il–Kwon,"

164

NOTES TO PAGES 108–114

May 8, 1975, Folder "President Ford Memcons (1)," National Security Adviser's Files, NSC East Asia and Pacific Affairs Staff Files, Box 16, GRFL.

137. Hayes 1991, 60.

138. Cha 1999, 146–49.

139. Lanoszka 2018, 127–29; Cable, Mike Armacost to Deputy Secretary of Defense Claytor.

140. Memorandum of Conversation, November 22, 1974, *FRUS*, 1969–1976, vol. E–12, doc. 258; Information Memorandum from Bergold to Rumsfeld, Washington, March 16, 1976, *FRUS*, 1969–1976, vol. E–12, doc. 275.

141. Nam 1986, 79; McLaurin 1988, 179; Lanoszka 2018, 121–25.

142. Telegram 2685 from the Embassy in the Republic of Korea to the Department of State, April 18, 1975, *FRUS*, 1969–1976, vol. E–12, doc. 267.

143. Monteiro and Debs 2017.

144. Ludvik 2018.

5. "Is Iceland Blackmailing Us?"

1. Agreement between the United States and Iceland for the termination of the defense agreement of July 1, 1941, *FRUS*, Diplomatic Papers, 1945, vol. 4, Iceland.

2. The Consul in Iceland to the Secretary of State, March 11, 1948, *FRUS*, 1948, vol. 3, doc. 33; The Ambassador in Norway to the Secretary of State, May 18, 1948, *FRUS*, 1948, vol. 3, doc. 98.

3. The Minister in Iceland to the Secretary of State, December 11, 1948, *FRUS*, 1948, vol. 3, doc. 193; The Minister in Iceland to the Director of the Office of European Affairs, August 18, 1948, *FRUS*, 1948, vol. 3, doc. 438; The Secretary of State to the Secretary of Defense, September 10, 1948, *FRUS*, 1948, vol. 3, doc. 439.

4. Sandars 2000, ch. 3; Memorandum of the Ninth Meeting of the Working Group Participating in the Washington Exploratory Talks on Security, August 9, 1948, *FRUS*, 1948, vol. 3, doc. 135; Memorandum of the Thirteenth Meeting of the Working Group Participating in the Washington Exploratory Talks on Security, September 2, 1948, *FRUS*, 1948, vol. 3, doc. 144; Memorandum by the Participants in the Washington Security Talks, July 6 to September 9, Submitted to Their Respective Governments for Study and Comment, September 9, 1948, *FRUS*, 1948, vol. 3, doc. 150; The Acting Secretary of State to the United States Special Representative in Europe), December 3, 1948, *FRUS*, 1948, vol. 3, doc. 190.

5. Memorandum of Conversation, February 14, 1949, *FRUS*, 1949, vol. 4, doc. 67.

6. Minutes of the Third Meeting of the Washington Exploratory Talks on Security, July 7, 1948, 10 a.m., *FRUS*, 1948, vol. 3, doc. 114; Policy Statement of the Department of State, August 23, 1949, *FRUS*, 1949, vol. 4, doc. 393.

7. Duke 1989, 181–86; Mazarr et al. 2018, 147–52.

8. Sandars 2000, 76. See also National Security Council Report, May 20, 1957, *FRUS*, 1955–1957, vol. 27, doc. 179.

9. The Minister in Iceland to the Secretary of State, December 11, 1948, *FRUS*, 1948, vol. 3, doc. 193.

10. The Secretary of State to the Legation in Iceland, January 27, 1949, *FRUS*, 1949, vol. 4, doc. 40.

11. The Minister in Iceland to the Secretary of State, February 8, 1949, *FRUS*, 1949, vol. 4, doc. 54.

12. Memorandum of Conversation, by the Secretary of State, March 14, 1949, *FRUS*, 1949, vol. 4, doc. 107; Memorandum of Conversation, by the Counselor of the Department of State, March 14, 1949, *FRUS*, 1949, vol. 4, doc. 108; Memorandum of Conversation, March 15, 1949, *FRUS*, 1949, vol. 4, doc. 114; Memorandum of Conversation, March 17, 1949, *FRUS*, 1949, vol. 4, doc. 120; Report by the Executive Secretary of the National Security Council to the Council, July 29, 1949, *FRUS*, 1949, vol. 4, doc. 173; Policy Statement of the Department of State, August 23, 1949, *FRUS*, 1949, vol. 4, doc. 393.

13. Policy Statement of the Department of State, August 23, 1949, *FRUS*, 1949, vol. 4, doc. 393.

NOTES TO PAGES 114–117

14. Policy Statement Prepared in the Department of State, May 15, 1950, *FRUS*, 1950, vol. 3, doc. 651; Telegram from the United States Delegation at the NATO Heads of Government Meeting to the Department of State, December 17, 1957, *FRUS*, 1955–1957, vol. 4, doc. 75.

15. The Minister in Iceland to the Secretary of State, January 17, 1951, *FRUS*, 1951, vol. 4, doc. 205.

16. Memorandum of the Ninth Meeting of the Working Group Participating in the Washington Exploratory Talks on Security, August 9, 1948, *FRUS*, 1948, vol. 3, doc. 135; Memorandum of the Thirteenth Meeting of the Working Group Participating in the Washington Exploratory Talks on Security, September 2, 1948, *FRUS*, 1948, vol. 3, doc. 144; Memorandum of the Fourteenth Meeting of the Working Group Participating in the Washington Exploratory Talks on Security, September 7, 1948, *FRUS*, 1948, vol. 3, doc. 147.

17. The Ambassador in Belgium to the Secretary of State, November 29, 1948, *FRUS*, 1948, vol. 3, doc. 188.

18. The Ambassador in Sweden to the Secretary of State, January 5, 1951, *FRUS*, 1951, vol. 4, doc. 1; Editorial Note, *FRUS*, 1951, vol. 4, doc. 68.

19. The Ambassador in Sweden to the Secretary of State, January 5, 1951, *FRUS*, 1951, vol. 4, doc. 1; The Administrator for Economic Cooperation to the ECA Mission in Iceland, March 17, 1951, *FRUS*, 1951, vol. 4, doc. 215; The Minister in Iceland to the Secretary of State, April 18, 1951, *FRUS*, 1951, vol. 4, doc. 217; The Secretary of State to the Legation in Iceland, April 20, 1951, *FRUS*, 1951, vol. 4, doc. 218; The Minister in Iceland to the Secretary of State, April 22, 1951, *FRUS*, 1951, vol. 4, doc. 219.

20. Memorandum of Conversation, by the Director of the Office of British Commonwealth and Northern European Affairs, March 10, 1952, *FRUS*, 1952–1954, vol. 6, doc. 688; Memorandum by the Executive Secretary of the National Security Council to the National Security Council, July 12, 1954, *FRUS*, 1952–1954, vol. 6, doc. 705.

21. Policy Statement Prepared in the Department of State, May 15, 1950, *FRUS*, 1950, vol. 3, doc. 651.

22. National Security Council Report, May 20, 1957, *FRUS*, 1955–1957, vol. 27, doc. 179.

23. Jervis 1980.

24. Johannesson 2004, 117–18; The Minister in Iceland to the Secretary of State, January 17, 1951, *FRUS*, 1951, vol. 4, doc. 205; Memorandum by the Executive Secretary of the National Security Council to the National Security Council, July 12, 1954, *FRUS*, 1952–1954, vol. 6, doc. 705.

25. Memorandum of Conversation, January 20, 1951, *FRUS*, 1951, vol. 4, doc. 206; Memorandum of Conversation, by the Minister in Iceland, February 12, 1951, *FRUS*, 1951, vol. 4, doc. 208; The Minister in Iceland to the Secretary of State, February 21, 1951, *FRUS*, 1951, vol. 4, doc. 210; The Minister in Iceland to the Secretary of State, February 27, 1951, *FRUS*, 1951, vol. 4, doc. 211; The Minister in Iceland to the Secretary of State, March 4, 1951, *FRUS*, 1951, vol. 4, doc. 213.

26. The Minister in Iceland to the Secretary of State, April 6, 1951, *FRUS*, 1951, vol. 4, doc. 216; Editorial Note, *FRUS*, 1951, vol. 4, doc. 220.

27. Memorandum of Conversation, January 20, 1951, *FRUS*, 1951, vol. 4, doc. 206; The Minister in Iceland to the Secretary of State, February 21, 1951, *FRUS*, 1951, Vol. v, doc. 210; National Security Council Report, May 20, 1957, *FRUS*, 1955–1957, vol. 27, doc. 179.

28. Trachtenberg 1999, 151–52.

29. Policy Statement of the Department of State, August 23, 1949, *FRUS*, 1949, vol. 4, doc. 393.

30. The Chargé in Iceland to the Secretary of State, April 18, 1947, *FRUS*, 1947, vol. 3, doc. 536; Editorial Note, *FRUS*, 1947, vol. 3, doc. 538; The Chargé in Iceland to the Secretary of State, September 1, 1947, *FRUS*, 1947, vol. 3, doc. 539.

31. Memorandum by the Director of the Office of British Commonwealth and Northern European Affairs to the Assistant Secretary of State for European Affairs, November 25, 1953, *FRUS*, 1952–1954, vol. 6, doc. 695.

32. Memorandum by the Director of the Office of British Commonwealth and Northern European Affairs to the Operations Coordinator, May 28, 1954, *FRUS*, 1952–1954, vol. 6, doc. 704; National Security Council Report, May 20, 1957, *FRUS*, 1955–1957, vol. 27, doc. 179.

NOTES TO PAGES 117–125

33. The Minister in Iceland to the Secretary of State, June 21, 1951, *FRUS*, 1951, vol. 4, doc. 222.

34. Telegram From the United States Delegation at the North Atlantic Council Ministerial Meeting to the Department of State, December 13, 1956, *FRUS*, 1955–1957, vol. 4, doc. 47; Memorandum by the Executive Secretary of the National Security Council to the National Security Council, July 12, 1954, *FRUS*, 1952–1954, vol. 6, doc. 705; Memorandum by the Operations Coordinating Board Working Group on Iceland to the Board Assistants of the Operations Coordinating Board, December 7, 1954, *FRUS*, 1952–1954, vol. 6, doc. 706.

35. Memorandum by the Director of the Office of British Commonwealth and Northern European Affairs to the Assistant Secretary of State for European Affairs, November 25, 1953, *FRUS*, 1952–1954, vol. 6, doc. 695.

36. Memorandum by the Operations Coordinating Board Working Group on Iceland to the Board Assistants of the Operations Coordinating Board, December 7, 1954, *FRUS*, 1952–1954, vol. 6, doc. 706.

37. Memorandum by the Executive Secretary of the National Security Council to the National Security Council, July 12, 1954, *FRUS*, 1952–1954, vol. 6, doc. 705.

38. Johannesson 2004, 118–19; Memorandum by the Director of the Office of British Commonwealth and Northern European Affairs to the Operations Coordinator, May 28, 1954, *FRUS*, 1952–1954, vol. 6, doc. 704; Memorandum by the Executive Secretary of the National Security Council to the National Security Council, July 12, 1954, *FRUS*, 1952–1954, vol. 6, doc. 705.

39. *FRUS*, 1952–1954, vol. 6, docs. 696–703, 706.

40. Letter from Secretary of State Dulles to Foreign Minister Cunha, April 7, 1956, *FRUS*, 1955–1957, vol. 27, doc. 151.

41. National Security Council Report, May 20, 1957, *FRUS*, 1955–1957, vol. 27, doc. 179; Telegram from the United States Delegation at the NATO Heads of Government Meeting to the Department of State, December 17, 1957, *FRUS*, 1955–1957, vol. 4, doc. 75.

42. National Security Council Report, May 20, 1957, *FRUS*, 1955–1957, vol. 27, doc. 179.

43. National Security Council Report, May 20, 1957, *FRUS*, 1955–1957, vol. 27, doc. 179; Northern European Chiefs of Mission Conference, London September 19–21, 1957, undated, *FRUS*, 1955–1957, vol. 4, doc. 253; Telegram from the United States Delegation at the North Atlantic Council Ministerial Meeting to the Department of State, December 13, 1956, *FRUS*, 1955–1957, vol. 4, doc. 48.

44. Johannesson 2004, 120; Memorandum of a Conversation, Department of State, Washington, October 24, 1957, *FRUS*, 1955–1957, vol. 4, doc. 58; Report by the Operations Coordinating Board, June 25, 1958, *FRUS*, 1958–1960, vol. 7 (pt. 2), doc. 293; Report by the NSC Planning Board, December 29, 1960, *FRUS*, 1958–1960, vol. 7 (pt. 2), doc. 298.

45. Preliminary Notes of the Operations Coordinating Board Meeting, May 7, 1958, *FRUS*, 1958–1960, vol. 7 (pt. 2), doc. 292; Report by the Operations Coordinating Board, June 25, 1958, *FRUS*, 1958–1960, vol. 7 (pt. 2), doc. 293.

46. Memorandum from the Assistant Secretary of State for European Affairs to Secretary of State Dulles, September 3, 1958, *FRUS*, 1958–1960, vol. 7 (pt. 2), doc. 294.

47. Report by the Operations Coordinating Board, June 25, 1958, *FRUS*, 1958–1960, vol. 7 (pt. 2), doc. 293; Report by the NSC Planning Board, December 29, 1960, *FRUS*, 1958–1960, vol. 7 (pt. 2), doc. 298.

48. Johannesson 2004, 121–22.

Conclusion

1. Olson and Zeckhauser 1966; Morrow 1991.

2. Ninkovich 2004, 123. Nixon and Kissinger saw the center-right Christian Democrats as more reliable partners than Brandt's Social Democrats, with Nixon remarking, "I don't want to hurt our friends in Germany by catering to that son of a bitch [Brandt]" (Klitzing 2009, 103) and "any non-socialist government would be better" (Juneau 2011, 284).

3. Schwartz 2003, 147–49.

4. Powaski 1994, 80; Lanoszka 2018, 74–76.

NOTES TO PAGES 126–128

5. Schwartz 2003, 140–41; Sayle 2019, 133.

6. Welfield 1988, 295–99, 317, 335. The United States feared leftist influence in Japan, and on several occasions during the 1950s and 1960s it provided financial and other support to conservative Japanese politicians. A Department of State Guidelines Paper in early 1962 noted that "rule by the Socialists . . . would not only completely reverse the present trend of U.S.-Japan relations but could also precipitate a major and decisive power shift in Asia toward the Communist bloc with other Asian nations also swinging to a Communist-oriented neutralism." The ambassador to Japan noted in a July 1965 letter to Secretary of State Rusk that "the leadership of the ruling Liberal-Democratic Party" kept Japan aligned with the United States, but he warned that a growth of left-wing influence could jeopardize this. A State Department study in 1974 similarly concluded that "a left-wing government in Japan . . . would probably be inclined to abrogate the Security Treaty." National Security Council Report, April 9, 1955, *FRUS*, 1955–1957, vol. 23, 52–62; Memorandum from the Assistant Secretary of State for Far Eastern Affairs (Robertson) to the Secretary of State, January 7, 1957, *FRUS*, 1955–1957, vol. 23, 240–44; Editorial Note, *FRUS*, 1964–1968, vol. 29 (pt. 2), 1; Memorandum from the Ambassador to Japan (Reischauer) to Secretary of State Rusk, *FRUS*, 1964–1968, vol. 29 (pt. 2), 105; Memorandum from Richard Finn to Winston Lord, "Study on Forces at Work in Japan," April 23, 1974, Folder "Japan—NSSM 172 (5)," National Security Adviser's Files, NSC East Asia and Pacific Affairs Staff Files, Box 4, GRFL, 41; Department of State Guidelines Paper, undated [early 1962], *FRUS*, 1961–1963, vol. 22, 731.

7. Samuels 2007, 31–35; Smith 2019, 52–53.

8. Welfield 1988, 283–84, 292, 311–14, 320–23, 329.

9. Reischauer to Harriman, October 22, 1962, *FRUS*, 1961–1963, vol. 22, 745; Memorandum of Conversation between President Johnson and President Pak, November 1, 1966, *FRUS*, 1964–1968, vol. 29 (pt. 1), 205–7.

10. Greene 1975, 11; Welfield 1988, 329.

11. Curtis 1970, 863.

12. Summary Paper Prepared by the Interdepartmental Group for East Asia, August 2, 1971, *FRUS*, 1969–1976, vol. 19 (pt. 2), 237; Paper Prepared by the Interdepartmental Group for East Asia, undated, *FRUS*, 1969–1976, vol. 19 (pt. 2), 328.

13. Berger 1998, 98–101, 110–23.

14. Berger 1998, 101–4, 110–23; Cha 1999, 69–70; Komine 2014, 100–102, 110–11, 120.

15. Greene 1975, 78–87; Komine 2014, 100–102.

16. Nam 1986, 125, 156–57; Yong Lee 2011, 405–9, 416–17; Gul Hong 2011, 505–6.

17. Memorandum of Conversation, June 12, 1975, *FRUS*, vol. E–12, doc. 269; Telegram 9567 from Embassy in the Republic of Korea to the Department of State, December 3, 1976, *FRUS*, vol. E–12, doc. 290; National Security Council Meeting, "SALT," December 2, 1974, Box 1, National Security Adviser, National Security Council Meetings File, 1974–77, GRFL.

18. Oberdorfer 1997, 37–41; Y. Kim 2011, 459–60.

19. The Minister in Iceland to the Secretary of State, February 8, 1949, *FRUS*, 1949, vol. 4, doc. 54; Report by the Executive Secretary of the National Security Council to the Council, July 29, 1949, *FRUS*, 1949, vol. 4, doc. 173.

20. Minutes of the Twelfth Meeting of the Washington Exploratory Talks on Security, February 8, 1949, 3 p.m., *FRUS*, 1949, vol. 4, doc. 56; Policy Statement Prepared in the Department of State, May 15, 1950, *FRUS*, 1950, vol. 3, doc. 651; National Security Council Report, May 20, 1957, *FRUS*, 1955–1957, vol. 27, doc. 179; Northern European Chiefs of Mission Conference, London, September 19–21, 1957, *FRUS*, 1955–1957, vol. 4, doc. 252.

21. Minutes of the Sixteenth Meeting of the Washington Exploratory Talks on Security, March 7, 1949, 3 p.m., *FRUS*, 1949, vol. 4, doc. 92.

22. Memorandum by the Executive Secretary of the National Security Council to the National Security Council, July 12, 1954, *FRUS*, 1952–1954, vol. 6, doc. 705.

23. Policy Statement Prepared in the Department of State, May 15, 1950, *FRUS*, 1950, vol. 3, doc. 651.

24. The Administrator for Economic Cooperation to the ECA Mission in Iceland, March 17, 1951, *FRUS*, 1951, vol. 4, doc. 215; The Minister in Iceland to the Secretary of State, April 18, 1951,

NOTES TO PAGES 128–132

FRUS, 1951, vol. 4, doc. 217; The Secretary of State to the Legation in Iceland, April 20, 1951, *FRUS*, 1951, vol. 4, doc. 218; The Minister in Iceland to the Secretary of State, April 22, 1951, *FRUS*, 1951, vol. 4, doc. 219; Editorial Note, *FRUS*, 1951, vol. 4, doc. 221.

25. Johannesson 2004, 119–20. Report by the NSC Planning Board, December 29, 1960, *FRUS*, 1958–1960, vol. 7, doc. 298.

26. Memorandum by the Operations Coordinating Board Working Group on Iceland to the Board Assistants of the Operations Coordinating Board, December 7, 1954, *FRUS*, 1952–1954, vol. 6, doc. 706; Memorandum by the Executive Secretary of the National Security Council to the National Security Council, July 12, 1954, *FRUS*, 1952–1954, vol. 6, doc. 705; National Security Council Report, May 20, 1957, *FRUS*, 1955–1957, vol. 27, doc. 179.

27. Zimmermann 2002, 192–93, 199, 201–3.

28. Schwartz 2003, 163–64.

29. Welfield 1988, 296–300, 314–20, 332–38; Komine 2014, 110–14; Smith 2019, 40–41.

30. Blankenship 2021.

31. Johnson 1981, 7–9, 21–23, 38–40, 45–46; Nelson and Lepgold 1986; Nelson 1986, ch. 3; Mastny and Byrne 2005, 5, 80, 84; Crump 2015, 25–30.

32. Mastny and Byrne 2005, 9–10; Crump 2015, 20–33, 148.

33. Johnson 1981, 19–26, 29–33; Nelson 1986, ch. 4; Palmer and Reisinger 1990; Selvage 2008; Mastny 2008; Crump 2015.

34. Johnson 1981, 2–3, 8–11, 21–23, 26, 42; Mastny 2008, 144–5; Crump 2015, 27–28, 39–40.

35. Mastny 1998, 232–35; Mastny and Byrne 2005, 28–39, 84–90, 192–214, 264–69, 323–29; Mastny 2008, 148–50; Crump 2015, 134–48, 154–55, 160–62, 260–62, 265–66, 276–80.

36. Johnson 1981, 12–13, 17–19, 30–31, 39; Mastny and Byrne 2005, 47–49, 427–34; Mastny 2008, 147–53.

37. Johnson 1981, 6, 37–40, 45–46; Schweller and Wohlforth 2000, 86–90; Mastny and Byrne 2005, 537–40, 546–50, 559–61, 605–6; Zubok 2009, 267–70, 289–306, 321–24; Zubok 2021, 15–18, 20–22, 44–50; Christian Nünlist 2016. "Cold War Generals: The Warsaw Pact Committee of Defense Ministers, 1969–90." Parallel History Project on Cooperative Security, 2016, https://www.php.isn.ethz.ch/lory1.ethz.ch/collections/coll_cmd/introductiond6c9.html?navinfo=14565.

38. Goncharenko 1998; Zhang 1998, 193–200.

39. Westad 1998, 11–20; Weathersby 1998, 102, 109–10.

40. Westad 1998; Li and Xia 2014.

41. Friedman 2015, 26.

42. Westad 1998, 18–29; Goncharenko, 1998, 152–60; Zhang 1998, 200–17.

43. Radchenko 2009; Crump 2015; Friedman 2015, ch. 1.

44. "NATO Secretary General Visits Washington D.C.," NATO, June 2, 2022, https://www.nato.int/cps/en/natohq/news_196095.htm.

45. Meijer and Brooks 2021.

46. Christina Mackenzie, "Seven European Nations Have Increased Defense Budgets in One Month. Who Will Be Next?," Breaking Defense, March 22, 2022, https://breakingdefense.com/2022/03/seven-european-nations-have-increased-defense-budgets-in-one-month-who-will-be-next/; "Defence Expenditure of NATO Countries (2014–2021)," Public Diplomacy Division, NATO, June 27, 2021, https://www.nato.int/nato_static_fl2014/assets/pdf/2022/6/pdf/220627-def-exp-2022-en.pdf.

47. Jaroslaw Adamowski, "Estonia increases defense spending to buy air defense systems, more weapons," *Defense News*, March 25, 2022, https://www.defensenews.com/global/europe/2022/03/25/estonia-increases-defense-spending-to-buy-air-defense-systems-more-weapons/; "Lithuania to Ramp Up Military Spending, PM Says," *Reuters*, March 7, 2022, https://www.reuters.com/world/europe/lithuania-ramp-up-military-spending-pm-says-2022-03-07/; Tim Stickings, "Nato Member Latvia to Raise Military Spending to 2.5% of GDP," *The National*, March 30, 2022, https://www.thenationalnews.com/world/europe/2022/03/30/nato-member-latvia-to-raise-military-spending-to-25-of-gdp/; Ana-Roxana Popescu, "Poland to Increase Defence Spending to 3% of GDP from 2023," *Janes*, March 4, 2022, https://www.janes.com/defence-news/news-detail/poland-to-increase-defence-spending-to-3-of-gdp

NOTES TO PAGES 132–133

-from-2023; "Poland to Raise Defence Spending to 5% of GDP, Highest Level in NATO, Says Ruling Party Chief," *Notes from Poland*, July 18, 2022, https://notesfrompoland.com/2022/07/18/poland-to-raise-defence-spending-to-5-of-gdp-highest-level-in-nato-says-ruling-party-chief/. Greece's defense spending is so high in part because of its rivalry in Turkey, but also because it uses its military as a public works program and spends a substantial portion of its budget on personnel. Diego Urteaga, "Greece Boosts Its Defence Budget Because of the Threat from Turkey," *Atalayar*, January 11, 2021, https://atalayar.com/en/content/greece-boosts-its-defence-budget-because-threat-turkey; Jeremy Bender, "Greece's Military Budget Is Getting Bigger Even as the Country's Economy Lurches towards Mayhem," *Business Insider*, June 29, 2015, https://www.businessinsider.com/why-greeces-military-budget-is-so-high-2015-6.

48. "Who's Really Sending Aid to Ukraine?" *Wall Street Journal*, June 16, 2022, https://www.wsj.com/articles/whos-really-helping-ukraine-voloymyr-zelensky-france-emmanuel-macron-russia-11655410110.

49. Jonathan Masters and Will Merrow, "How Much Aid Has the U.S. Sent Ukraine? Here Are Six Charts," Council on Foreign Relations, December 16, 2022, https://www.cfr.org/article/how-much-aid-has-us-sent-ukraine-here-are-six-charts.

50. Christina Mackenzie, "Seven European Nations Have Increased Defense Budgets in One Month. Who Will Be Next?" *Breaking Defense*, March 22, 2022; Steven Keil and Martin Quencez, "Will the War in Ukraine Lead to Real Transatlantic Security Burden Sharing?" German Marshall Fund, March 22, 2022, https://www.gmfus.org/news/will-war-ukraine-lead-real-transatlantic-security-burden-sharing.

51. Ivan Krastev and Mark Leonard, "Peace versus Justice: The Coming European Split over the War in Ukraine," European Council on Foreign Relations, June 15, 2022, https://ecfr.eu/publication/peace-versus-justice-the-coming-european-split-over-the-war-in-ukraine/.

52. Tom Kington, "Italy Aims to Reach NATO Defense Spending Target by 2028, Four Years Late," *Defense News*, April 1, 2022, https://www.defensenews.com/global/europe/2022/04/01/italy-aims-to-reach-nato-defense-spending-target-by-2028-four-years-late/.

53. Melanie Amann et al., "Why Has Germany Been So Slow to Deliver Weapons?" *Der Spiegel*, June 3, 2022, https://www.spiegel.de/international/germany/olaf-scholz-and-ukraine-why-has-germany-been-so-slow-to-deliver-weapons-a-7cc8397b-2448-49e6-afa5-00311c8fedce.

54. Lukas Paul Schmelter and Bastian Matteo Scianna, "It's Time for Olaf Scholz to Walk His Talk," *Foreign Policy*, August 9, 2022, https://foreignpolicy.com/2022/08/09/scholz-germany-zeitenwende-ukraine-russia-war-bundeswehr-nato-defense-military-security/; Sophia Besch and Liana Fix, "Don't Let Zeitenwende Get Derailed," *War on the Rocks*, November 21, 2022, https://warontherocks.com/2022/11/dont-let-zeitenwende-get-derailed/.

55. Deni 2021, ch. 3.

56. "Germany Wavers on Military Spending," *Wall Street Journal*, May 8, 2022, https://www.wsj.com/articles/germany-wavers-on-military-spending-defense-berlin-olaf-scholz-ukraine-russia-nato-11651258628; Katrin Bennhold and Steven Erlanger, "Ukraine War Pushes Germans to Change. They Are Wavering," *New York Times*, April 12, 2022, https://www.nytimes.com/2022/04/12/world/europe/germany-russia-ukraine-war.html; Torben Schutz, Joseph Verbovszky, and Heiko Borchert, "Beware of Potemkin: Germany's Defense Rethink Risks Reinforcing Old Habits," *War on the Rocks*, April 11, 2022, https://warontherocks.com/2022/04/beware-of-potemkin-germanys-defense-rethink-risks-reinforcing-old-habits/; Laurenz Gehrke and Hans von der Burchard, "German Government and Opposition Agree on €100B Defense Spending Bill," *Politico*, May 30, 2022, https://www.politico.eu/article/germany-government-opposition-agree-100bn-defense-spending-bill/; Aylin Matle, "Making the Sea Change Real: What Germany and Allies Can Do," *War on the Rocks*, May 30, 2022, https://warontherocks.com/2022/05/making-the-sea-change-real-what-germany-and-allies-can-do/; Carlo Martuscelli, "Germany to Miss 2 Percent NATO Defense Spending Target: Think Tank," *Politico*, August 15, 2022, https://www.politico.eu/article/germany-to-miss-2-percent-nato-defense-spending-target-think-tank/; Sophia Besch and Liana Fix, "Don't Let Zeitenwende Get Derailed," *War on the Rocks*, November 21, 2022, https://warontherocks.com/2022/11/dont-let-zeitenwende-get-derailed/; Steven Erlanger, "When It Comes to Building Its Own

170

NOTES TO PAGES 133–134

Defense, Europe Has Blinked," *New York Times*, February 4, 2023, https://www.nytimes.com /2023/02/04/world/europe/europe-defense-ukraine-war.html.

57. Noemie Bisserbe, "France to Increase Defense Spending in Response to Russian Invasion," *Wall Street Journal*, March 2, 2022, https://www.wsj.com/livecoverage/russia-ukraine -latest-news-2022-03-02/card/france-to-increase-defense-spending-in-response-to-russian -invasion-56tWtAkB1kXUByKZ1Bvy; Christina Mackenzie, "France, UK Pledge Big Increases in Defense Spending for Coming Years," *Breaking Defense*, September 28, 2022, https:// breakingdefense.com/2022/09/france-uk-pledge-big-increases-in-defense-spending-for -coming-years/; Tim Martin, "UK Delays Defense Spending Increase, Raising Fears 3% GDP Target Will Be Axed," *Breaking Defense*, November 17, 2022, https://breakingdefense.com/2022 /11/uk-delays-defense-spending-increase-raising-fears-3-gdp-target-will-be-axed/; Clea Caulcutt, "Macron Proposes Major Boost to French Defense Spending Amid Ukraine War," *Politico*, January 20, 2023, https://www.politico.eu/article/emmanuel-macron-ukraine-war-volody myr-zelenskyy-major-boost-to-french-defense-spending/.

58. Deni 2021, chs. 2, 4.

59. Gesine Weber, "A Case for French Leadership on Ukraine," *War on the Rocks*, March 8, 2022, https://warontherocks. com/2022/03/a-case-for-French-leadership-on-ukraine/; "Russia Must Not Be Humiliated despite Putin's 'Historic' Mistake, Macron Says," Reuters, June 4, 2022, https://www.reuters.com/world/europe/russia-must-not-be-humiliated-despite-putins -historic-mistake-macron-2022-06-04/.

60. Sayle 2019, chs. 2–3, 6.

61. Bozo 2015.

62. Vucetic 2011.

63. O'Hara 2003; Hughes and Robb 2013.

64. "NATO's Military Presence in the East of the Alliance," NATO, June 1, 2022, https:// www.nato.int/cps/en/natohq/ topics_136388.htm; Matina Stevis-Gridneff, "NATO Doubles Its Battlegroups in Eastern Europe Ahead of Multiple Summits," *New York Times*, March 23, 2022, https://www.nytimes.com/2022/03/23/world/europe/nato-troops-ukraine.html; Kelly A. Grieco and Alec Evans, "Biden Should Nudge Europeans to Lead NATO," *Defense News*, March 22, 2022, https://www.defensenews.com/global/europe/2022/03/22/biden-should -nudge-europeans-to-lead-nato/; Gordon Lubold, David S. Cloud, and Lindsay Wise, "Ukraine War Complicates Biden Administration's Military Strategy on China and Russia," *Wall Street Journal*, March 21, 2022, https://www.wsj.com/articles/biden-administrations-military-strategy -juggles-russia-concerns-china-threat-11647872415; NATO, "Madrid Summit Declaration," June 29, 2022, https://www.nato.int/cps/en/natohq/official_texts_196951.htm.

65. Kyle Rempfer, "Troops Sent to Bolster NATO Begin Turnover as US Mulls Larger Footprint in Europe," *Army Times*, May 13, 2022, https://www.armytimes.com/news/pentagon -congress/2022/05/13/troops-sent-to-bolster-nato-begin-turnover-as-us-mulls-larger -footprint-in-europe/; Michael D. Shear and Steven Erlanger, "As NATO Announces Extra Troops in Europe, Biden Says It Will Be 'Ready for Threats in All Directions,'" *New York Times*, June 29, 2022, https://www.nytimes.com/live/2022/06/29/world/russia-ukraine-war-news#nato -will-sharply-increase-the-number-of-troops-it-keeps-on-standby; William Gallo, "After Russia's Ukraine Invasion, Baltics Push for Permanent NATO Presence," *Voice of America*, March 23, 2022, https://www.voanews.com/a/after-russia-s-ukraine-invasion-baltics-push-for-permanent -nato-presence-/6497246.html; Missy Ryan, Michael Birnbaum, Paul Sonne, and Steve Hendrix, "On NATO's Vulnerable Eastern Edge, Baltic Nations Face High Stakes in Ukraine Crisis," *Washington Post*, March 20, 2022, https://www.washingtonpost.com/national-security/2022/03 /20/ukraine-baltics-nato-russia/.

66. "Who's Really Sending Aid to Ukraine?" *Wall Street Journal*, June 16, 2022, https://www .wsj.com/articles/whos-really-helping-ukraine-voloymyr-zelensky-france-emmanuel -macron-russia-11655410110.

67. Natasha Bertrand, "NATO Officials Say Plan to Boost High Response Force to 300,000 'Still a Work in Progress,'" CNN, June 30, 2022, https://www.cnn.com/2022/06/30/politics /nato-high-readiness-force/index.html.

NOTES TO PAGES 134–140

68. Meijer and Brooks 2021.

69. Brian Blankenship, "Control versus Cost-Sharing: The Dilemma at the Heart of NATO," *War on the Rocks*, August 7, 2018, https://warontherocks.com/2018/08/control-vs-cost-sharing-the-dilemma-at-the-heart-of-nato/.

70. Schake 1998; Posen 2006; Shifrinson 2020; Rachel Rizzo, "The United States Should Rally behind European Strategic Autonomy," European Leadership Network, October 29, 2018, https://www.europeanleadershipnetwork.org/commentary/the-united-states-should-rally-behind-strategic-autonomy/; Ronja Kempin and Barbara Kunz, "Washington Should Help Europe Achieve Strategic Autonomy, Not Fight It," *War on the Rocks*, April 12, 2018, https://warontherocks.com/2018/04/washington-should-help-europe-achieve-strategic-autonomy-not-fight-it/; Steven Erlanger, "Europe Vows to Spend More on Defense, but U.S. Still Isn't Happy," *New York Times*, June 6, 2019, https://www.nytimes.com/2019/06/06/world/europe/us-defense-spending-nato.html.

71. Hunter 2002, 33–34.

72. David M. Herszenhorn, "Biden's Team Wants EU Allies to Get Real on 'Strategic Autonomy,'" *Politico*, November 19, 2021, https://www.politico.eu/article/joe-biden-us-eu-strategic-autonomy-brussels-g20/.

73. Portions of this paragraph are drawn from Blankenship 2021 (723) with permission from *Security Studies*.

74. Tago 2007; 2008; Kreps 2010; Henke 2019.

75. Zyla 2015, 2016, 2018.

76. Kertzer and Rathbun 2015. I thank Josh Kertzer for this suggestion.

77. Morrow 1994.

78. Gannon 2021.

79. Snyder 1997; Fearon 1997; Benson 2012; Posen 2014; Narang and Mehta 2019; Olson and Zeckhauser 1966; Sandler 1993; Martínez Machain and Morgan 2013; Posen 2014; Jakobsen and Jakobsen 2018.

80. See also Blankenship 2020; Kuo and Blankenship 2021.

81. For a similar point, see Lanoszka 2015.

82. Olson and Zeckhauser 1966; Gilpin 1981.

83. Gholz, Press, and Sapolsky 1997; Posen 2014; MacDonald and Parent 2018.

84. Norrlof 2010; Brooks, Ikenberry, and Wohlforth 2012.

85. On the importance of combining threats and assurances, see Davis 2000; Carnegie 2015; Kydd and McManus 2015; and Cebul, Dafoe, and Monteiro 2021.

86. Blankenship 2020.

87. Schelling 1966.

88. Pfundstein Chamberlain 2016.

89. Portions of the next two paragraphs are drawn from Blankenship 2021 (723–24) with permission from *Security Studies*.

90. Deni 2021.

91. Cooley and Nexon 2020.

92. Olson and Zeckhauser 1966.

References

Allen, Michael A., Julie VanDusky-Allen, and Michael E. Flynn. 2016. "The Localized and Spatial Effects of US Troop Deployments on Host-State Defense Spending." *Foreign Policy Analysis* 12 (4): 674–94.

Anders, Therese, Christopher J. Fariss, and Jonathan N. Markowitz. 2020. "Bread before Guns or Butter: Introducing Surplus Domestic Product (SDP)." *International Studies Quarterly* 64 (2): 392–405.

Art, Robert J. 1996. "Why Western Europe Needs the United States and NATO." *Political Science Quarterly* 111 (1): 1–39.

Bak, Daehee. 2018. "Alliance Proximity and Effectiveness of Extended Deterrence." *International Interactions* 44 (1): 107–31.

Barnett, Michael N. 1996. "Identity and Alliances in the Middle East." In *The Culture of National Security*, edited by Peter Katzenstein, 400–47. New York: Columbia University Press.

Barnett, Michael N., and Jack S. Levy. 1991. "Domestic Sources of Alliances and Alignments: The Case of Egypt, 1962–73." *International Organization* 45 (3): 369–95.

Bearce, David H., Kristen M. Flanagan, and Katharine M. Floros. 2006. "Alliances, Internal Information, and Military Conflict among Member-States." *International Organization* 60 (3): 595–625.

Beckley, Michael. 2015. "The Myth of Entangling Alliances: Reassessing the Security Risks of U.S. Defense Pacts." *International Security* 39 (4): 7–48.

Beckley, Michael. 2018. *Unrivaled: Why America Will Remain the World's Sole Superpower*. Ithaca, NY: Cornell University Press.

Bennett, Andrew, Joseph Lepgold, and Danny Unger. 1994. "Burden-Sharing in the Persian Gulf War." *International Organization* 48 (1): 39–75.

Bennett, D. Scott. 1997. "Testing Alternative Models of Alliance Duration, 1816–1984." *American Journal of Political Science* 41 (3): 846–78.

Benson, Brett V. 2012. *Constructing International Security: Alliances, Deterrence, and Moral Hazard*. New York: Cambridge University Press.

REFERENCES

Benson, Brett V., Adam Meirowitz, and Kristopher W. Ramsay. 2014. "Inducing Deterrence through Moral Hazard in Alliance Contracts." *Journal of Conflict Resolution* 58 (2): 307–35.

Berger, Thomas. 1993. "From Sword to Chrysanthemum: Japan's Culture of Antimilitarism." *International Security* 17 (4): 119–50.

Berger, Thomas. 1998. *Cultures of Antimilitarism: National Security in Germany and Japan*. Baltimore, MD: Johns Hopkins University Press.

Biddle, Stephen. 2004. *Military Power: Explaining Victory and Defeat in Modern Battle*. Prince- ton, NJ: Princeton University Press.

Bitzinger, Richard A. 1989. *Assessing the Conventional Balance in Europe, 1945–1975*. Santa Monica, CA: RAND Corporation.

Blackwill, Robert D., and Jeffrey W. Legro. 1989. "Constraining Ground Force Exercises of NATO and the Warsaw Pact." *International Security* 14 (3): 68–98.

Blankenship, Brian. 2020. "Promises under Pressure: Statements of Reassurance in U.S. Al- liances." *International Studies Quarterly* 64 (4): 1017–30.

Blankenship, Brian. 2021. "The Price of Protection: Explaining Success and Failure of U.S. Alliance Burden-Sharing Pressure." *Security Studies* 30 (5): 691–724.

Blankenship, Brian, and Erik Lin-Greenberg. 2022. "Trivial Tripwires? Military Capabilities and Alliance Reassurance." *Security Studies* 31 (1): 92–117.

Blechman, Barry M., and Stephen S. Kaplan. 1978. *Force without War: U.S. Armed Forces as a Political Instrument*. Washington, DC: Brookings Institution.

Boulding, Kenneth E. 1962. *Conflict and Defense: A General Theory*. New York: Harper & Row.

Boutton, Andrew. 2019. "Coup-Proofing in the Shadow of Intervention: Alliances, Moral Hazard, and Violence in Authoritarian Regimes." *International Studies Quarterly* 63:43–57.

Bove, Vincenzo, Leandro Elia, and Petros G. Sekeris. 2014. "US Security Strategy and the Gains from Bilateral Trade." *Review of International Economics* 22 (5): 863–85.

Bozo, Frédéric. 2015. "'I feel more comfortable with you': France, the Soviet Union, and German Reunification." *Journal of Cold War Studies* 17 (3): 116–58.

Brady, Steven J. 2004. "The U.S. Congress and German-American Relations." In *The United States and Germany in the Era of the Cold War, 1945–1990*, vol. 1, *1945–1968*, edited by Detlef Junker, 133–40. New York: Cambridge University Press..

Brooks, Stephen G., G. John Ikenberry, and William C. Wohlforth. 2012. "Don't Come Home, America: The Case against Retrenchment." *International Security* 37 (3): 7–51.

Budge, Ian, and Richard I. Hofferbert. 1990. "Mandates and Policy Outputs: U.S. Party Platforms and Federal Expenditures." *American Political Science Review* 84 (1): 111–31.

Bueno de Mesquita, Bruce, James D. Morrow, Randolph M. Siverson, and Alastair Smith. 1999. "An Institutional Explanation of the Democratic Peace." *American Political Science Review* 93 (4): 791–807.

Bueno de Mesquita, Bruce, and Alastair Smith. 2007. "Foreign Aid and Policy Concessions." *Journal of Conflict Resolution* 51 (2): 251–84.

Caldwell, Dan. 2009. "The Legitimation of the Nixon-Kissinger Grand Design and Grand Strategy." *Diplomatic History* 33 (4): 633–52.

Campbell, Kurt M., and Tsuyoshi Sunohara. 2004. "Japan: Thinking the Unthinkable." In *Nuclear Tipping Point: Why States Reconsider Their Nuclear Choices*, edited by Kurt M. Campbell, Robert Einhorn, and Mitchell Reiss, 218–53. Washington, DC: Brookings Institution Press.

Cappella Zielinski, Rosella. 2016. *How States Pay for Wars*. Ithaca, NY: Cornell University Press.

Carnegie, Allison. 2015. *Power Plays: How International Institutions Reshape Coercive Diplomacy*. New York: Cambridge University Press.

Catalinac, Amy L. 2010. "Why New Zealand Took Itself Out of ANZUS: Observing 'Opposition for Autonomy' in Asymmetric Alliances." *Foreign Policy Analysis* 6 (3): 317–38.

Cebul, Matthew D., Allan Dafoe, and Nuno P. Monteiro. 2021. "Coercion and the Credibility of Assurances." *Journal of Politics* 83 (3): 975–91.

Cesa, Marco. 2010. *Allies yet Rivals: International Politics in 18th-Century Europe*. Stanford, CA: Stanford University Press.

Cha, Victor D. 1999. *Alignment despite Antagonism: The United States-Korea-Japan Security Triangle*. Stanford, CA: Stanford University Press.

Cha, Victor D. 2016. *Powerplay: The Origins of the American Alliance System in Asia*. Princeton, NJ: Princeton University Press.

Chanley, Virginia A. 1999. "U.S. Public Views of International Involvement from 1964 to 1993: Time-Series Analyses of General and Militant Internationalism." *Journal of Conflict Resolution* 43 (1): 23–44.

Chapman, Terrence. 2011. *Securing Approval: Domestic Politics and Multilateral Authorization for War*. Chicago: University of Chicago Press.

Chapman, Terrence L., Patrick J. McDonald, and Scott Moser. 2015. "The Domestic Politics of Strategic Retrenchment, Power Shifts, and Preventive War." *International Studies Quarterly* 59 (1): 133–44.

Choi, Lyong. 2018. "Human Rights, Popular Protest, and Jimmy Carter's Plan to Withdraw U.S. Troops from South Korea." *Diplomatic History* 41 (5): 933–58.

Christensen, Thomas J. 2011. *Worse than a Monolith: Alliance Politics and Problems of Coercive Diplomacy in Asia*. Princeton, NJ: Princeton University Press.

Christensen, Thomas J., and Jack Snyder. 1990. "Chain Gangs and Passed Bucks: Predicting Alliance Patterns in Multipolarity." *International Organization* 44 (2): 137–68.

Clark, David H., Benjamin O. Fordham, and Timothy Nordstrom. 2011. "Preying on the Misfortune of Others: When Do States Exploit Their Opponents' Domestic Troubles?" *Journal of Politics* 73 (1): 248–64.

Clark, David H., Timothy Nordstrom, and William Reed. 2008. "Substitution Is in the Variance: Resources and Foreign Policy Choice." *American Journal of Political Science* 52 (4): 763–73.

Cohen, Raphael S., and Gabriel M. Scheinmann. 2014. "Can Europe Fill the Void in U.S. Military Leadership?" *Orbis* 58 (1): 39–54.

Cooley, Alexander, and Daniel Nexon. 2020. *Exit from Hegemony: The Unraveling of the American Global Order*. New York: Oxford University Press.

Crawford, Timothy W. 2003. *Pivotal Deterrence: Third-Party Statecraft and the Pursuit of Peace*. Ithaca, NY: Cornell University Press.

Crawford, Timothy W. 2021. *The Power to Divide: Wedge Strategies in Great Power Competition*. Ithaca, NY: Cornell University Press.

Creswell, Michael H., and Dietrich H. Kollmer. 2013. "Power, Preferences, or Ideas? Explaining West Germany's Armaments Strategy, 1955–1972." *Journal of Cold War Studies* 15 (4): 55–103.

REFERENCES

Crump, Lauren. 2015. *The Warsaw Pact Reconsidered: International Relations in Eastern Europe, 1955–1969*. New York: Routledge.

Curran, James. 2014. "The Dilemmas of Divergence: The Crisis in American-Australian Relations, 1972–1975." *Diplomatic History* 38 (2): 377–408.

Curran, James. 2015. *Unholy Fury: Whitlam and Nixon at War*. Victoria, Australia: Melbourne University Press.

Curtis, Gerald. 1970. "The 1969 General Election in Japan." *Asian Survey* 10 (10): 859–71.

Darby, Michael R. 1982. "The Price of Oil and World Inflation and Recession." *American Economic Review* 72 (4): 738–51.

Davis, James W. 2000. *Threats and Promises: The Pursuit of International Influence*. Baltimore, MD: Johns Hopkins University Press.

Deni, John R. 2021. *Coalition of the UnWilling and UnAble: European Realignment and the Future of American Geopolitics*. Ann Arbor: University of Michigan Press.

DiGiuseppe, Matthew, and Paul Poast. 2018. "Arms versus Democratic Allies." *British Journal of Political Science* 48 (4): 981–1003.

DiGiuseppe, Matthew, and Patrick E. Shea. 2021. "Alliances, Signals of Support, and Military Effort." *European Journal of International Relations* 27 (4): 1067–89.

Dorussen, Han, Emil J. Kirchner, and James Sperling. 2009. "Sharing the Burden of Collective Security in the European Union." *International Organization* 63 (4): 789–810.

Douglas, Jake A. 2014. "Commitment without Control: The Burdensharing Dilemma in the US- Japan Alliance." BA thesis, College of William and Mary.

Doyle, Michael W. 1986. "Liberalism and World Politics." *American Political Science Review* 80 (4): 1151–69.

Driver, Darrell. 2016. "Burden Sharing and the Future of NATO: Wandering between Two Worlds." *Defense & Security Analysis* 32 (1): 4–18.

Duffield, John. 1995. *Power Rules: The Evolution of NATO's Conventional Force Posture*. Stanford, CA: Stanford University Press.

Duke, Simon. 1989. *United States Military Forces and Installations in Europe*. New York: Stockholm International Peace Research Institute.

Dumbrell, John. 1996. "The Johnson Administration and the British Labour Government: Vietnam, the Pound, and East of Suez." *Journal of American Studies* 30 (2): 211–31.

Eichenberg, Richard. 1996. *Public Opinion and National Security in Western Europe*. Ithaca, NY: Cornell University Press.

Fang, Songying, Jesse C. Johnson, and Brett Ashley Leeds. 2014. "To Concede or to Resist? The Restraining Effect of Military Alliances." *International Organization* 68 (4): 775–809.

Fang, Songying, and Kristopher W. Ramsay. 2010. "Outside Options and Burden Sharing in Non- binding Alliances." *Political Research Quarterly* 63 (1): 188–202.

Fazal, Tanisha. 2007. *State Death: The Politics and Geography of Conquest, Occupation, and Annexation*. Princeton, NJ: Princeton University Press.

Fearon, James D. 1994. "Domestic Political Audiences and the Escalation of International Dis- putes." *American Political Science Review* 88 (3): 577–92.

Fearon, James D. 1997. "Signaling Foreign Policy Interests: Tying Hands versus Sinking Costs." *Journal of Conflict Resolution* 41 (1): 68–90.

Fearon, James D. 1998. "Bargaining, Enforcement, and International Cooperation." *International Organization* 52 (2): 269–305.

Flores-Macias, Gustavo A., and Sarah E. Kreps. 2017. "Borrowing Support for War: The Effect of War Finance on Public Attitudes toward Conflict." *Journal of Conflict Resolution* 61 (5): 997–1020.

Fordham, Benjamin O. 2011. "Who wants to be a major power? Explaining the expansion of foreign policy ambition." *Journal of Peace Research* 48 (5): 587–603.

Foster, Dennis M. 2008. "Comfort to Our Adversaries? Partisan Ideology, Domestic Vulnerability, and Strategic Targeting." *Foreign Policy Analysis* 4 (4): 419–436.

Fox, Annette Baker. 1959. *The Power of Small States: Diplomacy in World War II*. Chicago: University of Chicago Press.

Friedberg, Aaron L. 1988. *The Weary Titan: Britain and the Experience of Relative Decline, 1895–1905*. Princeton, NJ: Princeton University Press.

Friedman, Jeremy. 2015. *Shadow Cold War: The Sino-Soviet Competition for the Third World*. Chapel Hill: University of North Carolina Press.

Fuhrmann, Matthew. 2020. "When Do Leaders Free-Ride? Business Experience and Contributions to Collective Defense." *American Journal of Political Science* 64 (2): 416–431.

Fuhrmann, Matthew, and Sarah E. Kreps. 2010. "Targeting Nuclear Programs in War and Peace: A Quantitative Empirical Analysis, 1941–2000." *Journal of Conflict Resolution* 54 (6): 831–59.

Gannon, Andrés. 2021. "Use Their Force: Interstate Security Alignments and the Distribution of Military Capabilities." PhD diss., University of California, San Diego.

Gartzke, Erik, and Kristian S. Gleditsch. 2004. "Why Democracies May Actually Be Less Reliable Allies." *Amerian Journal of Political Science* 48 (4): 775–95.

Gaubatz, Kurt T. 1996. "Democratic States and Commitment in International Relations." *International Organization* 50 (1): 109–39.

Gavin, Francis J. 2004. *Gold, Dollars, and Power: The Politics of International Monetary Relations, 1958–1971*. Chapel Hill: University of North Carolina Press.

Gavin, Francis J. 2012. *Nuclear Statecraft: History and Strategy in America's Atomic Age*. Ithaca, NY: Cornell University Press.

Gavin, Francis J. 2015. "Strategies of Inhibition: U.S. Grand Strategy, the Nuclear Revolution, and Nonproliferation." *International Security* 40 (1): 9–46.

Gelpi, Christopher. 1999. "Alliances as Instruments of Intra-Allied Control." In *Imperfect Unions: Security Institutions over Time and Space*, edited by Helga Haftendorn, Robert O Keohane, and Celeste A Wallander, 107–39. New York: Clarendon Press.

Gelpi, Christopher, Peter D. Feaver, and Jason Reifler. 2009. *Paying the Human Costs of War: American Public Opinion and Casualties in Military Conflicts*. Princeton, NJ: Princeton University Press.

George, Alexander L., and Andrew Bennett. 2005. *Case Studies and Theory Development in the Social Sciences*. Cambridge, MA: MIT Press.

Gerzhoy, Eugene. 2015. "Alliance Coercion and Nuclear Restraint: How the United States Thwarted West Germany's Nuclear Ambitions." *International Security* 39 (4): 91–129.

Gholz, Eugene, Daryl G. Press, and Harvey M. Sapolsky. 1997. "Come Home, America: The Strategy of Restraint in the Face of Temptation." *International Security* 21 (4): 5–48.

REFERENCES

Gilli, Andrea, and Mauro Gilli. 2019. "Why China Has Not Caught Up Yet: Military- Technological Superiority and the Limits of Imitation, Reverse Engineering, and Cyber Espionage." *International Security* 43 (3): 141–89.

Gilpin, Robert. 1971. "The Politics of Transnational Economic Relations." *International Organization* 25 (3): 1971.

Gilpin, Robert. 1981. *War and Change in World Politics*. 1st ed. Cambridge, MA: Cambridge University Press.

Gleditsch, Kristian S. 2002. "Expanded Trade and GDP Data." *Journal of Conflict Resolution* 46 (5): 712–24.

Goncharenko, Sergei. 1998. "Sino-Soviet Military Cooperation." In *Brothers in Arms: The Rise and Fall of the Sino-Soviet Alliance, 1945–1963*, edited by Odd Arne Westad, 141–64. Palo Alto, CA: Stanford University Press.

Green, Michael. 1995. *Arming Japan: Defense Production, Alliance Politics, and the Postwar Search for Autonomy*. New York: Columbia University Press.

Green, Michael. 2017. *By More than Providence: Grand Strategy and American Power in the Asia Pacific since 1783*. New York: Columbia University Press.

Greene, Fred. 1975. *Stresses in U.S.-Japanese Security Relations*. Washington, DC: Brookings Institution Press.

Gul Hong, Sung. 2011. "The Search for Deterrence: Park's Nuclear Option." In *The Park Chung Hee Era: The Transformation of South Korea*, edited by Pyong-guk Kim and Ezra F. Vogel, 483–510. Cambridge, MA: Harvard University Press.

Ha, Joseph M., and John Guinasso. 1980. "Japan's Rearmament Dilemma: The Paradox of Recovery." *Pacific Affairs* 53 (2): 245–68.

Haas, Mark L. 2005. *The Ideological Origins of Great Power Politics, 1789–1989*. Ithaca, NY: Cornell University Press.

Haas, Mark L. 2014. "Ideological Polarity and Balancing in Great Power Politics." *Security Studies* 23 (4): 715–53.

Haftendorn, Helga. 1996. "The Nuclear Dilemmas of the Alliance: Revision of Strategy and the Nuclear Dilemma of NATO." In *NATO and the Nuclear Revolution: A Crisis of Credibility, 1966–1967*, edited by Helga Haftendorn, 111–99. New York: Oxford University Press.

Haftendorn, Helga, Robert O. Keohane, and Celeste Wallander, eds. 1999. *Imperfect Unions: Security Institutions over Time and Space*. Oxford: Oxford University Press.

Handel, Michael I. 1990. *Weak States in the International System*. 2nd ed. Portland, OR: Frank Cass.

Harrison, Hope M. 2005. *Driving the Soviets up the Wall: Soviet-East German Relations, 1953–1961*. Princeton, NJ: Princeton University Press.

Hayes, Peter. 1991. *Pacific Powderkeg: American Nuclear Dilemmas in Korea*. Lexington, MA: Lexington Books.

Haynes, Kyle. 2015. "Decline and Devolution: The Sources of Strategic Military Retrenchment." *International Studies Quarterly* 59 (3): 490–502.

Henke, Marina E. 2019. *Constructing Allied Cooperation: Diplomacy, Payments, and Power in Multilateral Military Coalitions*. Ithaca, NY: Cornell University Press.

Herring, George C. 1998. "Tet and the Crisis of Hegemony." In *1968: The World Transformed*, edited by Carole Fink, Philipp Gassert, and Detlef Junker, 31–53. New York: Cambridge University Press.

REFERENCES

Hirschman, Albert O. 1945. *National Power and the Structure of Foreign Trade*. Berkeley: University of California Press.

Horowitz, Michael C. 2010. *The Diffusion of Military Power: Causes and Consequences for International Politics*. Princeton, NJ: Princeton University Press.

Howorth, Jolyon, and John T. S. Keeler, eds. 2003. *Defending Europe: The EU, NATO, and the Quest for European Autonomy*. New York: Palgrave Macmillan.

Hughes, R. Gerald, and Thomas Robb. 2013. "Kissinger and the Diplomacy of Coercive Linkage in the 'Special Relationship' between the United States and Great Britain, 1969–1977." *Diplomatic History* 37 (4): 861–905.

Hunt, Richard A. 2015. *Melvin Laird and the Foundation of the Post-Vietnam Military, 1969–1973*. Washington, DC: Historical Office, Office of the Secretary of Defense.

Hunter, Robert E. 2002. *The European Security and Defense Policy: NATO's Companion—or Competitor?* Santa Monica, CA: RAND Corporation.

Hunzeker, Michael A., and Alexander Lanoszka. 2016. "Landpower and American Credibility." *Parameters* 45 (4): 17–26.

Izumikawa, Yasuhiro. 2018. "Binding Strategies in Alliance Politics: The Soviet-Japanese-US Diplomatic Tug of War in the Mid-1950s." *International Studies Quarterly* 62 (1): 108–20.

Jakobsen, Jo, and Tor G. Jakobsen. 2018. "Tripwires and Free-Riders: Do Forward-Deployed US Troops Reduce the Willingness of Host-Country Citizens to Fight for Their Country?" *Contemporary Security Policy* 40 (2): 1–30.

Jang, Se Young. 2016. "The Evolution of US Extended Deterrence and South Korea's Nuclear Ambitions." *Journal of Strategic Studies* 39 (4): 502–20.

Jervis, Robert L. 1976. *Perception and Misperception in International Politics*. Princeton, NJ: Princeton University Press.

Jervis, Robert L. 1980. "The Impact of the Korean War on the Cold War." *Journal of Conflict Resolution* 24 (4): 563–92.

Jervis, Robert L. 1989. *The Meaning of the Nuclear Revolution*. Ithaca, NY: Cornell University Press.

Jervis, Robert L. 1997. *System Effects: Complexity in Political and Social Life*. Princeton, NJ: Princeton University Press.

Jo, Dong-Joon, and Erik Gartzke. 2007. "Determinants of Nuclear Weapons Proliferation." *Journal of Conflict Resolution* 51 (1): 167–94.

Johannesson, Gudni Th. 2004. "To the Edge of Nowhere? U.S.-Icelandic Defense Relations during and after the Cold War." *Naval War College Review* 57 (3/4): 115–37.

Johnson, A. Ross. 1981. *The Warsaw Pact: Soviet Military Policy in Eastern Europe*. Santa Monica, CA: RAND Corporation.

Juneau, Jean-François. 2011. "The Limits of Linkage: The Nixon Administration and Willy Brandt's Ostpolitik, 1969–72." *International History Review* 33 (2): 277–97.

Kaplan, Lawrence. 1999. *The Long Entanglement: NATO's First Fifty Years*. Westport, CT: Praeger.

Kelleher, Catherine A. 1975. *Germany and the Politics of Nuclear Weapons*. New York: Columbia University Press.

Kennedy, Paul M. 1987. *The Rise and Fall of the Great Powers: Economic Change and Military Conflict from 1500 to 2000*. New York: Random House.

179

REFERENCES

Kertzer, Joshua D., and Brian C. Rathbun. 2015. "Fair Is Fair: Social Preferences and Reciprocity in International Politics." *World Politics* 64 (4): 613–55.

Khanna, Jyoti, and Todd Sandler. 1997. "Conscription, Peace-Keeping, and Foreign Assistance: NATO Burden-Sharing in the Post–Cold War Era." *Defence and Peace Economics* 8 (1): 101–21.

Khanna, Jyoti, Todd Sandler, and Hirofumi Shimizu. 1998. "Sharing the Financial Burden for U.N. and NATO Peacekeeping, 1976–1996." *Journal of Conflict Resolution* 42 (2): 176–95.

Kim, Seung-Young. 2001. "Security, Nationalism, and the Pursuit of Nuclear Weapons and Missiles: The South Korean Case, 1970–82." *Diplomacy & Statecraft* 12 (4): 53–80.

Kim, Tongfi. 2011. "Why Alliances Entangle but Seldom Entrap States." *Security Studies* 20 (3): 350–77.

Kim, Tongfi. 2016. *The Supply Side of Security: A Market Theory of Military Alliances.* Stanford, CA: Stanford University Press.

Kim, Yong-Jick. 2011. "The Security, Political, and Human Rights Conundrum, 1974–1979." In *The Park Chung Hee Era: The Transformation of South Korea*, edited by Pyong-guk Kim and Ezra F. Vogel, 457–82. Cambridge, MA: Harvard University Press.

King, Gary, Robert O. Keohane, and Sidney Verba. 1994. *Designing Social Inquiry.* Princeton, NJ: Princeton University Press.

Kissinger, Henry. 1979. *White House Years.* Boston: Little, Brown.

Klingemann, Hans-Dieter, Richard Hofferbert, and Ian Budge. 1994. *Parties, Politics, and Democracy.* Boulder, CO: Westview Press.

Klitzing, Holger. 2009. "To Grin and Bear It: The Nixon Administration and Ostpolitik." In *Ostpolitik, 1969–1974: European and Global Responses*, edited by Carole Fink and Bernd Schaefer, 80–110. New York: Cambridge University Press.

Komine, Yukinori. 2014. "Whither a 'Resurgent Japan': The Nixon Doctrine and Japan's Defense Buildup, 1969–1976." *Journal of Cold War Studies* 16 (3): 88–128.

Krebs, Ronald R., and Jennifer Spindel. 2018. "Divided Priorities: Why and When Allies Differ over Military Intervention." *Security Studies* 27 (4): 575–606.

Kreps, Sarah E. 2010. *Coalitions of Convenience: United States Military Interventions after the Cold War.* New York: Oxford University Press.

Kreps, Sarah E. 2018. *Taxing Wars: The American Way of War Finance and the Decline of Democracy.* New York: Oxford University Press.

Kuo, Raymond. 2021. *Following the Leader: International Order, Alliance Strategies, and Emulation.* Palo Alto, CA: Stanford University Press.

Kuo, Raymond, and Brian Blankenship. 2021. "Deterrence and Restraint: Do Joint Military Exercises Escalate Conflict?" *Journal of Conflict Resolution* 66 (1): 3–31.

Kydd, Andrew H. 1997. "Sheep in Sheep's Clothing: Why Security Seekers Do Not Fight Each Other." *Security Studies* 7 (1): 114–55.

Kydd, Andrew H., and Roseanne W. McManus. 2015. "Threats and Assurances in Crisis Bargaining." *Journal of Conflict Resolution* 61 (2): 325–38.

Lake, David A. 1999. *Entangling Relations: American Foreign Policy in Its Century.* Princeton, NJ: Princeton University Press.

Lake, David A. 2007. "Escape from the State of Nature: Authority and Hierarchy in World Politics." *International Security* 32 (1): 47–79.

REFERENCES

Lake, David A. 2009. *Hierarchy in International Relations*. Ithaca, NY: Cornell University Press.

Lanoszka, Alexander. 2015. "Do Allies Really Free-Ride?" *Survival* 57 (3): 133–52.

Lanoszka, Alexander. 2018. *Atomic Assurance: The Alliance Politics of Nuclear Proliferation*. Ithaca, NY: Cornell University Press.

Lanoszka, Alexander. 2022. *Military Alliances in the Twenty-First Century*. London: Polity.

Large, David Clay. 1996. *Germans to the Front: West German Rearmament in the Adenauer Era*. Chapel Hill: University of North Carolina Press.

Lee, James. 2020. "US Grand Strategy and the Origins of the Developmental State." *Journal of Strategic Studies* 43 (5): 737–61.

Lee, Jong-Sup, and Uk Heo. 2002. *The U.S.-South Korean Alliance, 1961–1988: Free-Riding or Bargaining?* Lewiston, NY: Edwin Mellen.

Leeds, Brett Ashley. 2003a. "Alliance Reliability in Times of War: Explaining State Decisions to Violate Treaties." *International Organization* 57 (4): 801–27.

Leeds, Brett Ashley. 2003b. "Do Alliances Deter Aggression? The Influence of Military Alliances on the Initiation of Militarized Interstate Disputes." *American Journal of Political Science* 47 (3): 427–39.

Leeds, Brett Ashley, and Sezi Anac. 2005. "Alliance Institutionalization and Alliance Performance." *International Interactions* 31 (3): 183–202.

Leeds, Brett Ashley, Andrew G. Long, and Sara McLaughlin Mitchell. 2000. "Reevaluating Alliance Reliability: Specific Threats, Specific Promises." *Journal of Conflict Resolution* 44 (5): 686–99.

Leeds, Brett Ashley, Michaela Mattes, and Jeremy S. Vogel. 2009. "Interests, Institutions, and the Reliability of International Commitments." *American Journal of Political Science* 53 (2): 461–76.

Leeds, Brett Ashley, Jeffrey Ritter, Sara Mitchell, and Andrew Long. 2002. "Alliance Treaty Obligations and Provisions, 1815–1944." *International Interactions* 28 (3): 237–60.

Leeds, Brett Ashley, and Burcu Savun. 2007. "Terminating Alliances: Why Do States Abrogate Agreements?" *Journal of Politics* 69 (4): 1118–32.

Lepgold, Joseph. 1990. *The Declining Hegemon: The United States and European Defense, 1960–1990*. New York: Praeger.

Levy, Jack S., and William R. Thompson. 2010. "Balancing on Land and at Sea: Do States Ally against the Leading Global Power?" *International Security* 35 (1): 7–43.

Li, Danhui, and Yafeng Xia. 2014. "Jockeying for Leadership." *Journal of Cold War Studies* 16 (1): 24–60.

Lieber, Keir A., and Daryl G. Press. 2020. *The Myth of the Nuclear Revolution: Power Politics in the Atomic Age*. Ithaca, NY: Cornell University Press.

Lieberman, Evan S. 2005. "Nested Analysis as a Mixed-Method Strategy for Comparative Research." *American Political Science Review* 99 (3): 435–52.

Lind, Jennifer M. 2004. "Pacifism or Passing the Buck? Testing Theories of Japanese Security Policy." *International Security* 29 (1): 92–121.

Liska, George. 1962. *Nations in Alliance*. Baltimore, MD: Johns Hopkins University Press.

Litwak, Robert S. 1986. *Detente and the Nixon Doctrine: American Foreign Policy and the Pursuit of Stability, 1969–1976*. New York: Cambridge University Press.

REFERENCES

Long, Andrew G., and Brett Ashley Leeds. 2006. "Trading for Security: Military Alliances and Economic Agreements." *Journal of Peace Research* 43 (4): 433–51.

Ludvik, Jan. 2018. "Closing the Window of Vulnerability: Nuclear Proliferation and Conventional Retaliation." *Security Studies* 28 (1): 87–115.

Lundestad, Geir. 2003. *The United States and Western Europe since 1945*. New York: Oxford University Press.

MacDonald, Paul K., and Joseph M. Parent. 2018. *Twilight of the Titans: Great Power Decline and Retrenchment*. Ithaca, NY: Cornell University Press.

Martínez Machain, Carla, and T. Clifton Morgan. 2013. "The Effect of US Troop Deployment on Host States' Foreign Policy." *Armed Forces & Society* 39 (1): 102–23.

Mastanduno, Michael. 1992. *Economic Containment: CoCom and the Politics of East-West Trade*. Ithaca, NY: Cornell University Press.

Mastanduno, Michael. 2009. "System Maker and Privilege Taker: U.S. Power and the International Political Economy." *World Politics* 61 (1): 121–54.

Mastny, Vojtech. 1998. "'We are in a bind': Polish and Czechoslovak Attempts at Reforming the Warsaw Pact, 1956–1969." In *Cold War Flashpoints*, Cold War International History Project, 230–50. Washington, DC: Woodrow Wilson International Center for Scholars.

Mastny, Vojtech. 2008. "The Warsaw Pact: An Alliance in Search of a Purpose." In *NATO and the Warsaw Pact: Intra-Bloc Conflicts*, edited by Mary Ann Heiss and S. Victor Papacosma, 141–60. Kent, OH: Kent State University Press.

Mastny, Vojtech, and Malcolm Byrne, eds. 2005. *A Cardboard Castle? An Inside History of the Warsaw Pact, 1955–1991*. New York: Central European University Press.

Mattes, Michaela. 2012. "Reputation, Symmetry, and Alliance Design." *International Organization* 66 (4): 679–707.

Mazarr, Michael J., Arthur Chan, Alyssa Demus, Bryan Frederick, Alireza Nader, Stephanie Pezard, Julia A. Thompson, and Elina Treyger. 2018. *What Deters and Why: Exploring Requirements for Effective Deterrence of Interstate Aggression*. Santa Monica, CA: RAND Corporation.

McLaurin, Ronald D. 1988. "Security Relations: Burden-Sharing in a Changing Security Environment." In *Alliance under Tension: The Evolution of South Korean--U.S. Relations*, by Manwoo Lee, Ronald D. McLaurin, and Chung-in Moon, 157–90. Boulder, CO: Westview Press.

McLean, David. 2001. "Australia in the Cold War: A Historiographical Review." *International History Review* 23 (2): 299–321.

McManus, Roseanne W. 2014. "Fighting Words: The Effectiveness of Statements of Resolve in International Conflict." *Journal of Peace Research* 51 (6): 726–40.

McManus, Roseanne W. 2018. "Making It Personal: The Role of Leader-Specific Signals in Extended Deterrence." *Journal of Politics* 80 (3): 982–95.

Mearsheimer, John J. 1983. *Conventional Deterrence*. Ithaca, NY: Cornell University Press.

Mearsheimer, John J. 2001. *The Tragedy of Great Power Politics*. New York: W. W. Norton.

Meijer, Hugo, and Stephen G. Brooks. 2021. "Illusions of Autonomy: Why Europe Cannot Provide for Its Security If the United States Pulls Back." *International Security* 45 (4): 7–43.

Miller, Nicholas L. 2014. "Nuclear Dominoes: A Self-Defeating Prophecy?" *Security Studies* 23 (1): 33–73.

Monteiro, Nuno P. 2014. *Theory of Unipolar Politics*. New York: Cambridge University Press.

Monteiro, Nuno P., and Alexandre Debs. 2017. *Nuclear Politics: The Strategic Causes of Proliferation*. New York: Cambridge University Press.

Moon, Chung-in. 1988. "Influencing Washington: An Analysis of the South Korean Lobby in the United States." In *Alliance under Tension: The Evolution of South Korean-U.S. Relations*, by Manwoo Lee, Ronald D. McLaurin, and Chung-in Moon, 103–27. Boulder, CO: Westview Press.

Morgan, Patrick M. 1983. *Deterrence: A Conceptual Analysis*. 2nd ed. Beverly Hills, CA: Sage.

Morrow, James D. 1991. "Alliances and Asymmetry: An Alternative to the Capability Aggregation Model of Alliances." *American Journal of Political Science* 35 (4): 904–33.

Morrow, James D. 1994. "Alliances, Credibility, and Peacetime Costs." *Journal of Conflict Resolution* 38 (2): 270–97.

Morrow, James D. 2000. "Alliances: Why Write Them Down?" *Annual Review of Political Science* 3:63–83.

Mueller, John E. 1973. *War, Presidents, and Public Opinion*. New York: Wiley.

Murdoch, James C., and Todd Sandler. 1984. "Complementarity, Free Riding, and the Military Expenditures of NATO Allies." *Journal of Public Economics* 25 (1): 83–101.

Nam, Joo-Hong. 1986. *America's Commitment to South Korea: The First Decade of the Nixon Doctrine*. New York: Cambridge University Press.

Narang, Neil, and Rupal N. Mehta. 2019. "The Unforeseen Consequences of Extended Deterrence: Moral Hazard in a Nuclear Client State." *Journal of Conflict Resolution* 63 (1): 218–50.

Nelson, Daniel N. 1986. *Alliance Behavior in the Warsaw Pact*. Boulder, CO: Westview Press.

Nelson, Daniel N., and Joseph Lepgold. 1986. "Alliances and Burden-Sharing: A NATO-Warsaw Pact Comparison." *Defense Analysis* 2 (3): 205–24.

Nelson, Keith L. 2019. *The Making of Détente*. Baltimore, MD: Johns Hopkins University Press.

Nichter, Luke A. 2015. *Richard Nixon and Europe: The Reshaping of the Postwar Atlantic World*. New York: Cambridge University Press.

Niksch, Larry A. 1981. "U.S. Troop Withdrawal from South Korea: Past Shortcomings and Future Prospects." *Asian Survey* 21 (3): 325–41.

Ninkovich, Frank A. 2004. "The United States and the German Question, 1949–1968." In *The United States and Germany in the Era of the Cold War, 1945–1990*, vol. 1, *1945–1968*, edited by Detlef Junker, 118–24. New York: Cambridge University Press.

Nixon, Richard. 1971. *United States Foreign Policy for the 1970s: Building for Peace*. New York: Harper & Row.

Norrlof, Carla. 2010. *America's Global Advantage: US Hegemony and International Cooperation*. New York: Cambridge University Press.

Oatley, Thomas. 2015. *A Political Economy of American Hegemony: Buildups, Booms, and Busts*. New York: Cambridge University Press.

Oberdorfer, Don. 1997. *The Two Koreas: A Contemporary History*. New York: Basic Books.

REFERENCES

O'Hara, Glen. 2003. "The Limits of US Power: Transatlantic Financial Diplomacy under the Johnson and Wilson Administrations, October 1964–November 1968." *Contemporary European History* 12 (3): 257–78.

Olson, Mancur. 1965. *The Logic of Collective Action: Public Goods and the Theory of Groups*. Cambridge, MA: Harvard University Press.

Olson, Mancur, and Richard Zeckhauser. 1966. "An Economic Theory of Alliances." *Review of Economics and Statistics* 48 (3): 266–79.

Oneal, John R. 1990. "The Theory of Collective Action and Burden Sharing in NATO." *International Organization* 44 (3): 379–402.

Oneal, John R., and Mark A. Elrod. 1989. "NATO Burden Sharing and the Forces of Change." *International Studies Quarterly* 33 (4): 435–56.

Owen, John, IV. 1997. *Liberal Peace, Liberal War: American Politics and International Security*. Ithaca, NY: Cornell University Press.

Owsiak, Andrew P., and Derrick V. Frazier. 2014. "The Conflict Management Efforts of Allies in Interstate Disputes." *Foreign Policy Analysis* 10 (3): 243–64.

Palmer, Glenn. 1990a. "Alliance Politics and Issue Areas: Determinants of Defense Spending." *American Journal of Political Science* 34 (1): 190–211.

Palmer, Glenn. 1990b. "Corralling the Free Rider: Deterrence and the Western Alliance." *International Studies Quarterly* 34 (2): 147–64.

Palmer, Glenn, Tamar London, and Patrick Regan. 2004. "What's Stopping You? The Sources of Political Constraints on International Conflict Behavior in Parliamentary Democracies." *International Interactions* 30 (1): 1–24.

Palmer, Glenn, and William Reisinger. 1990. "Defense Allocations in Eastern Europe: Alliance Politics and Leadership Change." *International Interactions* 16 (1): 33–47.

Pelt, Mogens. 2006. *Tying Greece to the West: US-West German-Greek Relations 1949–1974*. Copenhagen: Museum Tusculanum Press.

Peters, Dirk. 2010. *Constrained Balancing: The EU's Security Policy*. New York: Palgrave Macmillan.

Pfundstein Chamberlain, Dianne. 2016. *Cheap Threats: Why the United States Struggles to Coerce Weak States*. Washington, DC: Georgetown University Press.

Plümper, Thomas, and Eric Neumayer. 2015. "Free-Riding in Alliances: Testing an Old Theory with a New Method." *Conflict Management and Peace Science* 32 (2): 247–68.

Poast, Paul. 2019. *Arguing about Alliances: The Art of Agreement in Military-Pact Negotiations*. Ithaca, NY: Cornell University Press.

Posen, Barry R. 2006. "European Union Security and Defense Policy: Response to Unipolarity?" *Security Studies* 15 (2): 149–86.

Posen, Barry R. 2014. *Restraint: A New Foundation for U.S. Grand Strategy*. Ithaca, NY: Cornell University Press.

Powaski, Ronald E. 1994. *The Entangling Alliance: The United States and European Security, 1950–1993*. Westport, CT: Greenwood Press.

Pressman, Jeremy. 2008. *Warring Friends: Alliance Restraint in International Politics*. Ithaca, NY: Cornell University Press.

Putnam, Robert D. 1988. "Diplomacy and Domestic Politics: The Logic of Two-Level Games." *International Organization* 42 (3): 427–60.

Radchenko, Sergey. 2009. *Two Suns in the Heavens: The Sino-Soviet Struggle for Supremacy, 1962–1967*. Stanford, CA: Stanford University Press.

REFERENCES

Rapp-Hooper, Mira. 2015. "Absolute Alliances: Extended Deterrence in International Politics." PhD diss., Columbia University.

Rapp-Hooper, Mira. 2020. *Shields of the Republic: The Triumph and Peril of America's Alliances*. Cambridge, MA: Harvard University Press.

Rector, Chad. 2009. *Federations: The Political Dynamics of Cooperation*. Ithaca, NY: Cornell University Press.

Reed, William, and Daina Chiba. 2010. "Decomposing the Relationship between Contiguity and Militarized Conflict." *American Journal of Political Science* 54 (1): 61–73.

Reiter, Dan. 2014. "Security Commitments and Nuclear Proliferation." *Foreign Policy Analysis* 10 (1): 61–80.

Reiter, Dan, and Allan C. Stam. 2002. *Democracies at War*. Princeton, NJ: Princeton University Press.

Rockoff, Hugh. 2012. *America's Economic Way of War: War and the U.S. Economy from the Spanish-American War to the Persian Gulf War*. New York: Cambridge University Press.

Rosato, Sebastian. 2015. "The Inscrutable Intentions of Great Powers." *International Security* 39 (3): 48–88.

Russett, Bruce. 1990. "Economic Decline, Electoral Pressure, and the Initiation of International Conflict." In *Prisoners of War? Nation-States in the Modern Era*, edited by Charles Gochman and Ned Sabrosky, 123–40. Lexington, MA: Lexington Books.

Russett, Bruce. 1994. *Grasping the Democratic Peace: Principles for a Post–Cold War World*. Princeton, NJ: Princeton University Press.

Samuels, Richard J. 2007. *Securing Japan: Tokyo's Grand Strategy and the Future of East Asia*. Ithaca, NY: Cornell University Press.

Sandars, Christopher T. 2000. *America's Overseas Garrisons: The Leasehold Empire*. New York: Oxford University Press.

Sandler, Todd. 1993. "The Economic Theory of Alliances: A Survey." *Journal of Conflict Resolution* 37 (3): 446–83.

Sandler, Todd. 2017. "International Peacekeeping Operations: Burden-Sharing and Effectiveness." *Journal of Conflict Resolution* 61 (9): 1875–97.

Sandler, Todd, and John F. Forbes. 1980. "Burden Sharing, Strategy, and the Design of NATO." *Economic Inquiry* 18 (3): 425–44.

Sandler, Todd, and Hirofumi Shimizu. 2014. "NATO Burden Sharing 1999–2010: An Altered Alliance." *Foreign Policy Analysis* 10 (1): 43–60.

Sayle, Timothy Andrews. 2019. *Enduring Alliance: A History of NATO and the Postwar Global Order*. Ithaca, NY: Cornell University Press.

Schake, Kori. 1998. "NATO after the Cold War, 1991–1995: Institutional Competition and the Collapse of the French Alternative." *Contemporary European History* 7 (3): 379–407.

Schelling, Thomas. (1966) 2008. *Arms and Influence*. New Haven, CT: Yale University Press.

Schmitz, David F. 1999. *Thank God They're on Our Side: The United States and Right-Wing Dictatorships, 1921–1965*. Chapel Hill: University of North Carolina Press.

Schroeder, Paul W. 1976. "Alliances, 1815–1945: Weapons of Power and Tools of Management." In *Historical Dimensions of National Security Problems*, edited by Klaus Knorr, 247–86. Lawrence: University Press of Kansas.

REFERENCES

Schuessler, John M., and Joshua R. Shifrinson. 2019. "The Shadow of Exit from NATO." *Strategic Studies Quarterly* 13 (3): 38–51.

Schultz, Kenneth A. 1998. "Domestic Opposition and Signaling in International Crises." *American Political Science Review* 92 (4): 829–44.

Schwartz, Thomas Alan. 2003. *Lyndon Johnson and Europe: In the Shadow of Vietnam.* Cambridge, MA: Harvard University Press.

Schweller, Randall L., and William C. Wohlforth. 2000. "Power Test: Evaluating Realism in Response to the End of the Cold War." *Security Studies* 9 (3): 60–107.

Seawright, Jason. 2016. *Multi-method Social Science: Combining Qualitative and Quantitative Tools.* New York: Cambridge University Press.

Sechser, Todd. 2018. "Reputations and Signaling in Coercive Bargaining." *Journal of Conflict Resolution* 62 (2): 318–45.

Selden, Zachary. 2013. "Balancing against or Balancing with? The Spectrum of Alignment and the Endurance of American Hegemony." *Security Studies* 22 (2): 330–64.

Selvage, Douglas. 2008. "The Warsaw Pact and the German Question, 1955–1970: Conflict and Consensus." In *NATO and the Warsaw Pact: Intra-Bloc Conflicts*, edited by Mary Ann Heiss and S. Victor Papacosma, 178–92. Kent, OH: Kent State University Press.

Senese, Paul D. 2005. "Territory, Contiguity, and International Conflict: Assessing a New Joint Explanation." *American Journal of Political Science* 49 (4): 769–79.

Shifrinson, Joshua R. Itzkowitz. 2018. *Rising Titans, Falling Giants: How Great Powers Exploit Power Shifts.* Ithaca, NY: Cornell University Press.

Shifrinson, Joshua R. Itzkowitz. 2020. "Eastbound and Down: The United States, NATO Enlargement, and Suppressing the Soviet and Western European Alternatives, 1990–1992." *Journal of Strategic Studies* 43 (6/7): 1–31.

Simmons, Robert R. 1978. *The Pueblo, EC-121, and Mayaguez Incidents: Some Continuities and Changes.* Baltimore, MD: Occasional Papers/Reprints in Contemporary Asian Studies.

Singer, J. David. 1987. "Reconstructing the Correlates of War Dataset on Material Capabilities of States, 1816–1985." *International Interactions* 14 (1): 115–32.

Siverson, Randolph M., and Joel King. 1980. "Attributes of National Alliance Membership and War Participation, 1815–1965." *American Journal of Political Science* 24 (1): 1–15.

Smith, Sheila A. 2019. *Japan Rearmed: The Politics of Military Power.* Cambridge, MA: Harvard University Press.

Snyder, Glenn. 1965. "The Balance of Power and the Balance of Terror." In *The Balance of Power*, edited by Paul Seabury, 184–201. San Francisco: Chandler.

Snyder, Glenn H. 1997. *Alliance Politics.* Ithaca, NY: Cornell University Press.

Starr, Harvey. 2005. "Territory, Proximity, and Spatiality: The Geography of International Conflict." *International Studies Review* 7 (3): 387–406.

Stein, Arthur A. 1984. "The Hegemon's Dilemma: Great Britain, the United States, and the International Economic Order." *International Organization* 38 (2): 355–86.

Stravers, Andrew. 2021. "Pork, Parties, and Priorities: Partisan Politics and Overseas Military Deployments." *Conflict Management and Peace Science* 38 (2): 156–77.

Suhrke, Astri, and Charles E. Morrison. 1977. "Carter and Korea: The Difficulties of Disengagement." *World Today* 33 (10): 366–75.

REFERENCES

Sungjoo, Han. 1980. "South Korea and the United States: The Alliance Survives." *Asian Survey* 20 (11): 1075–86.

Swenson-Wright, John. 2005. *Unequal Allies? United States Security and Alliance Policy toward Japan, 1945–1960.* Stanford, CA: Stanford University Press.

Tago, Atsushi. 2007. "Why Do States Join US-Led Military Coalitions? The Compulsion of the Coalition's Missions and Legitimacy." *International Relations of the Asia-Pacific* 7 (2): 179–202.

Tago, Atsushi. 2008. "Is There an Aid-for-Participation Deal? U.S. Economic and Military Aid Policy to Coalition Forces (Non)Participants." *International Relations of the Asia Pacific* 8 (3): 379–98.

Tago, Atsushi. 2014. "Too Many Problems at Home to Help You: Domestic Disincentives for Military Coalition Participation." *International Area Studies Review* 17 (3): 262–78.

Talmadge, Caitlin. 2015. *The Dictator's Army: Battlefield Effectiveness in Authoritarian Regimes.* Ithaca, NY: Cornell University Press.

Thies, Wallace J. 2003. *Friendly Rivals: Bargaining and Burden-Shifting in NATO.* Armonk, NY: M. E. Sharpe.

Trachtenberg, Marc. 1999. *A Constructed Peace: The Making of the European Settlement, 1945–1963.* Princeton, NJ: Princeton University Press.

Trachtenberg, Marc. 2012. *The Cold War and After: History, Theory, and the Logic of International Politics.* Princeton, NJ: Princeton University Press.

Treisman, Daniel. 2004. "Rational Appeasement." *International Organization* 58 (2): 345–73.

Uslu, Nasuh. 2003. *The Turkish-American Relationship between 1947 and 2003: The History of a Distinctive Alliance.* Hauppauge, NY: Nova Science Publishers.

Van Hooft, Paul. 2020. "All-In or All-Out: Why Insularity Pushes and Pulls American Grand Strategy to Extremes." *Security Studies* 29 (4): 701–29.

Vasconcelos, Alvaro. 1988. "Portuguese Defence Policy: Internal Politics and Defence Commitments." In *NATO's Southern Allies: Internal and External Challenges,* edited by John Chipman, 86–139. New York: Routledge.

Volpe, Tristan. 2018. "Threatening Proliferation: The Goldilocks Principle of Bargaining with Nuclear Latency." In *Coercion: The Power to Hurt in International Politics,* edited by Kelly M. Greenhill, and Peter Krause, 312–30. New York: Oxford University Press.

Vucetic, Srdjan. 2011. "Bound to Follow? The Anglosphere and US-Led Coalitions of the Willing, 1950–2001." *European Journal of International Relations* 17 (1): 27–49.

Walt, Stephen M. 1987. *The Origins of Alliances.* Ithaca, NY: Cornell University Press.

Walt, Stephen M. 2009. "Alliances in a Unipolar World." *World Politics* 61 (1): 86–120.

Waltz, Kenneth N. 1979. *Theory of International Politics.* Boston: McGraw-Hill.

Weathersby, Kathryn. 1998. "Stalin, Mao, and the End of the Korean War." In *Brothers in Arms: The Rise and Fall of the Sino-Soviet Alliance, 1945–1963,* edited by Odd Arne Westad, 90–116. Palo Alto, CA: Stanford University Press.

Weitsman, Patricia A. 2004. *Dangerous Alliances: Proponents of Peace, Weapons of War.* Stanford, CA: Stanford University Press.

Welfield, John. 1988. *An Empire in Eclipse: Japan in the Post-War American Alliance System.* Atlantic Highlands, NJ: Athlone Press.

REFERENCES

Westad, Odd Arne. 1998. Introduction to *Brothers in Arms: The Rise and Fall of the Sino-Soviet Alliance, 1945–1963*, edited by Odd Arne Westad, 1–46. Palo Alto, CA: Stanford University Press.

Williams, Phil. 1985. *The Senate and U.S. Troops in Europe*. London: Macmillan.

Yarhi-Milo, Keren. 2014. *Knowing the Adversary: Leaders, Intelligence, and Assessment of Intentions in International Relations*. Princeton, NJ: Princeton University Press.

Yarhi-Milo, Keren, Alexander Lanoszka, and Zachary Cooper. 2016. "To Arm or To Ally? The Patron's Dilemma and the Strategic Logic of Arms Transfers and Alliances." *International Security* 41 (2): 90–139.

Yoda, Tatsuro. 2006. "Japan's Host Nation Support Program for the U.S.-Japan Security Alliance: Past and Prospects." *Asian Survey* 46 (6): 937–61.

Yong Lee, Min. 2011. "The Vietnam War: South Korea's Search for National Security." In *The Park Chung Hee Era: The Transformation of South Korea*, edited by Pyong-guk Kim and Ezra F. Vogel, 403–29. Cambridge, MA: Harvard University Press.

Yost, David S. 1985a. *France's Deterrent Posture and Security in Europe, Part I: Capabilities and Doctrine*. Adelphi Papers. London: International Institute for Strategic Studies.

Yost, David S. 1985b. *France's Deterrent Posture and Security in Europe, Part II: Strategic and Arms Control Implications*. Adelphi Papers. London: International Institute for Strategic Studies.

Zelizer, Julian E. 2010. "Congress and the Politics of Troop Withdrawal." *Diplomatic History* 34 (3): 529–41.

Zhang, Shu Guang. 1998. "Sino-Soviet Economic Cooperation." In *Brothers in Arms: The Rise and Fall of the Sino-Soviet Alliance, 1945–1963*, edited by Odd Arne Westad, 189–225. Palo Alto, CA: Stanford University Press.

Zimmermann, Hubert. 1996. "'They have got to put something in the family pot!': The Burden- Sharing Problem in German-American Relations, 1960–1967." *German History* 14 (3): 325–46.

Zimmermann, Hubert. 2002. *Money and Security: Troops, Monetary Policy, and West Germany's Relations with the United States and Britain, 1950–1971*. New York: Cambridge University Press.

Zimmermann, Hubert. 2009. "The Improbable Permanence of a Commitment: America's Troop Presence in Europe during the Cold War." *Journal of Cold War Studies* 11 (1): 3–27.

Zubok, Vladislav. 2009. *A Failed Empire: The Soviet Union in the Cold War from Stalin to Gorbachev*. Chapel Hill: University of North Carolina Press.

Zubok, Vladislav. 2013. "Lost in a Triangle: U.S.-Soviet Back-Channel Documents on the Japan Factor in Tripartite Diplomacy, 1969–1972." *Journal of Cold War Studies* 15 (2): 51–71.

Zubok, Vladislav. 2021. *Collapse: Fall of the Soviet Union*. New Haven, CT: Yale University Press.

Zyla, Benjamin. 2015. *Sharing the Burden? NATO and Its Second-Tier Powers*. Toronto: University of Toronto Press.

Zyla, Benjamin. 2016. "NATO Burden Sharing: A New Research Agenda." *Journal of International Organizations Studies* 7 (2): 5–22.

Zyla, Benjamin. 2018. "Transatlantic Burden Sharing: Suggesting a New Research Agenda." *European Security* 27 (4): 515–35.

Index

References to figures and tables are indicated by "f" and "t" following the page numbers.

abandonment threats: alliance control theory on, 5, 12, 16–17; conditional pressure and, 16–17; credibility of, 2, 5–8, 28, 55, 62, 88, 108–9, 120–21; external threat environment and, 21; geography and, 8, 22, 23, 45; to Japan, 67; resource constraints and, 28; to South Korea, 1, 84, 88, 105, 107–8, 122; susceptibility to, 21, 22, 109; to West Germany, 1, 45, 46, 50–52, 59–63. *See also* troop withdrawals

Acheson, Dean, 39, 93, 114

Adenauer, Konrad, 42, 44–46, 50

AD-70 (Alliance Defense for the Seventies) initiative, 62, 63

Afghanistan, Soviet invasion of (1979), 21

Albright, Madeleine, 135

alliance control theory, 12–34; on abandonment threats, 5, 12, 16–17; alternative explanations, 29–31; on assurances of support, 5, 16–17; on asymmetric alliances, 5, 12–17, 30; on burden-sharing dilemma, 12, 14–16; on burden-sharing pressure, 5, 12, 16–29, 67, 88; on external threat environment, 5, 12, 17, 20–23; on latent military power, 5, 12, 17–20, 30; on resource constraints, 5, 12, 17, 27–29; summary of case study findings, 122–29, 123t; testing arguments of, 31–34, 33f

Alliance Defense for the Seventies (AD-70) initiative, 62, 63

alliances: coercive, 7, 8; during Cold War, 129–32; defined, 7, 144n30; democratic politics and, 7, 8; duration of, 8–9; economic theory of, 29, 37, 111–12, 140; institutionalization of, 8, 144n45; as tools of restraint and control, 10. *See also* alliance control theory; asymmetric alliances; burden-sharing; patron states; treaties; *specific alliances*

Alliance Treaty Obligations and Provisions (ATOP) dataset, 14

Anders, Therese, 18

antimilitarism, 31, 67, 75, 122, 126–27

ANZUS (Australia-New Zealand-United States) alliance, 21, 26

arms control agreements with Soviet Union, 55–57, 78, 94

arms race, 56, 77–78, 93, 107, 131

Article 5 obligations (NATO), 14

Asian Development Bank, 72

assurances of support: alliance control theory on, 5, 16–17; burden-sharing dilemma and, 14; conditional pressure and, 16–17; external threat environment and, 9; free-riding driven by, 3, 136; for Japan, 66, 67, 72, 73, 83; nuclear weapons and, 8, 44, 46, 73; policy implications, 137–38; risk-taking due to, 143n15; for South Korea, 73, 91–92, 95, 96, 108–9; theoretical implications, 136; treaties as, 10, 13–14; troop deployments as, 9, 30, 66; for West Germany, 36, 44, 46, 50, 54, 59, 64, 124

189

INDEX

asymmetric alliances: alliance control theory on, 5, 12–17, 30; bargaining in, 5; burden-sharing in, 3, 5, 12–17, 129, 136; control vs. cost-sharing in, 6, 9–11, 140; defined, 7; free-riding in, 3, 10, 140; public goods theory on, 3, 29–30, 67, 122, 124. *See also* patron states

ATOP (Alliance Treaty Obligations and Provisions) dataset, 14

Australia: rivalry with Indonesia, 21; Vietnam War and, 26, 90

Australia-New Zealand-United States (ANZUS) alliance, 21, 26

autonomous foreign policy, 3, 13, 15, 19, 30, 44, 49, 77–78

balance of payments deficit, 36, 40–42, 47–48, 50–56, 61, 64, 80

balance of power, 27, 34–35, 37, 39, 122, 125–26

Ball, George, 46

bargaining: in asymmetric alliances, 5; burden-sharing through, 4, 5, 9, 13; coercion in, 4; leverage for, 10, 13, 19, 91

Beckley, Michael, 18

Benediktsson, Bjarni, 113, 114

Benign Neglect cases, 24t, 26, 32, 112, 119

Berlin Crisis, 40, 46, 47, 63, 139

Biddle, Stephen, 146n29

Biden, Joseph, 132, 135

Brandt, Willy, 37, 49, 56, 58, 61–63, 125, 167n2

Bretton Woods monetary system, 40–41

Brezhnev, Leonid, 130

Bulgaria: NATO battlegroups in, 134; in Warsaw Pact, 129–31

Bundeswehr, 36, 42, 46, 50

Bundy, McGeorge, 50

Bundy, William, 70–72, 75

burden-sharing: in asymmetric alliances, 3, 5, 12–17, 129, 136; bargaining and, 4, 5, 9, 13; coercive, 6, 12, 16–17, 37, 134, 140; defined, 2–3; dilemma of, 6, 12, 14–17, 65, 110, 129; future research directions, 135–36; Goldilocks problem and, 5, 20, 120–21; literature review, 3–4; in NATO, 4, 21, 29, 132–35; selective encouragement of, 15–16; structural limitations of, 138–39

burden-sharing pressure: alliance control theory on, 5, 12, 16–29, 67, 88; Cold War and, 23; conditional pressure, 16–17; domestic politics and, 30–31, 67, 122, 125–29; effectiveness of, 1, 2, 6; external threat environment and, 17, 20–26, 22f, 24t, 120–21, 134, 139; generalizability of findings on, 129–35; geography and, 22–23, 73, 121, 138–39; Iceland, predictions for, 111–12, 112t; ideal-type outcomes of, 23–26, 24t; Japan, predictions

for, 67–70, 68t, 70t, 76, 76t; latent military power and, 17–20, 23–26, 24t, 30, 34, 120; resource constraints and, 17, 27–29, 76, 93, 110, 120–21, 138–40; South Korea, predictions for, 88, 88t, 90t, 93, 93t, 102, 102t; susceptibility to, 23, 30, 32, 110, 121, 126, 138; troop deployments and, 2, 4, 34, 124; variation in use and success of, 1, 17–29, 120–21; West Germany, predictions for, 36–37, 37t, 41–42, 42t, 47, 48t, 55, 55t. *See also* abandonment threats

Carter, Jimmy, 1, 102, 105–8

Cautious Success cases, 24t, 25, 26, 32, 36

China: burden-sharing based on fear of, 139; détente with, 79, 85; in external threat environment, 34, 68, 88; foreign aid to, 131; Japan, restoration of diplomatic ties with, 78, 85; Nixon's visit to, 78, 83, 94, 99; nuclear capabilities of, 72, 73; opening of, 78, 79, 83, 95, 99; rapprochement with, 28, 55, 83, 94; self-reliance of, 132; Soviet relations with, 131–32

Christian Democratic Party (Germany), 49, 125, 167n2

CINC (Correlates of War Composite Index of National Capability), 18

Cod War (1958–1961), 119

coercion: alliances and, 7, 8; bargaining and, 4; barriers to, 86; burden-sharing and, 6, 12, 16–17, 37, 134, 140; economic, 109, 124, 135; leverage gained through, 30; military, 109, 110; with nonshared adversaries, 20; strategies for effectiveness, 137, 138; vulnerability to, 19

Cold War: alliances during, 129–32; burden-sharing pressure during, 23; Communist bloc expansion during, 21, 26; NATO's role, 4, 23, 35–36; South Korea as central front in, 87; US foreign aid during, 25

Communist bloc: détente with, 77, 94; expansion of, 21, 26, 53, 87, 89; Iceland and, 117, 118, 127–28; Japan and, 66, 68, 69, 71, 78; rapprochement with, 77, 78, 125, 139; South Korea and, 87, 97, 124; threat perceptions of, 31, 34, 78. *See also* Soviet Union

conditional pressure, 16–17

conservation of resources, 5, 55, 77

constraints. *See* political constraints; resource constraints

control vs. cost-sharing: in asymmetric alliances, 6, 10–11, 140; burden-sharing dilemma on, 6, 14, 15; in Japan, 86; patron state management of, 9, 120; in Warsaw Pact, 131; in West Germany, 42, 44–46, 64

190

Correlates of War Composite Index of
National Capability (CINC), 18
Cost Imposition cases, 24*t*, 25, 32, 88
cost-sharing. *See* control vs. cost-sharing
credibility of abandonment threats, 2, 5–8,
28, 55, 62, 88, 108–9, 120–21
Crimea, Russian annexation of (2014), 25, 133
Cuban Missile Crisis (1962), 46, 57, 58
Czechoslovakia: Soviet invasion of (1968),
47, 53, 57, 64, 139; in Warsaw Pact, 130

defense spending: debt financing of, 3, 28;
domestic pressures to reduce, 27, 28;
economic growth in relation to, 128, 133;
Estonia, 4, 132; France, 133; Germany,
132, 133, 138; Japan, 66–67, 73–75, 74*f*, 80,
84–85, 126–29; Latvia, 4, 132; Lithuania, 4,
132; by patron states, 4, 27; Poland, 4, 132,
133; Romania, 132; South Korea, 1, 4, 87,
100–102, 101*f*, 105–7, 109, 124, 128; United
Kingdom, 133; United States, 58, 142*f*;
by Warsaw Pact members, 130; West
Germany, 4, 36–37, 42, 43*f*, 54, 62, 126, 128
democratic politics and alliances, 7, 8
détente: with China, 79, 85; with Communist
bloc, 77, 94; in foreign policy reorientations,
55, 56; resource constraints and, 28, 29;
South Korean views of, 97; with Soviet
Union, 31, 47, 56, 58–59, 62, 64, 67, 125
Dillon, Douglas, 70
domestic politics: burden-sharing pressure
and, 30–31, 67, 122, 125–29; internal repression of, 99, 103, 127; troop withdrawals and, 60; warfare tolerance and, 28
Dulles, John Foster, 1

East Asia: détente in, 94; external threat
environment in, 34; Japan's role in
regional defense of, 68; Nixon Doctrine
on, 77; retrenchment concerns in, 76–77;
US commitments in, 48, 67, 73, 76–77, 91;
US-friendly governments in, 19. *See also
specific countries*
East Germany, 35, 56–58, 62, 129–31
economic assistance. *See* foreign aid
economic coercion, 109, 124, 135
economic growth: defense spending in
relation to, 128, 133; differential rates
of, 27; in Japan, 66, 80, 92, 128; resource
constraints as hindrance to, 13, 18, 48; in
South Korea, 25, 32, 87–90, 93, 94, 100,
102, 122. *See also* gross domestic product;
surplus domestic product
economic recessions, 30, 51, 128
economic theory of alliances, 29, 37, 111–12,
140
EDIP (European Defense Improvement
Program), 62, 63

Eisenhower, Dwight, 38–39, 44, 69, 116
Erhard, Ludwig, 47, 49–53, 61, 125–26,
128–29
Estonia: defense spending by, 4, 132;
military capabilities in, 25
Europe: balance of power in, 35, 39;
burden-sharing pressure on, 1; defense
policy for, 2, 4, 39, 135; economic growth
in, 92; external threat environment in, 34;
Marshall Plan for, 19; strategic autonomy
in, 134; US-friendly governments in, 19.
See also specific countries
European Defense Improvement Program
(EDIP), 62, 63
external threat environment: abandonment threats and, 21; alliance control
theory on, 5, 12, 17, 20–23; assurances of
support and, 9; burden-sharing pressure
and, 17, 20–26, 22*f*, 24*t*, 120–21, 134, 139;
geography and, 8, 22–23, 34, 68, 86, 88;
for Iceland, 112, 119, 128; indicators of,
21–22; for Japan, 34, 67–69, 84–86, 127;
for South Korea, 34, 88, 127; for West
Germany, 34, 35, 47, 63–64

Fariss, Christopher, 18
Favorable Bargaining cases, 24*t*, 25, 32, 88
Federal Republic of Germany (FRG). *See*
West Germany
First Cod War (1958–1961), 119
fishing industry, 115–19
Flexible Response doctrine (NATO), 40, 52,
130, 148n22
Ford, Gerald, 82, 102, 104–8
foreign aid: to China, 131; to Iceland, 26,
111, 115, 115*f*, 118, 119, 128; Marshall Plan
and, 19; to South Korea, 87, 90, 91, 95–97,
100–105, 101*f*; to West Germany, 25, 53, 65
foreign policy: autonomous, 3, 13, 15, 19,
30, 44, 49, 77–78; economic issues related
to, 54; of left-wing parties, 31, 126; public
opinion as influence on, 77; reorientations
in, 55–56, 58, 78–79. *See also* burden-
sharing pressure; détente; rapprochement
France: defense spending by, 133; military
downsizing by, 40; Multilateral Force
opposed by, 44; nuclear capabilities of,
19, 38; South Korean nuclear assistance
from, 107–8; West German relations with,
46, 48–49; withdrawal from NATO
military command, 4, 19, 49, 134
free-riding: acceptance of, 10, 15, 16;
assurances of support as driver of, 3, 136;
in asymmetric alliances, 3, 140; burden-
sharing dilemma and, 6, 15; by Iceland,
111–12, 124; Obama on, 1; retrenchment
for mitigation of, 137; on West German
defenses, 63

191

INDEX

FRG (Federal Republic of Germany). *See* West Germany
Fuhrmann, Matthew, 30
Fukuda, Takeo, 77, 82
Fulbright, William, 48

Gavin, Francis, 148n22
GDP. *See* gross domestic product
geography: abandonment threats and, 8, 22, 23, 45; burden-sharing pressure and, 22–23, 73, 121, 138–39; external threat environment and, 22–23, 34, 68, 86, 88; South Korean vulnerabilities and, 87–89, 110, 121; West German vulnerabilities and, 55, 63, 121
German Democratic Republic. *See* East Germany
Germany: antimilitarism in, 31, 126; defense spending by, 132, 133, 138; geostrategic waterways near, 147n99; unification of, 44, 57. *See also* East Germany; West Germany
Gilpatric, Roswell, 75
Goldilocks problem, 5, 20, 120–21
Great Society, 92
Greenland-Iceland-United Kingdom (GIUK) Gap, 111, 113
gross domestic product (GDP): in Iceland, 32, 115, 115f; in Japan, 32, 71t, 80; latent military power and, 18, 32; in South Korea, 32, 87–88, 100; US share of global GDP, 145f; in West Germany, 32, 35
Grudging Cheap-Riding cases, 24t, 26, 32, 67
Guam Doctrine. *See* Nixon Doctrine

Habib, Philip, 96–100, 105
Handel, Michael, 21
Hassel, Kai Uwe von, 45, 50
hegemon's dilemma, 144n26
host-nation support (HNS), 75
Humphrey, Hubert, 91
Hungary: NATO battlegroups in, 134; Soviet interventions in, 129

Iceland, 111–19; accession to NATO, 4, 111, 114; base access provided by, 26, 32, 111–13, 116–19; external threat environment for, 112, 119, 128; fishing industry in, 115–19; foreign aid to, 26, 111, 115, 115f, 118, 119, 128; free-riding by, 111–12, 124; GDP and SDP in, 32, 33f, 115, 115f; latent military power of, 34; left-wing parties in, 112, 115, 118, 127–28; population of, 32, 33f, 111; predictions for burden-sharing pressure on, 111–12, 112t; in strategic context, 111, 113–15, 147n99; troops stationed in, 34, 112, 116, 125

inflation: debt financing and, 3, 28; in Iceland, 115; stagflation, 54, 76, 103; in United Kingdom, 133; in United States, 54, 76, 92, 103, 142f
Iran, Joint Comprehensive Plan of Action with, 21
isolationism, 36, 48, 60, 63, 129

Jackson-Nunn Amendment of 1973, 61, 63
Japan, 66–86; abandonment threats made to, 67; antimilitarism in, 31, 67, 75, 126, 127; assurances of support for, 66, 67, 72, 73, 83; China, restoration of diplomatic ties with, 78, 85; constitution of, 4, 66, 68; control vs. cost-sharing in, 86; defense spending by, 66–67, 73–75, 74f, 80, 84–85, 126–29; economic growth in, 66, 80, 92, 128; external threat environment for, 34, 67–69, 84–86, 127; GDP and SDP in, 32, 33f, 71t, 80; latent military power of, 32, 33f, 67, 69, 122; left-wing parties in, 67, 68, 126, 168n6; nationalism in, 70, 72, 77, 79; Nixon Doctrine and, 26, 66–67, 77, 79, 83–84, 86, 121, 122; nuclear weapons and, 67, 69, 73, 77–81, 85–86; Okinawa, US control of, 73, 154n19; population of, 32, 33f, 69; predictions for burden-sharing pressure on, 67–70, 68t, 70t, 76, 76t; rearmament of, 26, 68, 69, 75, 81, 82, 85; Self-Defense Forces of, 68, 84–85, 126, 127; self-reliance of, 67, 69, 71, 75–76, 79–80, 84–85, 127–28; in strategic context, 68–69, 147n99; troops stationed in, 34, 66, 67, 93, 124; troop withdrawals from, 77, 126
Japanese Communist Party (JCP), 68, 126
Johnson, Alexis, 79, 81, 83, 85, 129
Johnson, Lyndon, 41, 47, 49–54, 70, 73, 77, 89–92
JSP (Social Democratic Party of Japan), 68, 126

Kennedy, John F., 1, 40–42, 44–46
Khrushchev, Nikita, 40, 130
Kiesinger, Kurt, 49, 52, 125, 129
Kim Il-Sung, 103, 106
Kissinger, Henry, 54, 61, 77, 79–85, 95–97, 100, 151n126, 167n2
Korean War: cease-fire negotiations in, 87; NATO response to, 114, 116; Soviet involvement in, 131; threat perceptions following, 39, 89, 112, 115, 119, 128. *See also* North Korea; South Korea
Kubo, Takuya, 84

Laird, Melvin, 53, 56, 59–60, 80, 83, 95–97, 99
Lake, David, 13
Lanoszka, Alexander, 3–4

latent military power: alliance control theory on, 5, 12, 17–20, 30; burden-sharing pressure and, 17–20, 23–26, 24*t*, 30, 34, 120; GDP and, 18, 32; great power status vs., 146n28; of Iceland, 34; of Japan, 32, 33*f*, 67, 69, 122; nonmaterial forms of, 146n29; population and, 18, 32, 33*f*; SDP and, 18, 32, 33*f*; of South Korea, 32, 33*f*; of West Germany, 32, 33*f*, 35, 44

Latvia, defense spending by, 4, 132

Leeds, Brett Ashley, 144n30

left-wing parties: efforts to reduce appeal of, 19, 115; foreign policy preferences of, 31, 126; in Iceland, 112, 115, 118, 127–28; in Japan, 67, 68, 126, 168n6; in West Germany, 37, 125

Liberal Democratic Party (LDP), 68, 78, 79, 83, 84, 126, 168n6

Lithuania, defense spending by, 4, 132

Long, Andrew G., 144n30

Lord, Winston, 78

Macron, Emmanuel, 15, 133

Mansfield, Mike, 32, 48–53, 56, 57, 63, 64

Mansfield Amendments, 48, 56, 61, 62

Mao Zedong, 132

Markowitz, Jonathan, 18

Marshall Plan, 19

McCloy, John, 52

McGhee, George, 49, 51

McNamara, Robert, 45, 50, 51, 70

Meyer, Armin, 82

Miki, Takeo, 84

military coercion, 109, 110

military exercises, 50, 95, 108, 124

military power. *See* latent military power

military spending. *See* defense spending

military troops. *See* troop deployments; troop withdrawals

misery index, 142*f*

Mitchell, Sara McLaughlin, 144n30

moral hazard, 136

Morrow, James, 13, 29–30, 122

Multilateral Force (MLF), 44

Mutual and Balanced Force Reductions (MBFR), 56, 59

Mutual Defense Treaty (MDT), 87, 91, 109

Mutual Security Treaty (MST), 66

Nakasone, Yasuhiro, 84, 127

National Commitments Resolution of 1969, 56

nationalism, 42, 49, 70, 72, 77, 79

NATO: Article 5 obligations, 14; burden-sharing in, 4, 21, 29, 132–35; during Cold War, 4, 23, 35–36; Flexible Response doctrine, 40, 52, 130, 148n22; French withdrawal from military command of,

4, 19, 49, 134; Korean War and, 114, 116; left-wing skepticism of, 112; nuclear weapons and, 38, 40, 44, 56; strategic challenges facing, 37; Ukraine invasion and, 132–35; Warsaw Pact conflicts with, 19, 34, 47, 129; West German military integration with, 16, 25, 36, 39, 45, 65. *See also specific member countries*

neo-isolationism, 48, 63

New Look approach, 38–39, 116

New Zealand: ANZUS alliance and, 21, 26; base access provided by, 26; refusal to host US nuclear-armed submarines, 20–21, 26; during Vietnam War, 90

Nixon, Richard: on Brandt, 167n2; defense spending under, 28, 58; foreign policy reorientation by, 55–56, 58; on regional role for Japan, 80, 82; resignation of, 102; on South Korean self-reliance, 95–97, 100, 105; on troop withdrawals, 57, 59–61, 63, 94; Vietnam War and, 54, 55, 66, 77, 92, 93; visit to China, 78, 83, 94, 99

Nixon Doctrine: Japan and, 26, 66–67, 77, 79, 83–84, 86, 121, 122; objectives of, 2, 26, 58, 66, 77, 94; South Korea and, 94, 95, 98, 105

North Atlantic Treaty Organization. *See* NATO

North Korea: deterrence strategies against, 87; in external threat environment, 32, 34, 88; military power of, 89, 89*t*, 106, 110; USS *Pueblo* abducted by, 92, 99; South Korea, provocations against, 29, 89, 92, 98, 127. *See also* Korean War

Nuclear Nonproliferation Treaty (NPT), 50, 78, 79, 83–84, 107

nuclear weapons: arms race, 56, 77–78, 93, 107, 131; assurances of support and, 8, 44, 46, 73; China and, 72, 73; as deterrence, 8, 19, 38, 41, 59, 73, 83; escalation threat and, 38, 45; Japan and, 67, 69, 73, 77–81, 85–86; NATO and, 38, 40, 44, 56; New Look approach on, 38, 116; proliferation of, 3–4, 14, 107; South Korea and, 102, 107–10, 121–22; Soviet Union and, 39, 41, 44, 58; stability-instability paradox of, 8; strategic challenges involving, 37; submarines armed with, 21, 26; West Germany and, 40, 44, 48, 50, 127

Obama, Barack, 1, 134

offset payments, 36, 44–47, 49–52, 54, 60–65, 125, 129

Olson, Mancur, 29, 122

Operation Paul Bunyan, 108

Organization of Petroleum Exporting Countries embargo (1973), 103

Ostpolitik, 56, 58, 126

INDEX

Packard, David, 81
Park Chung Hee, 91, 92, 95, 97–100, 103–8, 127
patron states: abandonment threats by, 2, 5–8; competing priorities of, 5, 120, 140; control vs. cost-sharing and, 9, 120; defense spending by, 4, 27. *See also* assurances of support; asymmetric alliances; burden-sharing pressure; resource constraints; *specific countries*
Poland: defense spending by, 4, 132, 133; NATO battlegroups in, 134; in Warsaw Pact, 129–31
political constraints, 27–28, 67, 88, 121, 126–27, 135
political parties. *See* left-wing parties; right-wing parties; *specific parties*
population: of Iceland, 32, 33*f*, 111; of Japan, 32, 33*f*, 69; latent military power and, 18, 32, 33*f*; of South Korea, 32, 33*f*, 90; of West Germany, 32, 33*f*, 35
Porter, William, 95, 97, 99
Portugal, overseas empire of, 23, 40
Progressive Party (Iceland), 118, 127
public goods theory, 3, 29–30, 67, 122, 124
USS *Pueblo* abduction (1968), 92, 99

rapprochement: with China, 28, 55, 83, 94; with Communist bloc, 77, 78, 125, 139; with Soviet Union, 28, 31, 44, 56, 58, 64, 125; West Germany on, 44, 49
rearmament: Japanese, 26, 68, 69, 75, 81, 82, 85; West German, 4, 25, 36, 39–46, 43*f*, 48–50, 52, 117–18
recessions, 30, 51, 128
REFORGER (Return of Forces to Germany) exercise, 50
Reischauer, Edward, 70–71
Republic of Korea (ROK). *See* South Korea
resource conservation, 5, 55, 77
resource constraints: abandonment threats and, 28; alliance control theory on, 5, 12, 17, 27–29; balance of payments deficit and, 36, 40–42, 47–48, 50–56, 61, 64, 80; burden-sharing pressure and, 17, 27–29, 76, 93, 110, 120–21, 138–40; economic growth hindered by, 13, 18, 48; Vietnam War and, 29, 32, 34, 51, 64, 67, 86–87, 93
retrenchment: domestic pressure for, 6, 28, 32, 34, 48, 55–58, 85, 93, 138; East Asian concerns regarding, 76–77; for mitigation of free-riding, 137; Vietnam War and, 32, 34, 48, 55, 66, 93. *See also* troop withdrawals
Return of Forces to Germany (REFORGER) exercise, 50
right-wing parties, 31, 112, 147n96
Rogers, William, 57, 80, 96, 97

ROK (Republic of Korea). *See* South Korea
Romania: defense spending by, 132; NATO battlegroups in, 134; in Warsaw Pact, 130–32
Rostow, Walt, 52, 54, 78, 92
Rumsfeld, Donald, 108
Rusk, Dean, 45–46, 49, 53, 66, 70–73
Russia: annexation of Crimea by (2014), 25, 133; burden-sharing based on fear of, 139; Ukraine invasion by (2022), 132–35. *See also* Soviet Union

SALT I and II (Strategic Arms Limitations Treaties), 56, 78
Sato, Eisaku, 72, 73, 78, 80, 83, 84
Schelling, Thomas, 138
Schlesinger, James, 96, 104–5, 108
Schmidt, Helmut, 56
Scholz, Olaf, 133
Schroeder, Gerhard, 49
SDP (surplus domestic product), 18, 32, 33*f*
SEATO (Southeast Asia Treaty Organization), 145n12
Self-Defense Forces (SDF), 68, 84–85, 126, 127
self-reliance: alliance control theory on, 12; benefits and risks of, 2, 9, 15, 17, 19, 137; of China, 132; of Japan, 67, 69, 71, 75–76, 79–80, 84–85, 127–28; latent military power and, 30; of South Korea, 88, 90, 93–100, 102–9, 121, 128; of West Germany, 36, 44, 49, 58, 64, 124
signals of support. *See* assurances of support
Sneider, Richard, 105–8
Snyder, Glenn, 8, 14
Social Democratic Party of Japan (JSP), 68, 126
Social Democrats (Iceland), 118
Social Democrats (West Germany), 49, 56, 125, 167n2
Socialist Party (Iceland), 112
Sonnenfeldt, Helmut, 61
Southeast Asia: communist expansion in, 21, 26; economic development in, 82; troops stationed in, 53. *See also specific countries*
Southeast Asia Treaty Organization (SEATO), 145n12
South Korea, 87–110; abandonment threats made to, 1, 84, 88, 105, 107–8, 122; assurances of support for, 73, 91–92, 95, 96, 108–9; defense spending by, 1, 4, 87, 100–102, 101*f*, 105–7, 109, 124, 128; economic growth in, 25, 32, 87–90, 93, 94, 100, 102, 122; external threat environment for, 34, 88, 127; foreign aid to, 87, 90, 91, 95–97, 100–105, 101*f*; GDP and SDP in, 32, 33*f*,

194

INDEX

87–88, 100; geographic vulnerability of, 87–89, 110, 121; latent military power of, 32, 33*f*; Nixon Doctrine and, 94, 95, 98, 105; North Korean provocations against, 29, 89, 92, 98, 127; nuclear weapons and, 102, 107–10, 121–22; population of, 32, 33*f*, 90; predictions for burden-sharing pressure on, 88, 88*t*, 90*t*, 93, 93*t*, 102, 102*t*; self-reliance of, 88, 90, 93–100, 102–9, 121, 128; in strategic context, 89, 147n99; susceptibility to burden-sharing pressure, 23; troops stationed in, 34, 87, 88, 93, 98*t*, 124; troop withdrawals from, 1, 77, 91–92, 94–99, 102–10, 122, 127, 159n15; in Vietnam War, 90–92, 122; Yushin Constitution, 99, 127. *See also* Korean War

Soviet Union: Afghanistan invasion by (1979), 21; alliances involving, 7, 129–32; arms control agreements with, 55–57, 78, 94; Berlin Crisis and, 40, 46, 47, 63, 139; Chinese relations with, 131–32; Cuban Missile Crisis and, 46, 57, 58; Czechoslovakia invasion by (1968), 47, 53, 57, 64, 139; détente with, 31, 47, 56, 58–59, 62, 64, 67, 125; in external threat environment, 32, 34, 63–64, 68, 85, 88; Icelandic relations with, 117, 118, 125; military power of, 37, 38*t*, 58, 130; Multilateral Force opposed by, 44; need for collective defense against, 36; nuclear capabilities of, 39, 41, 44, 58; rapprochement with, 28, 31, 44, 56, 58, 64, 125. *See also* Cold War; Communist bloc; Russia

stability-instability paradox, 8
stagflation, 54, 76, 103
Stalin, Joseph, 130–32
Stein, Arthur A., 144n26
Stikker, Dirk, 42
Strategic Arms Limitations Treaties (SALT I and II), 56, 78
Strauss, Franz Josef, 45
submarines, 21, 26, 111, 114, 132
Suh Jyong-chul, 103
support signals. *See* assurances of support
surplus domestic product (SDP), 18, 32, 33*f*

Tanaka, Kakuei, 80, 83, 84, 128, 129
Team Spirit military exercises, 108
threats. *See* abandonment threats; external threat environment
treaties: ambiguity within, 13–14; as assurances of support, 10, 13–14; design of, 10, 145n51. *See also specific treaties*
troop deployments: assurances of support through, 9, 30, 66; burden-sharing pressure and, 2, 4, 34, 124; in Iceland, 34, 112, 116, 125; in Japan, 34, 66, 67, 93, 124;

in Southeast Asia, 53; in South Korea, 34, 87, 88, 93, 98*t*, 124; during Vietnam War, 47; in West Germany, 34, 36, 37, 45, 50, 124
troop withdrawals: for coercive leverage, 30; domestic pressure for, 27, 29, 36, 47–49, 64; from Japan, 77, 126; opposition to, 44, 51, 57–58, 96; risks associated with, 17, 49–51; from South Korea, 1, 77, 91–92, 94–99, 102–10, 122, 127, 159n15; from West Germany, 1, 45, 46, 49–54, 56–63, 124, 129
Truman, Harry, 39
Trump, Donald, 1, 4, 15
Turkey: susceptibility to burden-sharing pressure, 23; West German provision of aircraft to, 62

Ukraine: Crimea annexation by Russia (2014), 25, 133; invasion by Russia (2022), 132–35
unemployment, 54, 76, 92, 103, 142*f*
Unfavorable Bargaining cases, 24*t*, 26
Union of Soviet Socialist Republics (USSR). *See* Soviet Union
United Kingdom: balance of payments deficit in, 52; burden-sharing pressure on, 1, 134; defense spending by, 133; fishing dispute with Iceland, 116–19; inflation in, 133; military downsizing by, 40; Multilateral Force opposed by, 44; nuclear capabilities of, 38
United Nations Law of the Sea Conference, 119
US-Soviet Agreement on the Prevention of Nuclear War, 56, 78
USSR (Union of Soviet Socialist Republics). *See* Soviet Union

Vance, Cyrus, 92
Vietnam War: casualties resulting from, 92, 103; costs of, 36, 47–48, 54–55, 66, 76–77, 85, 88, 92–93, 159n22; criticisms of US conduct in, 26; political impact of, 102; resource constraints and, 29, 32, 34, 51, 64, 67, 86–87, 93; retrenchment and, 32, 34, 48, 55, 66, 93; South Korean involvement in, 90–92, 122

Walt, Stephen, 144n30
warfare: deterrence strategies, 8, 10; domestic politics and, 28; economic consequences of, 27–28; Japanese constitution on, 68; resource constraints and, 27, 29, 32, 34, 47–48, 51. *See also specific conflicts*
War Powers Act of 1973, 56
Warsaw Pact, 19, 34–35, 41, 47, 60, 64, 129–32
weapons of mass destruction. *See* nuclear weapons

195

INDEX

West Germany, 35–65; abandonment threats made to, 1, 45, 46, 50–52, 59–63; accession to NATO, 36; assurances of support for, 36, 44, 46, 50, 54, 59, 64, 124; Bundeswehr and, 36, 42, 46, 50; control vs. cost-sharing in, 42, 44–46, 64; defense spending by, 4, 36–37, 42, 43f, 54, 62, 126, 128; economic recession in, 51, 128; in era of diminished resources, 54–63; external threat environment for, 34, 35, 47, 63–64; foreign aid to, 25, 53, 65; GDP and SDP in, 32, 33f, 35; geographic vulnerability of, 55, 63, 121; latent military power of, 32, 33f, 35, 44; left-wing parties in, 37, 125; military integration with NATO command, 16, 25, 36, 39, 45, 65; nationalism in, 42, 49; nuclear weapons and, 40, 44, 48, 50, 127; offset payments from, 36, 44–47, 49–52, 54, 60–65, 125, 129; *Ostpolitik* in, 56, 58, 126; population of, 32, 33f, 35; predictions for burden-sharing pressure on, 36–37, 37t, 41–42, 42t, 47, 48t, 55, 55t; rearmament of, 4, 25, 36, 39–46, 43f, 48–50, 52, 117–18; self-reliance of, 36, 44, 49, 58, 64, 124; in strategic context, 37–39; susceptibility to burden-sharing pressure, 23; troops stationed in, 34, 36, 37, 45, 50, 124; troop withdrawals from, 1, 45, 46, 49–54, 56–63, 124, 129; US resource and domestic constraints affecting, 46–54

Yoshida Doctrine, 68, 126
Yushin Constitution (South Korea), 99, 127

Zeckhauser, Richard, 29, 122

Milton Keynes UK
Ingram Content Group UK Ltd.
UKHW011951111023
430421UK00006B/45/J